NOTARIZING FOR INTERNATIONAL USE

Notarizing for International Use

A Guide for American Notaries, Attorneys and Public Officials

PETER ZABLUD
Notary Public

Director of Notarial Studies
Victoria University – Melbourne

Chairman of the Board of Governors of
The Australian and New Zealand
College of Notaries

**THE
NOTARY
PRESS**™

First published in 2012

National Library of Australia Cataloguing-in-Publication entry:

Zablud, Peter.

Notarizing for International Use: a Guide for American Notaries, Attorneys and Public Officials / Peter Zablud.

ISBN: 9780958127127 (hbk.)

Includes bibliographical references and index.

Notaries – United States – Power of Attorney – Affidavits – Declarations (Law) – Marine Protests – Legalization.

347.74016

Design and typography by Rob Walker.
Edited by Neil Conning.
Index by Max McMaster.
Printed in Australia by Ligare Pty. Ltd.

Published by
The Notary Press™ a division of Psophidian Pty. Ltd. (ACN 073 303 330).
415 Bourke Street, Melbourne,
Victoria, Australia, 3000.
Website: www.notarypress.com
email: sales@notarypress.com

DISCLAIMER

The purpose of this book is to provide information concerning notarizations performed by American notaries for international use and must not be construed as being the provision of legal or other professional advice to anyone. If legal or other professional advice is warranted or required, the services of an appropriate professional should be sought. This book is not and does not purport to be a complete and exhaustive treatise on its subject matter. It may contain errors and omissions and information that was accurate at the time of publication, but which has subsequently changed or become outdated. The author, the publisher and everyone involved in the book's publication or distribution have no responsibility to any person who buys, reads or uses this book or who directly or indirectly relies in any way on any part of the text.

For Matthew and Joanne

PREFACE

While just a fraction of the billion or so notarizations performed each year within the United States for domestic purposes, the millions of documents notarized annually by American notaries for international use comprise the largest single cohort of documents emanating from any country on earth for use outside its borders.

Not only do they form a lynchpin of world trade and commerce, but they also include documents relied upon by hundreds of thousands of private individuals in the conduct of their international affairs and transactions.

When it comes to domestic notarization, American notaries are well served by the books and other materials readily available to guide them in the conduct of their office. The same cannot be said in relation to notarizing for international purposes. There is precious little published material dealing directly with the subject.

The primary purpose of this book is to help fill the gap.

Peter Zablud
January 2012

ACKNOWLEDGMENTS

I happily take this opportunity to acknowledge and thank a number of people who have helped me in the preparation of this book.

First, foremost and as always, is my wife Robyn, who tolerated the many early morning, evening and weekend hours I spent in our study and then once again typed a long and complex manuscript. You are such a special lady and I am glad to have this forum to publicly say thank you.

My old friend and mentor Gerry Nash was instrumental in the conception and publication of *Principles of Notarial Practice* (2005), which I am pleased to say has achieved extremely satisfactory sales in 21 countries. Gerry takes the view that therefore, he is the progenitor of this book as well. Who am I to disagree with him?

Thank you also to the librarian at Victoria Law School, Murray Greenway. A good librarian is hard to find and, once found, is a real treasure. Murray is a very good librarian indeed.

Many thanks to the National Notary Association's Vice-President of Notary Affairs, Charles (Chuck) Faerber and to the many notary administrators and their staffers who responded so promptly and generously to my emails and telephone calls when I had questions about practical aspects of American notarizations.

The tedious task of checking and amending the ever-changing details of U.S. authentication authorities and the hundreds of foreign embassies and consulates in the United States fell to Greer Meehan and then to Michelle Podbury. Thank you both most sincerely.

My editor, Neil Conning, my indexer, Max McMaster and my designer/typesetter, Rob Walker are all highly regarded professionals in their fields. I am extremely conscious how important their skills have been to the finished product and I thank them for their work. I also thank them for treating this book as more than just another job.

Finally, I thank my friends and colleagues at Victoria University, Melbourne; in particular the late John Harber Phillips, Frank Vincent, Sue Marshall and Laura Kretiuk, who have been so supportive of me and the notarial studies program that we conduct at the Sir Zelman Cowen Centre.

Contents

CHAPTER 1

Toward Ensuring Trustworthy Documents

> To put it simply, ... [records] ... possess enormous power. Records tells us who we are as people. They tell us our stories and they inform our culture and our history; they define political sovereignty and our rights, privileges and obligations in society; they provide evidence of government policies, decisions programmes and services which have impact upon our lives as citizens; they sustain and facilitate access to judicial process at law. In essence, records constitute the very foundation of civilisation.[1]

Since the invention of writing, records have been created, maintained and accumulated for both public and private purposes. However, it should always be remembered that

> the parchment on which ... [a statement] ... is inscribed is 'only the skin of a dead beast' on which 'the pen of the scrivener can note anything'.[2]

Reliability and authenticity

For obvious reasons, over the ages the makers of records and those who rely upon them have been vitally concerned to ensure the trustworthiness of their documents. If documents are to be trustworthy, they must have two qualities:

- **reliability**; and
- **authenticity**.

Reliability means that information in a document is an accurate representation of the facts in it.

Authenticity means that the document is what it purports to be (i.e. that it is genuine) and has not been tampered with or corrupted.[3]

---

1 From 'The Fine Art of Destruction', a speech delivered in Ottawa, Canada on 1 May 2000 by the former National Archivist of Canada, Ian E Wilson. <http//journals.sfu.ca/archivar/index.php/archivaria/article/view/13925>

2 Jean-Phillipe Levy, *The Evolution of Written Proof*, quoted by Heather MacNeil in *Trusting Records – Legal, Historical and Diplomatic Perspectives* (Kluwer Academic Publishers 2000), 8.

3 For a detailed discussion on the evolution of legal and historical methods for assessing the trustworthiness of records, see MacNeil, *Trusting Records.*

Care must be taken not to confuse 'authenticity' with 'reliability', or to assume that merely because a document is authentic that *ipso facto* the information in it is reliable.

For example, in the United States, most of the information appearing in death certificates issued by state authorities is provided by relatives of deceased persons. Not infrequently, errors occur in dates, spelling and the like. The fact that a fresh certificate may subsequently be issued in which an error has been corrected, does not mean that the first certificate was not authentic. Equally, a testamur of a 'degree' issued by a diploma mill can be 'authentic', even though the diploma mill is not an accredited university and its 'degrees' have no genuine value.

How much weight may be put on the contents of particular documents (i.e. their reliability) depends upon a variety of factors, including their authenticity. Ultimately, it comes down to a matter of evaluation and judgment by recipients and occasionally, to determination by a court.

Throughout history, the methods utilized by legal systems and sovereign entities to meet the challenge of ensuring the reliability and authenticity of their own records and those of their citizens have been many and varied. They have included the use of seals,[4] the registration of documents,[5] the testimony of witnesses,[6] and even the introduction of a branch of linguistic scholarship known as 'philology' which involved the study of the language, form and historical content of the documents which comprised the record.

The office of notary

Of all, the method that has stood the test of time has been the creation of the office of notary and the reposing of trust and confidence in the holders of the office and in their official activities.

The concept of the state authorizing independent specially trained professionals of undoubted integrity to prepare and archive reliable and authentic documents

---

4   Michael Clanchy, *From Memory to Written Record – England 1066 – 1307* (Blackwell Publishers 2nd ed 1993), 308-317.

5   From about the fourth century, the papal chancery kept registers of important church documents. In a *summa* dating from the last quarter of the 12th century, one Huguccio, who was apparently then the leading canonical authority on forgeries, recommended that where there was doubt about the authenticity of a decretal, resort should first be had to the papal registers. (C Duggan, *Twelfth Century Decretal Collections and their Importance in English History* (1963) Cited by Clanchy, above, 323).

6   Clanchy, above, 297.

    Nearly all English charters of the eleventh and twelfth centuries listed witnesses to the transactions recorded in them who, if necessary, could be called upon to swear to the veracity of the documents and to the transactions themselves. Witnesses varied in number from the King's unique *Testo me ipso* (witness, myself) to 123 individuals named in an Agreement made in Kent in 1176.

    Clanchy goes on to note that it was common for a scribe to conclude his list of witnesses with a phrase such as 'and may others who would take too long to enumerate', which, although useless for the purpose of future identification, nonetheless recorded the impressiveness of the occasion at the time. One Oxfordshire scribe dismissed the witnesses to a deed with the phrase 'whose names we have been prevented by tedium from writing'.

for itself and its citizens, arose in Roman times.[7] It developed in the city states of central and northern Italy and then found its way throughout Europe.[8] Two thousand years later, the notary as the holder of an office of absolute trust exists in one form or another in virtually every country of the world.[9] While differing in status, function and number from country to country, the common denominator uniting all notaries is the high level of trust accorded to them and their acts both at home and abroad.

Notaries are unlike any other functionaries. As the then Lord Chancellor of England, Lord Eldon said over 200 years ago, (and it is still true today):

> By the law of nations, a notary has credit everywhere.[10]

The civil law notariat

The notariat is at its most influential in those countries which adhere to the civil law legal system. Civil law is more widely distributed throughout the world than is the common law. It is the principal legal system in most of Europe, virtually all of Central and South America and significant parts of Asia and Africa. In North America, pockets of the civil law continue to flourish in Louisiana, Puerto Rico and Quebec.[11]

---

7   During the last years of the Roman Republic, a new form of shorthand invented by Cicero's private secretary, Marcus Tullius Tiro, which became known as *notae tironianae,* quickly found its way into common use among the Roman scribes. A scribe who became proficient in the new system because known as a *notarius.* Over time, the title came to be used by court officials in Rome who prepared resolutions, orders and other documents for sealing by the court.

The preparation of private documents such as wills, leases, partnership agreements and the like was the preserve of private professionals known as *tabelliones* (from the thin wax covered tablets known as *tabellae* on which letters and legal documents were written). The *tabelliones* employed scribes to take shorthand notes of clients' instructions.

It is not now known when and under what circumstances the professions of *notarius* and *tabellio* merged or when and why *tabelliones* generally became known as 'notaries' in Europe. The merger probably began in the late 11th century and was, for all practical purposes, completed in the mid 13th century.

8   For a brief history of the European notariat, see Peter Zablud, *Principles of Notarial Practice,* Psophidian Press, (2005), Ch 2.

9   Countries such as the Peoples' Republic of China and several of the middle eastern theocracies whose legal systems had developed along philosophical lines unrelated to European traditions, have now found it appropriate to introduce notaries into those systems.

For example, in 1975, in Saudi Arabia, the *Law of the Judiciary* established the office of notary in that country. Notaries are state employees (Article 95). Documents issued by notaries have 'dispositive power' and are admitted in evidence in court without additional proof and may not be contested except on the ground that they violate the requirements of the Shari'ah principles or that they are forged (Article 96).

In the People's Republic of China, a public notary system was created in the early 1950s. It was abolished in 1957 and reinstated in 1978. In 1982, the State Council of the PRC promulgated the *Interim Regulation on Public Notary Services* as the legislation regulating notaries in that country.

An instrument which has been drafted and executed by one of the PRC's notarial offices is akin to a public act. It is conclusive evidence that the recitals and agreements expressed in it are accurate reports of the parties' statements and agreements. It is also conclusive evidence that any fact that the instrument recites to have occurred in the presence of the notary did occur and any act recited to have been performed was performed. The faith and credit granted a notarized document has been called in socialist terms, 'a potent force for civilisation and order'. (Alex Low, *New South Wales Law Society Journal* March 1995, 44.

10 *Hutcheon v Mannington* (1802) 6 Ves 823.

11 For an introduction to the civil law, see Appendix 1 .

One of the distinguishing features of the civil law is the central role played by notaries within the system. Notarial acts prepared by notaries in 'authentic' or 'public' form are public documents which are automatically granted *publica fides* (public faith). [12] They therefore carry absolute probative force in relation to statements and matters recorded in them. [13] The status thus accorded by the state to notarial acts both reflects and is reflective of the status accorded to the notaries themselves.

As a necessary concomitant of the probative force given to authentic form notarial acts, civil law systems typically also grant them executory force. Where a notarial act records an agreement or obligation, the act itself is enforceable in the same manner as if it were a judgment of a court.[14]

In addition to acts in authentic form for domestic purposes, civil law notaries also prepare and complete notarial acts in 'private' form for international use in much the same way as those acts are prepared by common law notaries.[15]

In civil law jurisdictions, notarial practice is rightly considered to be a specialist field. Candidates invariably must gain specialist qualifications and usually must undertake periods of service as employees before being eligible for appointment. For example, French notaries qualify for appointment in one of two ways. Senior staff members of notarial offices who have passed a principal clerk's diploma examination and who have had at least nine years experience in a notarial office (at least six years of which have been after completion of the diploma) are eligible for appointment if they pass a special entry examination. Alternatively, a university graduate who has also obtained a *Diplomes d'etudes superieurs de droit notarial* may apply for appointment after completing two years (four semesters) of practical training in a notarial office and after passing various examinations at the end of each semester.

Within their jurisdictions, the civil law notaries, and in particular the European and Central and South American notaries, are seen and see themselves, as being an indispensable component of the legal profession. They tend to be highly visible and well regarded professionals at the apex of their respective

---

12 The attribution of *publica fides* by the state to its judicial and administrative documents, i.e. its 'public' documents, is one of the key indicia of sovereignty and is of the essence in the conduct of government. In that context, 'faith' means complete trust, confidence and credence.

13 Entrusting notaries with the creation and execution of documents which will attain public faith places considerable responsibility on their shoulders. For example, in Germany, the Civil Code requires the intervention of a notary in the land transfer procedure to attract and invoke the so called 'public faith' protection of #892 of the Code which is the main indefeasibility of title provision in the German system. Only acquisition of property through *juristic acts* (i.e. the acts of notaries) is protected by #892. Failure on the notary's part will remove the entire transaction, even when registered, from the protection of #892. (Murray Raff, *Private Property and Environmental Responsibility – A Comparative Study of German Real Property Law* (Kluwer Law International 2003) 227-229.

14 Enforceability may either be the result of specific legislation, as is the case in Belgium, France, Germany, Greece, the Netherlands and Portugal or of an agreement between the parties embodied in the instrument, as is the case in Italy.

15 See Chapter 2 for a discussion concerning notarial acts in 'authentic' or 'public' form and notarial acts in private form.

national legal systems. They usually enjoy state sanctioned monopolies in their areas of expertise and generally find themselves at the upper end of the income scale.[16]

The common law notariat

The status, power and function of the civil law notary is not replicated in those jurisdictions where the legal system is based on the common law.[17] The emphasis in the common law jurisdictions has long been on the presentation of oral evidence in courts.[18] The civil law notion of documents prepared and authenticated by notaries having absolute probative and executory force is completely unacceptable to the common law, as it flies directly in the face of the rule against hearsay.

Common law notaries, or more particularly English notaries, have been described as 'anomalous' figures within their legal system, whose importance is 'in the link ... [they provide] ... between the institutions of the common law system and those of the civil law.'[19]

Anomalies or not, in Australia, New Zealand and other similar common law jurisdictions, including England herself, notaries are almost always lawyers in private practice who, when acting as notaries, exercise a discrete but essential function of authenticating personal and commercial documents which are prepared or executed domestically specifically for production and use abroad.

The appointment of notaries in common law jurisdictions outside the United States and the level of education required of them has, for a long time, been very much a mixed bag. Canada is a classic example. Notaries in British Columbia are well trained and highly regulated, but need not be lawyers. In Alberta, no specific training is necessary and law students and persons over the age of 18 years who are Canadian citizens ordinarily resident in Alberta are eligible for appointment.

---

16 Civil law or 'latin' notaries are found in some 78 countries throughout Africa, Europe, Asia, Central and South America and the former Soviet bloc. In North America, latin notaries are also found in Quebec, Louisiana and Puerto Rico.

   For a comprehensive review of the development, nature and function of the latin notary, see Pedro A Malavet, *Counsel for the Situation: The Latin Notary, An Historical and Comparative Model*, Hastings International and Comparative Law Review Vol 19, No 3, Spring 1996, 389.

17 The common law jurisdictions include most of the members of the (British) Commonwealth of Nations and a number of other countries, including the United States and Ireland, which were formally British colonies or which fell within the British sphere of influence.

   There are a several countries in the Commonwealth of Nations, such as South Africa, Mauritius and Vanuatu where Britain was not previously the dominant or the sole colonial power. As a result, those countries have tended to have hybrid legal systems which, in turn, have produced notaries who in many ways are closer to latin notaries than they are to common law notaries.

18 See CR Cheney, *Notaries Public in England in the Thirteenth and Fourteenth Centuries* (Oxford University Press 1972), Ch 1.

19 NP Ready, *Brooke's Notary* (Sweet & Maxwell 13th ed 2009), 1.

   Explaining the importance of notaries in those terms is completely understandable in an English textbook, having regard to the long-standing agenda of the English notariat which seeks to promote the 'link' as part of the continuing process of endeavouring to elevate the status of English notaries to that of their civil law cousins in Europe.

All local members of the federal and provincial parliaments are automatically notaries, as are members of the judiciary. All of Ontario's 35,000 lawyers are entitled to apply for appointment and about half of them have done so. At the same time, Ontario has about 650 notaries who are not lawyers.

Until relatively recently, save in relation to scrivener notaries who genuinely were and are in a special and highly qualified class of their own, it was accepted in England and in most other common law countries that if a person were a senior practicing lawyer, once appointed he or she would readily be able to conduct a notarial practice armed only with a handful of precedents and years of experience as a legal practitioner.

Following the fall of the Berlin wall and the opening up of world trade and investment from the early 1990s, governments in the common law jurisdictions which had previously paid scant attention to notaries, began to appreciate that notaries perform an important role which both facilitates international trade and commerce and assists citizens with families and interests abroad in conducting their personal affairs with a greater degree of certainty and efficiency.

An increased understanding of the necessity for specialist education for notaries followed. In England and Wales, it is now compulsory for prospective notaries to complete a university Diploma in Notarial Practice. In the Australian state of Victoria, the passage of the *Public Notaries Act 2001* with its mandatory education requirement has resulted in prospective Victorian notaries being required to complete a Professional Certificate in Notarial Practice offered by Victoria University's Sir Zelman Cowen Centre in order to be qualified for appointment to office.[20]

Notaries in the USA

In America, a third and different category of notary arose; a ministerial officer with minimal power to exercise independent judgment, whose sworn duty it is to take acknowledgments, administer oaths and carry out a number of other acts, primarily for domestic purposes. It is thought that at the end of 2011, there were approximately 4.9 million people holding commissions as notaries in the United States.[21]

American notaries may be, but usually are not, lawyers. Typically, they are drawn from support staff in a wide range of professions and businesses with a preponderance from areas such as accountancy, banking, real estate broking, insurance and legal practice, all of which deal with the myriad of documents prepared, signed, filed and processed every day in the United States.[22] Domestically, notarization has become a key element in the conduct of

---

20 In consequence, Victorian notaries are now among the best trained and most highly qualified notaries in the common law world.

 For those notaries who wish to take their studies further, Victoria University will shortly be offering a degree of Master of Notarial Science.

21 For an overview of the origins and powers of American notaries, see Chapter 3.

22 In 2007, the National Notary Association estimated that approximately one billion documents were notarized each year in the United States. That figure is obviously increasing annually.

daily governmental, commercial and personal life, to the point where defective notarization can not only invalidate individual documents but in extreme cases, can also derail and invalidate entire transactions.[23]

Notaries are appointed by authority of state or territory legislation, generally by the Governor or Secretary of State. With the exception of Louisiana and Puerto Rico, where notaries are appointed indefinitely, notarial commissions are granted for fixed terms with a right of renewal. The average term is four years.[24] In most cases, qualifications are minimal. Typically, applicants must be over 18 years of age, be literate in English, be resident in the state or territory in which a commission is sought and be of good character, that is to say, not have any felony convictions at all or within a certain number of years before application. Increasingly, prospective notaries are required to undertake short courses of instruction followed by examinations before being eligible for appointment.

The special status of notaries in Louisiana and Puerto Rico

For historical reasons, two enclaves of civil law notaries are found in the United States; the first in the state of Louisiana and the second in the territory of Puerto Rico. Louisiana notaries are descended from French antecedents. They are given far reaching powers by the *Louisiana Civil Code*, including the power to prepare authentic acts in the traditional civil law manner. Puerto Rico is a civil law jurisdiction founded upon Spanish law. Its notaries are legal professionals who must be attorneys admitted to practice in Puerto Rico and who are authorized to practice as notaries by the Supreme Court of Puerto Rico.

U.S. military notaries

Among the array of public officials and consular officers entitled by US state and federal law to provide notarial services, there is a largely overlooked but nonetheless significant branch of the American notariat, namely that of the military notary.

All

- judge advocates, including reserve judge advocates when not in a duty status
- civilian attorneys serving as legal assistance officers
- adjutants, assistant adjutants and personnel adjutants, including reserve members when not in a duty status; and
- other members of the armed forces, including reserve members when not in a duty status, who are designated (from time to time) by regulations of the armed forces or by statute

have the general powers of a notary public and of a consul of the United States

---

23 Michael Closen and Thomas W Mulcahy, *Conflicts of Interest in Documents Authenticated by Attorney Notaries in Illinois*, Illinois Bar Journal (June 1999) 320 at n 23.

24 New York notaries are only appointed for two years. Notaries in California, South Dakota and West Virginia enjoy ten year terms, while Vermont notaries have terms which are effectively co-extensive with the terms of the superior court judges who appoint them.

in the performance of notarial acts for members of the armed forces and persons who are eligible for legal assistance from the military.[25]

Difficulties in acceptance of American notarizations

Lack of appropriate legal training and qualifications combined with the ministerial nature of the office and the limited range of powers usually granted to them have in the past and still continue to cause problems for American notaries when they intervene in international commercial transactions. Particularly in Europe, business people and government agencies are often troubled by the nature and status of American notaries. Not infrequently they decline to accept American notarizations.[26]

The 'civil law' notaries of Alabama and Florida

In response, in the late 1990s Alabama and Florida pioneered the appointment of a new class of American notary, the members of which must be lawyers of at least five years standing who have undergone specialist training. In addition to exercising the powers of ordinary notaries in their states, 'Civil Law' notaries as they are known are entitled to issue 'authentic' instruments for use in jurisdictions outside the United States. Regrettably, they remain very few in number and other jurisdictions have not followed suit.

The importance of American notaries internationally

Despite the problems their notarizations face and the criticisms often levelled at them, the importance of American notaries internationally should not be underestimated or lightly set aside. Some millions of documents emanate from the United States each year which are required for commercial, official and private purposes all over the world. The majority of those documents had need of notarial intervention before leaving the USA in order to have efficacy at their destinations. No amount of carping by critics at home or abroad alters the position.[27]

---

25 10 U.S.C. §1044A – Authority to act as a Notary.

    For further information about military notaries and their powers, training and responsibilities see *Army Regulation 27-55* (Effective 17 December 2003), published by the Department of Army, Washington DC, 17 November 2003.

    Also see *Manual of the Judge Advocate General* Ch IX Department of Navy (March 2004) which covers both Navy and Marine Corps and *Air Force Instruction* 51-504 (27 October 2003) as amended Ch 2 and *United States Coast Guard Commandant Instructions* 5801-4E October 26 2005.

    Statistics are difficult to find, but in November 2000, on the front page of its publication *From Counsel*, the Office of the Staff Judge Advocate of the U.S. Army Combined Arms Support Command, Fort Lee – Virginia, estimated that army, civilian and military personnel (then) notarized over 410,000 documents per annum.

26 For example, see Chapter 7 for a discussion as to the challenges faced by American notaries in relation to notarizing powers of attorney for use outside the United States.

27 Interestingly, the minimalist 'American' notarial certificate, much maligned by European civil law notaries has been adopted as a model by many countries with younger notarial cultures than those of Europe or England. For example, Vietnam, Laos, Cambodia, Thailand, South Korea and most of the Arab League nations all essentially look toward the traditional American style in the certifications they require from notaries abroad.

Notarial services provided by consular officers

Since the late 18th century, it has been the practice for consular officers acting within their consular districts to provide notarial services to their own nationals in relation to their personal and commercial affairs 'at home'. The practice is now enshrined in the *Vienna Convention on Consular Relations*. As at 31 December 2011, 173 nations, including the United States, were party to the Convention.[28]

Under the umbrella of the Convention, career consular officers and honorary consuls are all entitled to provide notarial services so long as the laws of the relevant receiving states do not forbid the activity. [29] Unfortunately, the Convention itself does not set out the extent of the notarial powers granted. It merely states that consular functions include, among other things, 'acting as a notary'.[30]

For a general explanation of the meaning of the function, it is necessary to turn to the International Law Commission's 1961 Commentaries on the Draft Articles of the (then) proposed Convention. The Commentaries note that:

(11)   The notarial functions are varied and may consist, for instance, in:

    (a)   Receiving in the consular offices, on board vessels and ships or on board aircraft having the nationality of the sending State, any statements which the nationals of the sending State may have to make;

    (b)   Drawing up, attesting and receiving for safe custody, wills and all unilateral instruments executed by nationals of the sending State;

    (c)   Drawing up, attesting and receiving for safe custody, deeds the parties to which are nationals of the sending State and nationals of the receiving State, or of a third State, provided that they do not relate to immovable property situated in the receiving State or to rights *in rem* attaching to such property;

    (d)   Attesting or certifying signatures, stamping, certifying or translating documents, in any case for which those formalities are requested by a person of any nationality for use in the sending State or in pursuance of the laws of that State. If an oath or a declaration in lieu of oath is required under the laws of the sending State, such oath or declaration may be sworn or made before the consular official;

(12)   ...

(13)   The administrative functions mentioned under paragraph (f) are determined by

---

28 The Convention was adopted by a United Nations Conference held in Vienna from 4 March to 22 April 1963. The United States was one of the 48 original signatories to the Convention on 24 April 1963. The Convention entered into force for the USA on 24 November 1969.

29 *Vienna Convention on Consular Relations*, Article 5(f).

    There is no law in the United States which forbids the activity.

30 Ibid.

the laws and regulations of the sending State. They may consist, for instance in:

(a) – (b)   ...

(c)   Certifying documents indicating the origin of goods, invoices and the like.[31]

In light of the limited powers of the American notariat and the problems with American notarizations periodically encountered abroad, consular officers in the United States, particularly those representing the interests of civil law jurisdictions, tend to provide a greater level of notarial services than do their counterparts in most other countries. As a rule, notarial services are provided by career consular officers. They are usually well trained and often have reasonably high skill levels. The same cannot always be said for honorary consuls who many times take up their posts for reasons not necessarily connected with a desire to provide services to nationals of the sending state.

Nonetheless, provided that consular services are limited to such things as completing authentic form documents prepared by notaries or lawyers abroad, witnessing the execution of documents, administering oaths and certifying copies, little harm can be done by consular officers dipping their toes into legal/ notarial waters. Unqualified consular officers who take it upon themselves to actually draft documents or modify precedents provided for consular use by the authorities of sending states are skating on extremely thin ice.

The challenge posed by e-commerce

The continuing growth of e-commerce, as well as the very nature of electronic records and the administrative context in which they exist, pose significant challenges to the notariat the world over and to the way notaries carry out their function. All things considered, the office of notary as such and the trust placed in it by states and the public do not immediately appear to be under serious threat. Even so, neither the longevity of the office nor the success and function of notarial intervention thus far are any guarantee of a long term future for notaries in the United States or elsewhere.

Ultimately,

> The validity and strength of ... [the notariat's] ... methods for assessing and ensuring record trustworthiness can only be judged ... in relation to the integrity and internal coherence of its procedures.[32]

If notaries are to continue to fulfill their traditional role in the new electronic world, they cannot afford to rest on their laurels. They and the organizations that represent them, together with the legislatures that govern them, must now take steps to ensure that the integrity and internal coherence of their practices and procedures move with the times and continue to meet communal needs and expectations.

---

31 *Yearbook of the International Law Commission*, 1961, Vol II, 96 and 97.

32 MacNeil, above, 114.

CHAPTER 2

NOTARIAL ACTS IN AUTHENTIC AND PRIVATE FORMS

Outside the United States, almost without exception,

- an **act** is an instrument that records a fact or something that has been said, done or agreed; and

- a **notarial act** is

  the act of a notary public authenticated by his signature and official seal, certifying the due execution in his presence of a deed, contract or other writing or verifying some fact or thing of which the notary has certain knowledge.[1]

When considering the notarization of documents for international use, it is necessary to distinguish a notarial act as defined above from a notarial act as typically defined in American legislation. In almost every United States jurisdiction, a notarial act is a function which a notary is authorized to perform, as opposed to a document or instrument which records that which the notary certifies has been done.[2]

Therefore, for example, in most countries the administration of an oath by a notary is an activity on the notary's part, but the recording of the administration of the oath in the jurat of an affidavit as certified by the notary's signature and seal, is a notarial act, albeit one of the simplest kind. On the other hand, within the United States, in the main, the administration of the oath is the notarial act and the jurat is merely a written statement confirming that the notarial act has occurred.

---

1   NP Ready, *Brooke's Notary* (Sweet & Maxwell 13th ed 2009), 75.

   Ready then goes on to say by way of explanation on the same page, 'Thus any certificate, attestation, note, entry, endorsement or instrument made or signed and sealed by a notary public in the execution of the duties of his office is a notarial act'.

   The former secretary of The Notaries' Society of England and Wales, A G (Tony) Dunford, has provided a useful alternative to the definition in *Brooke*. He defines a notarial act as being 'a record of some activity which is intended and or required to have some evidential status, or some legal or administrative force or effect or some commercial effect'. A G Dunford, *The General Notary*, (The Notaries Society 1999), 4.

2   Unlike a number of states which were once administered by civil law colonial powers, both Louisiana and Puerto Rico still follow their French and Spanish antecedents and make the distinction between notarial acts on the one hand and the powers and duties of notaries on the other. See generally, Louisiana Revised Statutes Title 35, *Notaries Public and Commissioners* and Laws of Puerto Rico Title 4, *Puerto Rico Notarial Act*.

Categories of notarial acts

In the civil law world and generally within common law jurisdictions other than the United States, all notarial acts necessarily fall into one of two categories, namely:

- **authentic** form acts; or

- other acts, known in most common law countries as **private** form acts.

Acts in 'authentic' or 'public' form

The concept of an act in authentic form, while fundamental to the civil law, is totally alien to the common law which had developed its methods of authenticating transactions from completely different theoretical premises to those upon which the civil law was founded.[3]

Also known as an act in 'public' form and occasionally, as an act in 'solemn' form, the notarial act in authentic form had its genesis in Italy in medieval times. It comprises a single narrative instrument, written by the notary in the first person, which sets out or perfects a legal obligation or records some fact or thing. Because it has been prepared by a notary, it is conclusive and has full probative value in civil law jurisdictions where notarial acts automatically have full recognition.

In civil law countries, an act in authentic form has special evidentiary status and is usually automatically evidence of the facts and statements it records unless it is deprived of authenticity by a rarely undertaken, long and complex judicial procedure. A notarial act in authentic form does not, however, have probative force in relation to the facts which the parties have declared to the notary without evidencing them. That part of the instrument can be rebutted by ordinary means of proof.

In addition to its probative force, an authentic form notarial act also has executory force; that is to say, an obligation or acknowledgment appearing in a notarially authenticated instrument is enforceable in the same way as if it were a judgment of the court, even though no proceedings have been brought before a court.

Save for American civil law notaries who comprise a special group very much in the minority, U.S. notaries do not have the power or authority to prepare or complete notarial acts in authentic form. This is so, even if the documents have actually been prepared abroad and sent to the United States for notarization.[4]

---

3   See generally, C R Cheney, *Notaries Public in England in the Thirteenth and Fourteenth Centuries* (Oxford University Press 1972).

4   Any American notary who wrongfully prepares or completes a notarial act in authentic form puts any transaction to which the document relates in immediate jeopardy. On one view, matters and things set out in the purported notarial act are a nullity *ab initio*, because American notaries other than civil law notaries do not have the training or status required to prepare or complete a notarial act in authentic form.

The elements of a notarial act in authentic form

A notarial act in authentic form

- begins with **a protocol** (preamble) which sets out introductory matters such as:
  - the notary's name and status;
  - the date and place of the notarial act;
  - the fact of the appearance of one or more persons (typically referred to as 'the appearer(s)') before the notary, often together with one or more witnesses;[5]
  - any capacity in which an appearer appears or is acting; and
  - the means by which the notary has verified any facts or statements set out in the act relating to the appearer(s)
- continues with the **corpus** (operative part) which
  - records any declarations made to the notary by the appearer(s) by way of
  - explanation or recital;
  - sets out, also by way of declaration by the appearer(s), the terms of the power of attorney, contract, arrangement, obligation or other legal act which is embodied in the instrument; and
  - refers to any annexures or documents produced to or by the appearer(s); and
- ends with an **eschatocal** (concluding statement) by the notary which states:
  - that the document was read over to and acknowledged by the appearer(s), and signed and, where applicable, sealed by the appearer(s) in the notary's presence and in the presence of any witnesses who are present; and
  - where appropriate or required, that all the requirements of the applicable local law relating to the formalities of execution of the document and its binding nature have been met.

The document is then signed by the appearer(s) in the notary's presence and in the presence of any witnesses who also sign the document in each other's presence and in the presence of the appearer(s). The notary then signs and

---

5   Civil law jurisdictions often require one or more witnesses to be present in addition to the notary when certain documents, typically documents relating to real estate and inheritance matters, are executed.

seals the executed document, although not necessarily in the presence of the appearer(s) or the witness(es), thereby making the document the notary's act.[6]

The notary's protocol

In civil law jurisdictions, each notary keeps his or her original notarial acts in what is known as a 'protocol' and provides appearers and other persons authorized by law with authentic certified copies.

In the common law jurisdictions outside the United States, when preparing an act in authentic form, notaries prepare a sufficient number of duplicate original documents to allow each appearer to have a fully executed original and to provide an original to be kept in the notarial protocol from which certified copies can be made if needed.[7]

Acts in private form

A notarial act in private form is a certificate signed and sealed by a notary which is endorsed upon or appended to another document not usually prepared by the notary. Typically it relates to or deals with one or more aspects of the document such as its genuine nature or validity, its legal status and legal consequences or more often, the execution of the document and the verification of the identity, capacity and authority of the person(s) executing it.

Although their origins may be less auspicious and their preparation less formal and ritualistic than their 'authentic' kin, notarial acts in private form have an important function in modern commercial life and must be prepared by a notary with proper care as to their content and with due concern as to the consequences which flow from any negligent misstatement which might appear.

---

6   Requirements as to form are regulated to a greater or lesser degree in most civil law jurisdictions. For example, in Quebec, the *Notaries Act 2000*, among other things, sets out rules for notarial acts including rules relating to errors and omissions (s 37), forms and abbreviations (s 45), added words, letters or signs and words crossed out (s 46), inserts and additions (ss 47, 48 & 49), signing (s 50), reading over (s 51) and place(s) of execution (ss 54 & 55).

Also see, for example, Part III, Title 1 of Malta's *Notarial Profession and Notarial Archives Act – Of formalities of Notarial Acts*, Article 51 of the *Notarial Law* of Italy and Chapter 9 of the Spanish Civil Code, *Reglamento Notarial*.

7   The law of evidence in common law countries prefers original documents for evidentiary purposes. Generally speaking, a copy of a document will not be admissible if an original of the document is available. In civil law jurisdictions, a notarially certified copy of a notarial act is itself a notarial act and is admissible in evidence.

Unfortunately, there is a tendency in some civil law quarters to think that acts in authentic form are the only true notarial acts and that the private form acts of the common law notaries are less worthy and of lower status as are, by extension, the common law notaries themselves.[8] Civil law notaries would do well to remember that a large proportion of the acts which they prepare are acts in private form, which are for production in jurisdictions outside their own. As with authentic acts, private form acts must be correctly and carefully prepared and completed.[9]

The place of the act

It is essential that the place of the notarial act be clearly stated, partly because notaries are only entitled to act within the geographical limits of their jurisdictions and partly because the place of the act must be recorded to establish its *lex actus*. American notarial practice does of course require the endorsement of an appropriate caption at the head of every notarial certificate which is prepared.

The notary's name

A notary's name must always appear on a notarial act. To avoid doubt, the name must be the same name which appears on the notary's seal of office. Provided a notary chooses and invariably uses the same 'professional' name, there is no need for those notaries who have two, three or more personal names to use them all on a seal or in a notarial act. Care should be taken by notaries to comply with their own state or territory legislation in relation to the use of personal and family names on documents and seals of office.

The date

A notarial act must bear the date of its making, which need not necessarily be the date of the activity which has been recorded. The date ought to be set out in words, or at very least, in a manner which makes it clear that the act has been made on a specific day of a specified month of a particular year.

Date formatting is not constant throughout the world. Although everywhere in the world dates display the day, month and year, there are significant differences between regional formats. For example, the date formats in Australia, the United States and Japan are different. In Australia, the date format is 'day, month, year'. In the United States, the date is usually in the format, 'month, day, year' save for formal legal documents which generally use the format 'day, month, year'. In Japan, the date format is 'year, month, day'. Problems with format are exacerbated when people only use numerical formats, for example '10/11/09'.

---

8   Dunford has observed that the essentials of public and private form notarial acts are, in reality, the same, but the difference between them lies in the purpose to which a particular act is to be put in the jurisdiction in which it is to be used (Dunford, above n 1, 45).

9   In the author's experience, civil law notaries are just as prone to error when preparing acts in private form as are their common law brethren.

Signature and seal

The notary's signature and seal are necessary formal requirements for every notarial act to be produced abroad, whether in authentic or private form.[10] All notaries must have their own distinctive seals. In parts of the United States, rubber stamps have become the norm. Good practice requires notarial seals to be embossing seals. The use of a wafer is not necessary, but it makes the impression of the embossing seal far easier to see.

Despite its history as an integral part of the notary's accoutrement, these days, nine of the states, namely, Connecticut, Kentucky, Louisiana, Maine, Michigan, New Jersey, New York, Rhode Island and Vermont, do not require notaries to have a seal of office.[11] Interestingly, the authorities in all of those states nonetheless encourage the use of a seal by notaries on documents which are to be produced outside the confines of the state and particularly for those notarized documents which are to be produced abroad.

Ink and ink color

Wherever possible, the signatures on notarial acts should be in indelible ink. A number of jurisdictions, including Barbados, Malaysia and South Africa, require signatures for most official purposes to be in black ink. Pencils, felt tipped pens and washable ink should never be used.

Acknowledgments

The quintessential notarial act in the United States is the taking of an 'acknowledgment' which is formal and official evidence of the proper execution of an instrument as a necessary precursor to admitting the instrument to public record.[12]

---

10 Until at least the early years of the 18th century, each civil law and English notary had his own individual hand drawn 'sign' which he rendered on the obverse sides of his more important notarial acts as a means of authentication. In addition to his sign, each notary also had his mark or 'paraph' which was used in conjunction with his signature. When documents were written in Latin, each notary generally used his own unique calligraphic form of the letter 'E' as the first capital 'E' in the expression *Et Ego* at the commencement of the eschatacol. Gradually, seals replaced signs as the preferred means of authentication until, by the 19th century, it had become standard practice for notaries to sign their notarial acts and affix their seals in conjunction with their signatures.

11 Delaware, Iowa, Massachusetts and Virginia had previously dispensed with the need for seals, but in recent years have returned to the fold as it were, and have legislated for the use of seals by notaries.

Since 1996, Florida notaries must use a rubber stamp either alone or with an embossing seal. The latter cannot, however, be used by itself.

South Carolina notaries must have seals. Although urged by the Secretary of State's office to use seals, especially on documents to be produced in another state or country, the absence of a seal does not render a notary's act invalid if the notary's title is affixed to the document. However, South Carolina notaries should always use a seal on documents they are notarizing for production abroad.

12 The acknowledgment has formed the basis of many notarial acts in countries such as the Philippines, Vietnam, Korea and Thailand, where American influence is keenly felt.

An **acknowledgment** is

A notarial act in which a notary public certifies that a signatory, whose identity is personally known to the notary public, or proven on the basis of satisfactory evidence has admitted, in the notary public's presence, to having voluntarily signed a document for its stated purposes.[13]

Acknowledgment also means

A declaration by a person that the person has executed an instrument for the purposes stated therein and if the instrument is executed in a representative capacity, that the person signed the instrument with proper authority and executed it as the act of a person or entity represented and identified therein.[14]

An acknowledgment must be distinguished from an 'attestation', which is the act of witnessing the execution of a document and then signing the document as a witness. In taking acknowledgments, American notaries do not act as witnesses to the execution of documents. If formal witnessing is required, that task typically falls to an independent person other than a notary.[15]

American notarial certificates

Within the United States, the forms of most notarial certificates (i.e. for present purposes 'notarial acts in private form') are prescribed by statute or recommended by notary administrators in the handbooks they publish.

Typically, notarial certificates are pre-printed on documents printed or prepared in the United States which are to be presented for notarization. All too often there is insufficient space left for the notary to properly complete and seal the certificate. On many occasions, the form of wording does not comply with the legislative requirement of the notary's home state or territory. In either case, a notary ought not be frightened to prepare an appropriate notarial certificate and append it to the underlying document or, if convenient, endorse it on the reverse side of a one-page document.

Leading commentator, Peter Van Alstyne has observed that:

An old myth has it that a notarization must appear on the same piece of paper where the customer's signature appears. The concept is illogical and without factual basis.

Attaching a notarial certificate to a customer's document has profound merit to it … By utilizing an attached notarial certificate, the message is given that it is a

---

13 *Connecticut Annotated Statutes* §3-94a, Notaries Public, Definitions.

14 *Illinois Compiled Statutes*, Ch 5 §312/6-101, Definitions.

15 In some U.S. jurisdictions, it is possible to 'prove' a deed as an alternative to obtaining a signatory's acknowledgment. The procedure is sometimes called 'probating' a deed and involves one or more of the attesting witnesses making an affidavit that the person whose signature was witnessed acknowledged the instrument in the presence of the affiant(s) and any other attesting witness(es). See for example *Colorado Revised Statutes,* Notaries Public §38-30-136 and *Iowa Code,* Iowa Law on Notarial Acts §558-31 and 558-32.

document separate and apart from the customer's documents. The notarization is not part of the customer's transaction. It stands alone as a certificate; it is a written testimony of the notary declaring the genuineness of the customer's signature.[16]

Secure attachment

When a notarial certificate is appended to another document, it is essential that it be securely attached in a manner which makes it impossible for the certificate to be removed without damaging both it and the document to which it is appended. Equally, it must not be possible to substitute, add or remove pages to either the notarial certificate, (if it be a certificate which exceeds a page in length) or to the document to which the certificate is appended. A notarial certificate should never merely be attached by a staple or glue to the document to which it relates.

Ideally, papers should be fastened together with a grommet or sewn or knotted ribbon, the ends of which are secured by a wafer upon which the notary's seal is impressed. Where appropriate, the notary should sign or initial each page of a document and impress his or her seal over or next to the initials or signature. It is always good practice for a notarial certificate to specifically refer to the number of pages of the document to which it is appended and to note that each page of the document has been signed or initialed and bears an impression of the notary's official seal for purposes of identification.[17]

Use of prescribed forms

Legislation in most states and territories allows notaries a reasonable amount of latitude in the preparation of certificates. As a rule, certificates must be 'substantially' in the prescribed forms. Adding a description of a document and referring to the number of pages it comprises usually does not offend against any substantial compliance rule. Neither does a statement by a notary to the effect that 'each page of the document has been initialled by me for purposes of identification'.[18]

Partly to reduce the possibility of notaries engaging in unauthorized practice of law and partly in recognition of the ministerial nature of the office, a number of states and territories impose restrictions on notaries in relation to the choice or wording of notarial certificates.

Occasionally there is a blanket ban on notaries exercising any discretion, but typically, the restrictions are directed towards notaries who are not attorneys and are formulated along lines to the effect that a non-attorney notary must not determine the type of certificate or wording to be used if certificate wording is not provided or indicated in a document.

---

16 Peter J Van Alstyne, *Van Alstyne's Notary Public Encyclopedia* (Wasatch Peaks Publishing, 2001), 19 and 20.

17 In reality, it is not possible to append a notarial certificate to a document in a completely 'tamper proof' manner. The aim is to append the certificate in a 'tamper evident' manner.

18 For example, see discussion about copy certification certificates in Chapter 6 at 85 and 86.

An exception to the 'non attorney' restriction is also usually allowed which enables a notary 'who is duly qualified, trained or experienced in a particular industry or field' to select, draft, complete or advise on a document or certificate related to that industry or field.[19]

---

19 American Samoa, Guam, Massachusetts, Mississippi, Nebraska, New Mexico, Northern Marianas, Rhode Island, Virginia and Washington all have varying formulations of such provisions in their legislation, handbooks or official advice to notaries.

In Texas, attorney notaries may choose or formulate a notarial certificate, but there is no exception granted to notaries who are 'duly qualified trained or experienced' in a particular industry or field.

In Alaska, Delaware, Indiana and Maryland, notaries have no discretion in relation to the choice or wording of certificates and may only complete certificates which have already been prepared by others.

CHAPTER 3

A MINISTERIAL OFFICE

When Christopher Columbus set sail for the New World on Friday 3 August 1492, the complement of the flagship included the royal notary, Rodrigo de Escobedo, whose sworn duty was to witness and record his admiral's noteworthy acts for posterity.[1] By so doing and by virtue of the *publica fides* reposed in him by his office, the legality of those acts, at least in the Spanish mind, was beyond question.

On coming ashore on the small island which he subsequently named 'San Salvador', Columbus enjoined his notary to witness his taking possession of the island for the Spanish King and Queen and to '[make] the declarations that were required ... [which] ... at more length ... [would be] ... contained in the testimonials made there in writing.'[2]

As they followed in Columbus' footsteps over the next 300 years, England and the major European powers all sponsored colonies in the Americas. Unsurprisingly, the colonists brought their religious beliefs, social customs, laws and institutions with them to smooth the way and provide the foundation for their new lives.

Among the institutions crossing the Atlantic from the civil law jurisdictions of Spain, Holland and France was that of the notary, which by the 16th century had become integral to the legal systems of those countries and therefore to the bureaucratic models they exported to their colonies.

The status, power and function of the civil law notariat was not however replicated in the common law jurisdiction of England, where law and government had developed largely independently of Roman law. While recognizing a need for notaries in limited circumstances, unlike their European counterparts, the first English colonists did not count any notaries among their number when embarking upon their expeditions.

---

1   Kathryn Burns, *Notaries Truth and Consequences*, The American Historical Review, Vol. 110, No. 2, April 2005, 350.

    Also see *1492 Crew Lists, Columbus's (sic) Crew on the First Voyage*.

    <www.immigrantships.net/v4/1400/u4/Santamaria_pinla_nina 1492.html>

2   Christopher Columbus, *The Diario of Christopher Columbus' First Voyage to America 1492-1493*, abstracted by Fray Bartolomé de las Cases, Oliver Dunn and James E. Kelley jr, ed and trans (Norman, Okla, 1989), 65. Cited and quoted by Kathryn Burns, above at 350.

Notaries in the European colonies

In pursuit of their colonial objectives in the Americas, centered upon a never ending search for gold, the Spanish

> ... arrived in the South East ... [of the United States] ... with a sober respect for the formalities of conquest, developed ... over centuries of reconquering Spain from the Moors and generations of experience in the New World. The sweatiest of entradas [*invasions*] into unknown territory was a matter of order and record, with banners flying and notaries at the ready.[3]

Spanish presence in south eastern North America ultimately lasted for more than three centuries, but their colonies tended to be sparsely populated with relatively few urban centers. Consequently, the need for notarial services for non-government purposes was small and the formidable Spanish notariat did not gain a lasting foothold.

The Dutch colonial adventure in North America was short (1609-1664) and largely confined to present day New York and parts of Delaware. The activities of notaries in New Netherlands had no discernible impact on the development of the notariat in the United States.[4]

French colonization originated in what is now Canada and spread southwards into the Mississippi river basin, the whole of which the explorer Rene-Robert Cavalier Sieur de La Salle claimed for France on 9 April 1682, and named 'La Louisianne' in honor of King Louis XIV. In 1803, the fledgling United States government under President Thomas Jefferson purchased 828,000 square miles of La Louisianne for a total price, including interest and the forgiving of debts by France, of $23,213,568.[5] Unlike the Spanish and the Dutch, the French left a legacy to the American notariat, namely the 'notaire' whose descendents hold office today in Louisiana.[6]

---

3   Amy Turner Bushnell, *Ruling the Republic of Indians in Seventeenth Century Florida*, an essay found in *Powhatans Mantle; Indians in the Colonial Southeast*, ed Geoffrey A Waselkov, Peter H Wood, M Thomas Hatley, (University of Nebraska Press, 2006), 195.

4   For an excellent insight into the Dutch colony which became New York, see Jaap Jacobs, *The Colony of New Netherland*, (Cornell University Press, 2009).

   Also see, Donna Merwick, *Death of a Notary*, (Cornell University Press, 2009) and *The Register of Salomon Lachaire, Notary Public of New Amsterdam 1661–1662, New York Historical Manuscripts Dutch*, ed Kenneth Scott and Kenn Stryker-Rodda (Genealogical Publishing Co. Baltimore, 1978).

5   Table 1.1 *Acquisition of the Public Domain 1781–1867*, published by the U.S. Government.

   The Louisiana Purchase doubled the size of the United States as it then was and represents approximately 23 percent of the territory of the United States today. Not only did it include the whole of what is now Louisiana west of the Mississippi river with the critically important port city of New Orleans as the center piece, but also all of present day Arkansas, Missouri, Iowa, Oklahoma, Kansas and Nebraska, parts of Minnesota south of the Mississippi river, most of North Dakota and South Dakota, north-east New Mexico, the northern part of Texas and those parts of Colorado, Montana and Wyoming east of the continental divide.

6   See C Alan Jennings, Richard P Bullock and Susan L Johnson, *Fundamentals of Louisiana Notarial Law and Practice*, (2009), published pursuant to LA R S 35:191.1(B)(2) by the Louisiana Secretary of State in co-operation with Louisiana State University.

Notaries in the English colonies

The lineage of the modern American notariat may be traced back to the notaries of the 13 English colonies which became the original states of the Union; in particular to the notaries of the New England colonies.[7] Initially, notaries were few and far between. Occasionally, but not often, they were appointed by the Court of Faculties of the Archbishop of Canterbury in England,[8] but, in the main, appointments were made by colonial governors or by the General Assemblies or General Courts of the various colonies.

Thomas Fugill appears to be the first person in the English colonies to have held the office of notary public. The Province of New Haven was established in 1638. On 25 October 1939, Fugill was appointed by the General Court of the Province as

> ... publique notary to attend the court and from time to time to keep a faithful record of all passages and conclusions of the court and of whatever else then or at other times shall by the court or magistrate be committed to him concerning the civil publique occasions of the plantation.[9]

At first, colonial notaries acted as recorders and record keepers for colonial administrators in the manner of the English ecclesiastical notaries, rather than as private professionals.[10] However, from the mid-1640s, as trade with the West Indies and England grew, the number of notaries steadily increased and their focus shifted to matters commercial. Within a relatively short time, protesting dishonored bills of exchange, preparing powers of attorney, charter-parties and bottomry bonds and noting marine protests became staple fare in New England and then in the newer colonies.

---

7 English colonization commenced in the late 16th century, when the Colony of Jamestown was established on a small river near Chesapeake Bay on the east coast of North America. The colonies grew steadily throughout the 17th and early 18th centuries, initially in 'New England' where the Connecticut Colony, the Plymouth Colony, the Massachusetts Bay Colony, the Province of New Hampshire and the Colony of Rhode Island developed into early commercial and trading centers with Boston as the principal port.

The English also absorbed the so-called 'Middle Colonies' comprising the present day States of New York, New Jersey, Pennsylvania and Delaware. Around the same time, they established new colonies in Maryland, Virginia, the Carolinas and Georgia.

For an overview of the history and role of notaries in the original 13 colonies, see John E Seth, *Notaries in the American Colonies*, 32 John Marshall Law Review (1998-1999), 863.

The notaries in the colonies were invariably men. The story of the gradual feminization of the office of notary from colonial times to the end of the 20th century is told by Deborah M Thaw in *The Feminisation of the Office of Notary Public : From Female Covert to Notaire Covert*, 31 John Marshall Law Review (1998), 703.

8 In 1533, the English parliament passed the *Ecclesiastical Licenses Act* pursuant to which the power of the Pope to appoint notaries in (then Catholic) England and in the dominions of the English Crown was removed and given to the Archbishop of Canterbury, who made appointments through his Court of Faculties. From that time onwards, the appointment of notaries in England has exclusively been within the gift of the Archbishop.

9 Quoted by Seth, above 876 ff.

10 Seth, above 876 ff.

Since Independence

Since Independence, the power to appoint notaries and regulate their activities has essentially rested with the states.[11] Authority for the federal government to appoint and regulate military notaries is derived from the power granted to Congress by the Constitution, 'To make Rules for the Government and Regulation of the land and naval forces'.[12]

On 5 March 1791, Pennsylvania enacted the first legislation in the United States appointing and granting powers to notaries.[13] Noting in its preamble that, 'the establishment of public notaries has been found useful in all commercial countries', the Act empowered the Governor to appoint six notaries for Philadelphia and three for the (then) remaining counties.[14]

The Act set out the powers of the new notaries with some particularity as follows:

Section III

That the said notaries, so commissioned as aforesaid and every of them shall have the power of administering oaths and affirmations according to law, in all matters belonging or incident to the exercise of their notarial office, and that all and every person and persons, that shall be legally convicted of wilfully and knowingly made or taken a false oath or affirmation before any notary or notaries, in any matter or matters within his or their official duty, shall suffer the pains and penalties of wilful and corrupt perjury.

Section IV

That the said notaries, and every of them, shall have the power to receive the proof or acknowledgment of all instruments of writing relating to commerce or navigation, such as bills of sale, bottomries, mortgages, and hypothecations of ships or vessels, charter-parties of affreightment, letters of attorney, and such other writings, as have been usually proved or acknowledged before notaries within this commonwealth, and also to make declarations, and testify the truth thereof under their seals of office, concerning all matters by them done in virtue of their respective offices.[15]

---

11 The Constitution is silent as to the appointment and regulation of notaries. However, as is made clear by the 10th Amendment – The States' Rights Amendment – (Ratified 15 December 1791), 'The powers not delegated to the United States by the Constitution, nor prohibited by it to the States, are reserved to the States respectively, or to the people.'

12 *U.S. Constitution*, Article 1, Section 8.

13 *An Act to Enable the Government to appoint Notaries Public, and for other purposes therein.* Recorded in the Commonwealth of Pennsylvania Law Book No. IV, 131.

   (John Bioren, Volume III, *Laws of the Commonwealth of Pennsylvania from the Fourteenth Day of October One Thousand Seven Hundred on the Twentieth Day of March One Thousand Eight Hundred and Ten* Philadelphia (1810).

14 Ibid, Section II.

   Pittsburgh businessman Isaac Craig was the first notary appointed under the Act.

15 Ibid.

Importantly, as a by-product of codifying the powers of its notaries, Pennsylvania provided a model for other states and territories to follow.[16]

A ministerial officer

Uniquely in the world, notaries today in the United States, as a class, are ministerial officers.[17] Their duties are of a ministerial nature.

> Whether a person is a ministerial officer depends not so much on the character of the particular act he or she is called upon to perform, or whether he or she exercises a judgment or discretion with reference to such act, as upon the general nature and scope of the duties devolving on him or her. If these are of a ministerial character, then the person charged with their performance is a ministerial officer.[18]

A notary's acts are ministerial acts. A ministerial act is

> ... commonly one that is simple, absolute and definite, arising under conditions admitted or proved to exist, and requiring merely the execution of a specific duty ... [as opposed to a judicial or discretionary act] ... which calls for the exercise of personal deliberation and judgment, which in turn entails examining the facts, reaching reasoned conclusions and acting on them in a way not specifically directed.[19]

As ministerial officers, notaries are obliged to carry out their duties strictly in accordance with statute, common law amplifications of the legislation and the materials and guidelines published by the relevant state or territory authorities. This does not mean that American notaries must leave their brains at the door when arriving at work each day. On the contrary. Carrying out the duties of a ministerial office always requires sensitivity and common sense. On occasion it involves the exercise of a degree of judgment and discretion.

As the Supreme Court of Nebraska observed over a century ago:

> If ministerial officers can perform nothing but ministerial acts, then it is hard to conceive of such officer, for some of the acts of every ministerial officer must require the exercise of judgment and discretion, which is the very antithesis of a ministerial act.[20]

---

16 For example, on 1 February 1803, the legislature of the Mississippi Territory (which included what is now Alabama) passed *An Act Concerning Notaries Public* which set out the powers of notaries virtually word for word as those powers were set out in the Pennsylvania Act. (Harry Toulmin, (Ginn & Curtis, 1828), *A Digest of the Laws of the State of Alabama*.)

17 See *Bernal v Fainter* 467 U.S. 216 (1984).

18 63C Am Jur 2d Public officers and Employees §21.

19 Supreme Court of Georgia, *Georgia Department of Transportation v Heller* 285 Ga (2009) 262 at 267.

20 *State v Loechner* 91 N.W. 874 (1902) at 876.

The Court went on to endorse the view expressed by the Supreme Court of Indiana in *Waldo v Wallace* 12 Ind 569 (1859) that, 'A judge will not be less a judicial officer because some duties he may have to perform are ... [ministerial] ... in character; nor will a ... [ministerial] ... officer become a judicial officer simply because some of his duties may be to some extent judicial in their character.'

However, as will be seen below and in the chapters which follow, the ministerial nature of American notarial powers and duties and the restrictions imposed on notaries in the exercise of their office often makes it extremely difficult, if not impossible, for them to meet the expectations of courts, legal professionals, public officials, bankers, patent and trademark attorneys and others abroad when notarizing documents for international use.

Powers of U.S. notaries

While the emphasis has changed over the years to meet the commercial requirements of the day, the basic statutory powers of U.S. notaries have remained remarkably consistent since the Pennsylvania legislators first sought to regulate their authority.

The evolution of the office during the 19th century saw some states conferring singular powers on their notaries. For example, at the turn of the 20th century:

- notaries in Alabama were empowered to 'collect delinquent taxes' and 'issue attachments' as well as 'to determine the offence of cruelty to animals;'[21]
- in Maine, notaries could grant warrants of survey on vessels;[22]
- Massachusetts notaries had power to give notice to owners of insecure building 'who live out of the Commonwealth';[23]
- in Missouri, notaries were entitled to 'perform the duties of register of boatmen';[24]
- notaries in Ohio had the power to imprison a witness for refusing to answer a question to a deposition; and
- in South Carolina, notaries were authorized to 'take renunciations of dower'.[25]

Most of those powers have since fallen by the wayside.

Nowadays, across the board, notaries in the United States have two absolutely fundamental powers:

- the power to take acknowledgments; and
- the power to administer oaths and affirmations.

Those powers are supplemented variously in each U.S. jurisdiction by

---

21 Edwards Mills John, *The American Notary and Commissioner of Deeds Manual*, (Callaghan & Company, 2nd ed, 1904), 15.
22 Ibid, 27.
23 Ibid, 28.
24 Ibid, 31.
25 Ibid, 40.
   That power is still on the South Carolina statute book, but for all practical purposes is in disuse.

authority to perform one or more other notarial acts, including:

- certifying copies of documents;
- witnessing or attesting signatures;
- receiving marine protests; and
- executing protests of negotiable instruments.[26]

The illusion of extraterritorial power

Legislation in New York, Nebraska and the District of Columbia purports to vest notaries in those jurisdictions with powers that operate extraterritorially. The formulations differ, but in essence, all three statutes provide that in addition to their ordinary powers, notaries may also

> ... exercise any powers or perform any acts for use and effect in other countries which according to the laws of those countries may be exercised or performed by notaries public.[27]

Much as the legislators might have wished to grant their own notaries power to prepare documents in America which would have the same legal force and effect in say, France or Germany, as would documents prepared by local notaries in those countries, New York, Nebraska and DC notaries simply do not have that power. American law cannot and does not operate extraterritorially in relation to foreign domestic legal practice or procedure. It cannot unilaterally bind foreign governments, courts and institutions any more than French or German statutes can unilaterally bind the United States government or American courts or institutions.[28]

A proper analysis of the position makes it clear that the latter references to notaries public in the relevant provisions of the three statutes are references to notaries holding office in each of the jurisdictions. They are not references to notaries holding office abroad. On that basis, the additional power given to New York, Nebraska and DC notaries has practical meaning and effect.

It is entirely a matter for the law of a foreign jurisdiction to determine whether or not the act of a notary from any other country will be recognised or have any efficacy within its borders. Take Australia as an example. Australian courts accept into evidence properly authenticated copies of private documents certified by foreign notaries. Therefore, copy documents certified by notaries in

---

26 For a comprehensive guide to notarial powers and notarization requirements for all United States jurisdictions, see Charles N Faerber, *U.S. Notary Reference Manual*, (National Notary Association, 10th ed, 2010). The manual is revised and published every two years.

27 *New York Executive Law*, Article 6, §135.

  Nebraska Revised Statutes, 64-107.

  Code of the District of Columbia, 1-1209 (The DC Code limits the countries where the purported power may be exercised to those 'in amity with the United States').

28 See generally, Stuart Dutson, *The Territorial Application of Statutes*, 22 Monash University Law Review (1996) and Alexander Layton and Angharad M Parry, *Extraterritorial Jurisdiction – European Responses*, 26 Houston Journal of International Law (2003-2004).

  Also see Pedro A Malavet, *The Foreign Notarial Legal Services Monopoly: Why Should We Care*, 31 John Marshall Law Review (1997 – 1998).

states such as Kansas and Oklahoma, where notaries are specifically authorized to do so, may readily be produced in Australia. In states such as Alaska and North Carolina, notaries are not empowered to certify copy documents at all. No amount of Australian legislation can authorize notaries in those jurisdictions to lawfully certify copy documents within their own states for any purpose in Australia.

On the other hand, notaries in Nebraska, New York and DC, although not authorized to certify copies of documents for domestic purposes, are entitled, by virtue of the unique provisions of their governing legislation, to certify copies of documents with impunity for production in Australia as well as in all other countries prepared to recognize American notarial acts of that nature.

The legislation creating 'civil law' notaries in Alabama and Florida, while directed towards empowering certain notaries in those states to prepare authentic form documents for production in civil law jurisdictions, is not as presumptuous as the New York, Nebraska or DC legislation. It merely gives specially qualified notaries the power to prepare authentic form documents. It is expected that the receiving states will accept those documents by virtue of their nomenclature and style and by virtue of the fact that they have been prepared by trained notaries who are also senior attorneys.

Where the statute is silent – enter the common law

Typically, statutes in the United States conferring powers on notaries are minimalist in style and offer little or no guidance as to the proper exercise of the powers. In those circumstances, save where other legislation is prescriptive, for example in relation to the administering of oaths and affirmations, or where guidelines are provided in materials published by notary administrators, recourse may be had to the common law to fill gaps in the legislation and where necessary, to assist in the proper conduct of the office. [29]

---

29 The common law is 'The part of English law that is applied by national courts, but is not fully prescribed by statute, purporting instead to be derived from ancient usage and judicial decisions. (*The New Shorter Oxford Dictionary*, (1993), entry for 'common law'.)

The first professor of law at Columbia College (1793–1798) and subsequently, Chief Justice of the New York Supreme Court and Chancellor New York, James Kent, described the common law as being, 'those principles, usages and rules of action applicable to the government and security of person and property which do not rest for their authority upon any express and positive declaration of the will of the legislature'.

Kent went on to say that:

'A great proportion of the rules and maxims which constitute the immense code of the common law grew into use by gradual adoption and received from time to time, the sanction of the courts of justice, without any legislative act or interference. It ... [is] ... the application of the dictates of natural justice and of cultivated reason to particular cases'.

(Lecture XXI *Commentaries on American Law*, (12th ed). Edited by OW Holmes Jr. 1873 Boston.

As to the relationship of the common law to statute, also see William N Eskridge, Jr, Philip P Frickey and Elizabeth Garrett, *Legislation and Statutory Interpretation* (2nd ed Foundation Press, 2006), 298 ff and Congressional Research Service Report, *Statutory Interpretation: General Principles and Recent Trends* (Updated August 31, 2008), 16-218.

The preparation of ship protests and the rules relating to their notarial certification and the associated entries in the notary's register provide a classic case in point. No U.S. legislation concerning the powers of notaries in relation to receiving marine protests gives any direction at all to notaries as to how to exercise their powers. Only the common law has the answers.[30]

Two of America's most highly regarded and influential experts on notarial law and practice have recently written a long and persuasive essay in support of the proposition that where statutes are silent in relation to notaries keeping journals or registers, the common law imposes a duty on them to do so.[31] For present purposes there is no need to rehearse their argument. Suffice to say that they endorse the place of the common law in modern American notarial practice as described above.

It is however important to note that in the United States, no tenet of the common law confers powers and authorities on notaries which are not conferred by statute. Even so, on occasion, wishful thinkers have looked to the history of the notariat and to common law in an attempt to find justification for claims that statutes are not conclusive in establishing notarial powers and determining their extent.

For example, in the late 1940s, New York Attorney Phanor James Eder advanced the extraordinary notion that in the light of the long history of the office of notary and the law existing in the colonies and wholly apart from the statutes governing the powers of notaries in the mid-20th century,

> the authority of notaries in the United States to execute powers of attorney ... [in public form] ... for production in civil law jurisdictions ... would seem indubitable.[32]

Eder then went on to advance an even more bizarre proposition that,

> The authority of a notary executing a power of attorney as a public instrument, under the law of nations, includes the power to certify the correctness of transcriptions or copies he makes of documents presented to him and the power to make or certify to (sic) translations.[33]

The unauthorized practice of law

When carrying out their duties, both generally and for international purposes, notaries must always be careful not to overstep the limits of their authority and accidentally stray into the unauthorized practice of law.

---

30 See Chapter 8 for a discussion concerning ship protests.

31 Michael L Closen and Charles N Faerber, *The Case That There is a Common Law Duty of Notaries Public to Create and Preserve Detailed Journal Records of their Official Acts*, 42 John Marshall Law Review, (2008-2009) 231.

32 *Powers of Attorney in International Practice*, (98 U Pa L Rev, 1949-1950), 840 at 844.

33 Ibid, 845.

It is easily done. For example, documents to be executed on behalf of American corporations for production in South Korea or Thailand, which have been prepared in those countries, usually include pre-printed certificates for the notary to sign to the effect that the corporation 'is a juristic [or "juridical"] person' and that the signatory 'is authorized to sign ... [the document] ... on its behalf.' On any occasion, both statements may well be true and the truth of both may well readily be ascertained. However, certificates of that nature constitute certificates of law. As such, they are beyond the power of most American notaries to provide.

As discussed in Chapter 7, many Latin American countries, including Mexico, insist upon comprehensive and wide ranging notarial certificates to be appended to simple powers of attorney for production within their jurisdictions. The required certificates constitute the provision of legal opinions, as is the case with the 'juristic person' certificates for South Korea and Thailand referred to above.

Only licensed attorneys or American civil law notaries should prepare and sign those certificates.

Where a certificate containing a legal opinion is prepared and completed by an attorney, a notary is then able to take and certify the attorney's acknowledgment or sworn statement. If the notary does otherwise and personally completes or signs the certificate as provided, then he or she has gone too far and has committed an offence.

Often enough, unauthorized practice of law is innocent and unintentional. Notaries, paralegals, accountants, realtors, bankers and insurance salespeople are prominent among those who most commonly violate the rules. Typically, they do so with the best of intentions.[34]

The problem is not new. In 1914, a Special Committee of the New York County Lawyers Association reported 'On the Unlawful Practice of Law by Corporations or Individuals (including Notaries).' The Committee found that:

> A great many notaries ... not lawyers, some of whom have not even served a clerkship in a law office, and have practically no knowledge whatever of the law, have solicited, undertaken, and received pay for the drawing of deeds, mortgages, contracts, wills, powers of attorney and other legal documents and papers and have inserted advertisements in newspapers and directories published in this city and elsewhere. ... The injury to the community is great, and some effort should be made to prevent it from the continuance of this evil practice.[35]

Notoriously difficult to define, the 'practice of law' is a right granted to attorneys upon admission to the bar of an American state or territory. One of the best known and most comprehensive definitions emanates from the Arizona Supreme Court which has stated that the practice of law comprises:

---

34 See generally, Sandra L Buhas, *Act Like a Lawyer, Be Judged Like a Lawyer: The Standard of Care for the Unlicensed Practice of Law*, 2007 Utah Law Review, 87.

35 *79 Central Law Journal*, (1914), 22 at 23.

    These days unscrupulous notaries are directing their efforts toward the Latin American immigrant communities by holding themselves out to be 'notarios' which is the equivalent of holding out to be lawyers.

... those acts, whether performed in court or in the law office which lawyers customarily have carried on from day to day through centuries ... [including but not limited to] ... one person assisting or advising another in the preparation of documents or writings which affect, alter or define legal rights; the direct or indirect giving of advice relative to legal rights or liabilities; the preparation for another of matters for courts, administrative agencies and other judicial or quasi-judicial bodies and officials as well as the acts of representation of another before such a body or officer.[36]

The unauthorized practice of law is prohibited by legislation in every United States jurisdiction, other than Arizona, which instead relies on the decision of its Supreme Court.[37] In most jurisdictions, it is a criminal offence with serious or flagrant breaches occasionally categorized as felonies.[38]

There are several useful publications which will help notaries keep clear of the unauthorized practice of law. For example, although directed to clerks of court and other court staff who provide telephone and over the counter service to the public, the Michigan Judicial Institute booklet *Legal Advice v Access to the Courts* contains a number of 'tips' and guidelines which will be of assistance.[39]

'Tips' include the following:

• Whenever you hear the word 'should', it is a tip that you are being asked for advice.

• Telling someone 'how' to do something does not usually cross the legal advice line. Telling someone what he/she 'should' do , does cross the legal advice line.

• Do not fill out forms *unless* there is a handicap or physical disability that prevents the person from filling out the form. If possible, it is recommended that an [independent] witness be present.[40]

Notaries who are also attorneys

A good many American attorneys are also notaries, but their status as lawyers does not confer additional powers on them when they act as notaries. Indeed, on one view, because they are attorneys, an even greater onus is placed on them to act 'according to Hoyle' when carrying out their notarial functions.

---

36 *State Bar of Arizona v Arizona Land and Title Trust Co.*, 366 P.2d 1, 14 (Ariz.1961).

37 See Jonathan Rose, *Unauthorized practice of Law in Arizona; A legal and political problem that won't go away*, 34 Ariz St L J 585 (2002).

38 See generally Deborah L Rhode, *The Delivery of Legal Services by Non Lawyers*, 4 Geo J Legal Ethics, 209 (1990-91).

39 The booklet has been endorsed by the Michigan Supreme Court as a model for providing information to the public.

40 The Michigan Judicial Institute has kindly given its consent to quote from its valuable publication. Also see Guiding Principal VI of *The Notary Public Code of Professional Responsibility,* (National Notary Association, November 1998).

To the extent that an attorney/notary is able to engage in the practice of law in relation to a notarial act, for example, by determining which certificate is to be used to evidence the act, he or she does so *qua* attorney and not *qua* notary.

Unless local legislation specifically empowers them to do so, being an attorney does not enable a notary to prepare and provide notarial certificates of a type and style for domestic or international use which are beyond the powers of ordinary notaries to provide.

E-notarization

Fully one-third of the National Notary Association's *Model Notary Act* (2010) is devoted to electronic notarization,[41] and with good reason. There is no doubt that for domestic purposes, e-notarization will be a significant part of the future for American notaries.

Driven by the needs of both government and business, the electronic age is now well and truly a reality in the United States. It is safe to predict that within the next 10 or 15 years, a large proportion, perhaps even the majority, of the billion or so documents currently notarized for domestic purposes in the USA each year will be signed and notarized electronically.[42]

E-notarization for international purposes

On the other hand, presently, electronic notarization by American notaries for international purposes is virtually non-existent. Which raises two basic questions. Firstly, when will e-notarization extend to documents to be used internationally and secondly, what will be the obligations of American notaries in that regard?

---

41 See Article III of the *Model Notary Act*, (2010) prepared and published as a public service by the National Notary Association.

42 U.S. notaries are served by a national legislative framework based upon the *Uniform Electronic Transaction Act* (UETA) and the enactment of the federal *Electronic Signatures in Global and National Commerce Act* (E-Sign), supplemented by legislation in a growing number of states specifically directed toward electronic notarization.

UETA was originally approved and recommended in 1999 by the National Conference of Commissioners on Uniform State Laws to provide a legal framework for the use of electronic records and signatories in government and commercial transactions. In the following 10 years, 47 states, DC, Puerto Rico and the Virgin Islands all adopted UETA. Illinois, New York and Washington did not do so, but each of those states has its own legislation dealing with electronic transactions.

On 30 June 2000, Congress enacted E-Sign (Public Law 106-229) to 'facilitate the use of electronic records and signatures in interstate or foreign commerce'. Section 101(g) of E-Sign specifically deals with notarizations and provides that 'If a statute, regulation, or other rule of law requires a signature or record relating to a transaction in or affecting interstate or foreign commerce to be notarized, acknowledged, verified or made under oath, that requirement is satisfied if the electronic signature of the person authorized to perform those acts, together with all other information required to be included by other applicable statute, regulation or rule of law, is attached to or logically associated with the signature or record'.

To answer the second question first. Article III of the *Model Notary Act* (2010) specifically addresses the role of notaries and the method of notarization in the electronic world. In parenthesis, it is noted that there is not, nor should there be, any distinction drawn between the duties of notaries for domestic and international purposes.

In their commentary at the commencement of the Article, the framers of the *Model Notary Act* (2010) are adamant that:

> The fundamental principles and processes of traditional notarization must apply ... [to electronic notarization] ... regardless of the technology used to create a signature. No principle is more critical to notarization than that a signer must appear in person before a duly commissioned notary public to affix or acknowledge the signature and be screened for identity, volition and basic awareness by the notary at the time of the notarial act.[43]

Importantly, the framers go on to say that contrary to popular understanding, electronic notarization does not mean 'remote' notarization with a notary in front of a computer at location 'A' and the principal before another computer at location 'B'.[44]

Virtually all American jurisdictions which have enacted legislation allowing e-notarization, support the NNA's position as expressed in the *Model Notary Act*. For example, while observing that 'currently the uses for electronic notarization are limited', the Colorado Secretary of State has posted the following statement on the 'Notary' page of the Department's official website:

> **Electronic notarization does not mean remote notarization.** As with all notarizations, the signer must appear in the physical presence of the notary to affirm, swear or acknowledge the document to be notarized.[45]

However, in a move which, at once, appears to be both forward looking and out of step with current thinking elsewhere in the United States, the Commonwealth of Virginia has recently amended the *Virginia Notary Act* with effect from 1 July 2012, to provide that in the case of electronic notarization, 'satisfactory evidence of identity' may be provided via 'video and audio conference technology' (i.e. remotely), subject to a number of very strict standards being met.[46]

---

43 Article III, *Model Notary Act*, (2010) 87.

44 Ibid.

45 <www.sos.state.co.us/pubs/notary/eNotary7.html>

   Also see by way of further example:

   New Mexico, *Frequently Asked Questions for e-Notarization*, Question #3

   North Carolina, *Electronic Notary Program Frequently Asked Questions*, Question 5

   Pennsylvania, Frequently Asked Questions about the Department of State's Electronic Notarization Program, 2 and 7

   Texas, *Frequently Asked Questions for Notaries Public*, Question #23 *Physical Appearance Requirement*

46 Code of Virginia §47.1-2 *Definitions*, (Definition of 'Satisfactory evidence of Identity')

   Also see *A Handbook for Virginia Notaries Public*, July 1, 2011, 9.

Given:

- the rigor and expense of the required standard of two-way live teleconferencing;

- the general lack of appropriate facilities;

- the time and effort likely to be involved in making necessary arrangements;

- the 'very high threshold for identity' imposed by the legislation;

- the amount and standard of record keeping involved; and

- the number of notaries available who are qualified to undertake 'standard' face to face e-notarization,

it is hard to see how remote electronic notarization as legislated in Virginia will ever be other than a marginal practice.

The real problem will be if, for 'convenience', Virginia or other jurisdictions adopting the Virginia model water down its strict requirements or if authorized notaries in Virginia or elsewhere honor those requirements in the breach.

Turning now to the first question. E-notarization for international purposes remains a pipe dream. Leaving aside the important associated issue of electronic authentication of electronic notarizations which is presently still in its infancy, there is no demand anywhere in the world for electronically notarized personal or commercial documents emanating from other countries to be circulated in electronic form.

In addition, international confidence in and acceptance of electronic notarization will only occur if the entire process is founded upon rock solid technical foundations. At its most fundamental level, this means that the systems used to support e-notarization must be interoperable, which presently they are not.

'Interoperability' is the ability of systems to share information and data in a reliable and secure manner. It is

> being able to accomplish end user applications using different types of computer systems, operating systems and application software, interconnected by different types of local and wide area networks.[47]

Unfortunately, despite massive investment in electronic communications technology by governments around the world, it appears that reliable and seamless interoperability of systems internationally is a long way off.[48]

---

47 James O'Brien and George M Maraka, *Introduction to Information Systems* (13th ed McGraw-Hill Irwin), 512.

48 See generally, Ali M Al-Khouri, *An Innovative Approach for E-Government Transformation*, International Journal of Managing Value and Supply Chains, Vol 2, no. 1 March 2011, 22.

CHAPTER 4

Oaths, Affirmations, Affidavits and Declarations

The power to administer oaths and affirmations and the right to receive affidavits for domestic purposes have long been within the statutory powers conferred on notaries in the United States. However, the ability of American notaries to administer oaths and affirmations and to receive affidavits and take declarations for use abroad actually stems from the legislation or practices of the foreign countries in which the affidavits or declarations are to be produced. Typically, notaries are specified as being among, and often prime among, the office holders approved by foreign jurisdictions to undertake the tasks outside their borders.[1]

Oaths

Oaths have been known since at least biblical times.[2] They have always been a feature of the common law landscape.[3] Their function was to ensure, under threat of divine sanction, that witnesses would tell the truth. In times past, the oath was not used to enhance the credibility of *viva voce* evidence; rather, it was a mode of proof in itself which constituted a complete procedure for the determination of the truth.[4]

---

1   The reverse is also true. The regulations as to persons outside the United States who may administer an oath or affirmation and receive an affidavit for use within the United States are fixed by the federal, state and territory governments. Invariably, foreign notaries are included in the list of approved officeholders.

2   For example, in *Genesis*, Ch 26 vv 28 and 29, it is recounted that Isaac and Abimelech swore oaths to each other. In *Genesis* Ch 47 vv 29 to 31, Jacob had his son Joseph swear that he would not bury him in Egypt. (*The Illustrated Jerusalem Bible*, ed M. Friedlander).

     In *Essays on Criminal Procedure* (1964), 16-79, Professor Helen Silving examines the origin and development of the oath in civil law systems and in Anglo-American law, and concludes that the oath has remained an atavistic survival of an ancient ritual – a primitive self-curse, which can be traced to a pre-religious, animistic period of culture.

3   For an overview of the oath and its use in civil law jurisdictions, see Law Reform Commission of Ireland, *Report on Oaths and Affirmations* (LRC 34-1990), Chapter 3 : *Some Comparative Aspects*.

4   Mark Weinberg, *The Law of Testimonial Oaths and Affirmations,* Monash University Law Review (Vol 3 November 1976, 28).

     Compurgation, which was an early method of trial, originally involved parties to a dispute swearing an oath as to the truth or falsity of the facts and being supported by a number of 'compurgators' or oath-helpers. From about the 12th century, the compurgators did not swear their oaths in relation to the matters at issue, but instead, in relation to their belief in the principal's oath.

When the common law ultimately dispensed with compurgation and other arcane modes of trial such as trial by battle and trial by ordeal in favour of the adversarial witness oriented trial, the testimonial oath took on a different role.[5]

Initially, only Christians were considered to have the religious belief necessary to swear oaths. Then, in 1668, in *Robeley v Langston*,[6] the court held that as the Old Testament was within the general words of *Sacrosancta Evangelia*, if Jews swore on the Old Testament, the necessary obligations and sanctions required by law would be sufficiently invoked.

The class of persons able to make oaths was further expanded by the landmark English court decision in *Omychund v Barker*.[7] The case related to the ability of persons of 'Gentoo' (i.e. Hindu) religion to give evidence on oath. In bringing down its decision, the court was at pains to definitively restate the common law rule that allowing a person to give evidence without first taking an oath was not possible because there could be no guarantee that the person would tell the truth.

The court then went on to say that it would be absurd for an infidel (i.e. a non-Christian) to 'swear according to the Christian oath which he does not believe', and that because the infidel believed in 'a God as the Creator of the Universe' who was 'a rewarder of those who do well and an avenger of those who do ill' and also believed in 'future rewards and punishments in the other world', he was therefore competent to take an oath in whichever manner would bind his conscience and religious convictions.[8]

---

5   Weinberg, above, 28.

   Weinberg also comments (at 28) that Coke, in his first *Institute*, rationalised the oath as enhancing the credibility of a witness, since if a witness testified on oath and was not immediately struck down, Divine judgment was pronouncing him to be a truth teller.

   The infamous Lord Chief Justice Jeffries took a more robust view of the function of an oath and the effect of the failure by a witness to tell the truth, as may be seen from his warning to the witness Mr. James Dunne in the *Trial of the Lady Alice Lisle for High Treason* (1685 11 How St Tr 326), viz;

   > ... consider that the Great God of Heaven and Earth before whose tribunal thou, and we, and all persons are to stand on the last day, will call thee to account for the rescinding of the truth and take vengeance of thee for every falsehood thou tellest ... for that God of Heaven may justly strike thee into eternal flames and make thee drop into the bottomless lake of fire and brimstone, if thou offer to deviate from the truth and nothing but the truth.

6   2 Keb 315.

7   1 Atk 22 (1744).

8   Being able to swear a witness by the method most binding on his conscience led to some unusual and bizarre oaths being approved by the courts in England and the Dominions. The Chinese 'chicken' oath which was a ritual attached to a Chinese secret society and not an oath at all was apparently performed in British Columbia in 1902 and involved the decapitation of a live rooster, followed by the incineration of the written oath.

   Another so-called 'oath' for Chinese witnesses, reference to which, embarrassingly, still may be found from time to time in text books, court bench books and manuals dealing with oaths, required the witness to break a saucer and then to incant, 'If I do not tell the truth, may my soul be cracked like this saucer.' In *My Sixty Years in the Law* (1936), F W Ashley recounts a story in which Avory J was presiding at the Liverpool Assizes in a case concerning hostilities between two Chinese gangs. Numerous Chinese witnesses were called and each of them gave evidence on oath after breaking a saucer in the witness box. When the last witness gave his evidence, he did so standing ankle deep in smashed crockery. (Cited in *Wigmore on Evidence* (3rd ed) para 1818).

The oath in the United States

When the colonies and later the states passed their first laws relating to oaths, they did so against a background of the English common law and in the light of *Omychund*. From the earliest days, the Judeo-Christian oath was the 'standard' oath typically administered throughout the country. However, the right to make any other religious oath which was binding on the maker's conscience gradually found its way into the laws of most states and territories either via their constitutions or by virtue of specific legislation.

The religious oath lost its privileged position in America in 1975 on the introduction of the *Federal Rules of Evidence*. Not only did those Rules immediately bind the extensive federal court network, but they also served as models for state courts. Within a relatively few years most state courts within the United States had adopted new rules, largely based on the federal model.

Rules 601 and 610 of the *Federal Rules of Evidence* set out the overall guidelines as to the competency of witnesses to give evidence and therefore to swear an oath or affirm.

Rule 601 provides that:

> Every person is competent to be a witness except as otherwise provided in these rules

In so providing, the Rule moderated the severity of the old common law which dictated that people without religious conviction and certain others, such as minors, were incompetent and therefore unable to take a witness' oath or testify.

Rule 610 provides that:

> Evidence of the belief or opinions of a witness on matters of religion is not admissible for the purpose of showing that by reason of their nature the witness' credibility is impaired or enhanced.[9]

Rule 603 deals with the requirement for each witness to swear or affirm that he or she will testify truthfully. Importantly, the Rule does not prescribe a particular form or oath or affirmation. It simply provides:

> Before testifying, every witness shall be required to declare that the witness will testify truthfully by oath or affirmation administered in a form calculated to awaken the witness' conscience and impress the witness' mind with the duty to do so.[10]

Despite its apparent simplicity, Rule 603 initially prompted not inconsiderable litigation in relation to the forms of oaths and affirmations which could lawfully be administered. Partly as a result of the litigation and partly because the Rules are not prescriptive, forms and ceremonies differ from state to state. Overall, with few exceptions, 'flexibility' and 'latitude' have become the watchwords in relation to the form and administration of oaths across the United States.

---

9   FED R EVID 610.

10 FED R EVID 603.

The Arizona Constitution, as updated on 14 April 2009, is indicative of the modern approach now taken. It provides that:

> The mode of administering an oath or affirmation shall be such as shall be most consistent with and binding upon the conscience of the person to whom such oath or affirmation may be administered.[11]

Only seven states still explicitly refer to the use of the Bible in their legislation concerning the administration of oaths.[12] But, in each of those states, legislation allows non-Christians or persons who have 'conscientious scruples against taking an oath' to either be sworn according to their own religious requirements or to affirm.

The use of religious texts

In 2002, the Law Reform Committee of the Parliament of Victoria in Australia, undertook a wide ranging inquiry into oaths and affirmations. The terms of reference included consideration of the significance of sacred texts to persons of particular faiths in relation to the taking of oaths.[13]

Several witnesses who gave evidence to the Committee noted that the ritual of swearing on a religious text is a Christian construct, transported (inappropriately in many cases) to other religions.[14] It was further noted that it is commonly assumed that the non-Christian religions each have single religious texts which may be used in the making of oaths in the same way as the Bible is used.

> In some religions, swearing on a religious text is meaningless or even offensive. For example, Sikhs do not regard the Granth as a holy book outside the Temple and would not regard a Granth produced in court as being binding on their conscience.[15]

Evidence was given by the Buddhist Council to the effect that Buddhism does not have a single religious text and that it is not customary (or even acceptable in the Tibetan Buddhist tradition) to swear an oath on a religious text.[16]

Representatives of the Islamic community made the point that it is actually not appropriate for Muslims to use the Qur'an when swearing an oath.

> The Muslim's oath then is an act performed in the name of God. It is also an act of worship that means that the individual must approach the act with absolute integrity. The validity of the oath and the obligation it imposes flow directly from the invocation of the name of God.

---

11 Arizona Constitution, Article 2.

12 Arkansas [ARK CODE ANN §16-2-101(a)], Delaware [DEL CODE ANN 10§5321], Kansas [KAN STAT ANN §54-102], New Jersey, [NJ STAT ANN §41:1-4], North Carolina [NC GEN STAT ANN §11-2], Pennsylvania [42 PA CONS STAT ANN §5901(a)], and Virginia [VA CODE ANN §49-10]

13 During the course of the Inquiry, it became clear that the central issue was the importance of an appropriate form of religious oath rather than the significance of a particular religious text. (*VPLR Inquiry Report* October 2003, 79).

14 *VPLR Inquiry Report* October 2002, 82.

15 Ibid, 80.

16 Ibid, 81.

Its force is not dependent on the association of the act of oath taking with the presence of a sacred text. A Muslim does not, and should not, be asked to 'swear on the Qur'an'. The use of the Qur'an in court for the purpose of administering the oath is therefore unnecessary.[17]

It appears that it is sufficient for a Muslim to swear in the name of Allah and that is probably not necessary to hold the Qur'an when making the oath. The fact that many Muslim witnesses choose to swear on the Qur'an despite it being religiously inappropriate was put down to the general perception in the courts that some sort of holy book should be used in association with the making of an oath. Faced with that expectation, it is likely that many Muslim witnesses have accommodated the practice for the sake of simplicity and convenience.[18]

The Committee also noted the importance to many people of swearing an oath in accordance with their religion as opposed to swearing an oath on a particular religious text.[19]

From a notary's viewpoint, the issues canvassed by the Committee and the evidence given to it are important reminders that it should never simply be assumed that someone seeking to make an affidavit holds a religious belief or is of a particular faith or is prepared to make an oath in a particular manner or at all. Even though most people in America will readily swear an oath on the Bible, it is always appropriate for a notary to clarify the position immediately upon being presented with an affidavit or other document which is to be sworn.

Affirmations

The principles enunciated in *Omychund v Barker* guided the English courts until well into the 19th century. Until parliament ultimately intervened, one of the side effects of that case was that atheists and agnostics were prohibited from giving evidence and serving as jurors, on the grounds that a person who had no religious belief could not swear an oath.[20]

In the end, the problems caused by the strict attitude of the common law were resolved in England by the introduction of the affirmation to tell the truth which was a formal and binding declaration made by a person without any reference to Divine authority, intervention or retribution.[21]

---

17 Ibid, 81-82.

18 Ibid, 82-83.

19 Ibid, 86 and 95.

20 Apparently John Locke and Thomas Jefferson also both agreed that atheists should be excluded from public office because as they would not swear an oath to God they were therefore untrustworthy. (UK *Judicial Studies Board Benchbook* Ch 7 para 7.2 – now superseded).

21 In 1696, members of the Religious Society of Friends (Quakers), who had long objected to taking oaths on the ground that the act of swearing was blasphemous, were permitted by legislation (3 and 4 Wm IV ch 49) to testify in court after having made a statutory affirmation in place of an oath.

In 1833, the *Quakers and Moravians Act* was passed in England which provided that, if 'Every person of the persuasion of the people called Quakers and every Moravian be permitted to make his or her solemn affirmation or declaration instead of taking an oath'.

Finally, In 1869, by the *Evidence Further Amendment Act* and then in 1888, by the *Oaths Act*, the ability to make an affirmation was extended in the first instance to anyone who declared that the taking of an oath was contrary to his or her religious belief, and then to 'non-believers' generally.

Each American state and territory has legislated for the making of an affirmation for all purposes where an oath would otherwise be required to be made. Importantly in each jurisdiction an affirmation has the same force and effect at law as does an oath and must 'be taken and administered with the utmost solemnity'.[22]

Whenever an affirmation is made, care should be taken to ensure that the words and expressions in the body of the affidavit, in the jurat, and in the exhibit notes do not give the impression that the affiant has taken an oath as opposed to making a solemn and sincere affirmation. For example, in the typical jurat, 'Subscribed to and sworn before me' etc., the word 'sworn' must be deleted and replaced by the word 'affirmed'.

Affidavits generally

Receiving an affidavit is a serious matter which ought not be taken lightly by notaries or others authorized by law to carry out that function. As Professor Michael Closen has observed,

> ... the notarial oath and affirmation administration function is widely misunderstood, disparaged and neglected. The fact is that at least eighty to ninety percent of the time notaries do not actually administer the oral oaths or affirmations which are supposed to be performed. The consequence of the failure of notaries to really administer such oaths or affirmations constitutes a disservice to document signers, to the third parties who rely upon notarized signatures and to the office of notary public.[23]

The formalities relating to the taking of oaths and receiving affidavits vary marginally from jurisdiction to jurisdiction in America, but the substantive procedures are the same. The following guidelines are generally applicable throughout the United States and in most common law jurisdictions. The guidelines are also generally applicable in relation to the taking of statutory declarations for production in present and past Commonwealth of Nations jurisdictions. (See pages 44 and 45 below).

No blanks

Affidavits must be legible and should contain no blank spaces which could be filled in at a later time.

Exhibits

All exhibits referred to in an affidavit must be complete and at hand when the affidavit is being sworn. An exhibit note must be endorsed and marked on each exhibit, even if exhibits are physically attached to the affidavit.

---

22 For example, see North Carolina General Statutes §11-1.

23 Michael L Closen, *To swear or not to swear document signers. The Default of Notaries Public and a Proposal to Abolish Oral Notarial Oaths,* 50 Buffalo Law Review (2012) 613 at 617).

The classic formulation for an exhibit note is:

> This is the exhibit marked 'A' produced and shown to [*Affiant*] at the time of swearing his affidavit before me this _____ day of _____ 20__.

....
Notary Public's signature and seal

Suspicion of illegal or improper purposes

Although a notary is under no obligation to investigate or even comment on the veracity of the contents of an affidavit, if for any reason the notary suspects that the affidavit is being made for illegal or improper purposes, then the notary is duty bound to refuse to receive it.

Corrections and re-swearing

Before an affidavit is made, any interlineations and corrections must be initialled in the adjacent margin by both the affiant and the notary. Where the affidavit contains any erasures, any words or figures which have been written over the erasure must also be rewritten in the adjacent margin and must be initialled by both the affiant and the notary. Even if there are no corrections or amendments in it, both the affiant and the notary should sign each page of an affidavit at its foot after the oath has been taken.

Once an affidavit has been sworn, no alteration can be made to it. If after it has been sworn it is found necessary to make an alteration, then the entire affidavit must be re-sworn and a new jurat confirming the re-swearing must be added. Although not technically necessary, it is usual to have the affiant sign the affidavit adjacent to or above the new jurat, after any alteration has been made and initialled. The first jurat must not be struck out. On re-swearing, each page of an affidavit should again be signed at the foot by the affiant and by the notary. There is no requirement to re-initial any previous alterations or mark any exhibits again.

If an affidavit is sworn again after a notarial certificate has been appended to it, a second certificate relating to the re-swearing must be appended. Otherwise, one notarial certificate can cover both the initial swearing and the subsequent re-swearing. An affidavit which was originally sworn in the presence of a particular notary need not necessarily be re-sworn in the presence of the same notary.

Where two notaries have been involved in the swearing and re-swearing of an affidavit, if legalization is necessary, it will be necessary to have both notaries' signatures and seals legalized. It will also be necessary to have both certificates legalized in cases where the same notary has prepared and appended two notarial certificates in relation to an affidavit where legalization is necessary before it can be used in the destination country.[24]

---

24 See Chapter 10.

Multiple affiants

If an affidavit is to be sworn by two or more affiants and if they both attend together before the notary, they should be sworn in turn and not in unison. Ideally, a separate jurat should be used for each affiant. However, if both or all affiants are sworn at the same time before the same notary, there is no reason why a single jurat cannot be used which states that the affidavit was sworn by both or all of the (named) affiants.

Affiants who are deaf or hearing impaired

Where a deaf person or someone with serious hearing difficulties is required to swear an affidavit, it is appropriate to obtain the assistance of an interpreter if the person is able to communicate in sign language. If an interpreter is not available or the person is unable to communicate in sign language, but is nonetheless literate, it is acceptable to administer the oath in writing after the person has read and signed the affidavit.

To do so either the affiant must write the oath out in his or her own hand or make an affirmative gesture or written affirmative response to the question 'Is this your true name and handwriting?' and to the appropriate adjuration.

The jurat should then be completed in the normal way. If an interpreter assists in the making of the affidavit, then the jurat should also refer to the interpreter's own oath and to the fact of the interpretation.

Affiants who are blind, sight impaired, illiterate or physically disabled

Affiants who are illiterate, blind or unable to read due to severe sight impairment, may be sworn after the affidavit and any exhibits have been read out to them in full. Subject to the notary being satisfied that the affiant has understood and approved the contents of the affidavit and any exhibits referred to in it, if the affiant is able to sign the affidavit, he or she should do so. Otherwise the affiant should make a mark.[25]

If the affiant is to make a mark, best practice is to have two independent witnesses present at the time, at least one of whom should subsequently swear an affidavit confirming the making of the mark.

The following jurat may be of assistance to notaries where local legislation or materials do not provide appropriate 'marksman' forms

> Sworn/Affirmed before me this _____ day of _____ 20__ by the Affiant who being unable to sign his/her name, made his/her mark in my presence and in the presence of the witnesses [*1st witness name*] and [*2nd witness name*] both personally known to me or satisfactorily identified.
>
> ....
> Notary's signature and seal
> My commission expires on _____

---

25 Illiterate persons have often been taught to sign their names. They should be allowed to do so if they are able, even if they have had their affidavits read over to them.

On the rare occasion when faced with an affiant who is unable to even hold a pen by virtue of some illness or injury or disability, it may be appropriate for the notary to sign for the affiant. If that is allowed by the relevant state or territory legislation, the following jurat may assist where local legislation or materials do not provide specific forms for the purpose.

> Sworn/Affirmed before me this _____ day of _____ 20__ by the Affiant and subscribed by me with the Affiant's name on behalf of, and at the direction of the affidavit in the presence of the affiant and the two witnesses [*1st witness name*] and [*2nd witness name*] both personally known to me or satisfactorily identified.
>
> ....
> Notary's signature and seal
> My commission expires on _____

Affidavits made on behalf of entities

Legal and commercial entities such as corporations, cooperatives, unions and the like cannot swear oaths or make affirmations. Where an affidavit by an entity is required, it can only be made by an appropriately authorized person on the entity's behalf.

In those circumstances, the affidavit should commence, as always, with the affiant's name and address. It should then include in the first paragraph a statement to the effect that the affiant holds a particular office or position with the entity and 'being authorized' makes the affidavit on behalf of the entity.[26]

Minors

There is no requirement that a person be of a particular age to swear an affidavit. Persons under the age of majority may swear affidavits, even though they are still minors in the eyes of the law.[27] In the unusual case of a minor under the age of 14 years being required to swear an affidavit, a notary's duty is to ensure that, before being sworn, the child not only understands the contents of the affidavit, but also is aware of and appreciates the importance of the oath and the need to tell the truth.[28]

---

26 The jurat is a standard jurat which does not mention the entity or the fact that the affiant makes the affidavit on the entity's behalf. Obviously, if an interpreter is used or the affiant is illiterate or suffers from an impairment, then an appropriate jurat setting out the circumstances must be used.

27 The age of majority varies from state to state. Typically, majority is 18 years of age, although in Alabama, Delaware and Nebraska, full age is 19 years. Mississippi is now the only state where majority is 21 years.

28 The notarial certificate appended to the affidavit should include statements as to the child's age and understanding of the affidavit, the oath and the need to tell the truth. In a number of states the certificate may only be prepared by an attorney.

Statutory declarations in Commonwealth of Nations jurisdictions

In Canada and England and in most of the other countries which are or were members of the Commonwealth of Nations (formerly known as the British Commonwealth),[29] affidavits are only used in court proceedings. In those countries where there is otherwise need for a solemn declaration which attracts penalties for perjury, a so-called 'statutory declaration' is used. There is no equivalent to this type of declaration in the United States.

American notaries are frequently required to take statutory declarations for use in Commonwealth countries, particularly for Canada. More often than not, the statutory declaration is in a pre-printed prescribed form, the significant amendment of which, particularly in the formal parts, could well render the form nugatory at the public office abroad at which it is ultimately to be filed.

For example, in Singapore, prospective company directors must make and file statutory declarations in prescribed forms, which, among other things, relate to whether they have been disqualified from acting as directors. The question arises as to whether or not a prospective company director who makes a statutory declaration for Singaporean purposes in the United States, is able to make a statutory declaration outside Singapore in accordance with Singaporean law.

There are different views as to whether or not a statutory declaration should be made in the manner and form prescribed by the law of the country where it is to be used or in the manner and form used in the place of making.

The principle *locus regit actum* ('the law of the location regulates that which is to be done' – literally 'the place governs the act') is well established in American law and is generally accepted in most common law jurisdictions. Based on that principle, the law of the place of signature is usually considered to be the appropriate law when determining the formal requirements for the execution of documents.

If that principle is correct in relation to statutory declarations, a declaration for use in Singapore must accord with the formal and technical requirements of the American state or territory in which it is made, despite the fact that it relates solely to Singapore company law.

The competing principle is that if the law of a particular country governing the substance of an instrument requires particular formality or solemnity for the instrument to have validity or be capable of registration, the formality or solemnity must be observed even if the contract or instrument is executed outside the country concerned.

If that principle is the correct principle to be applied, a statutory declaration for use in Singapore must accord with the prescribed Singapore form, despite the fact that it is made in the United States.

---

29 The Commonwealth of Nations is an international organization of 54 independent countries, most of which were once part of the British Empire. The full list of member countries may be found at <www.thecommonwealth.org>.

Unfortunately, there does not appear to be any legislative or other authority in the United States or elsewhere which can be relied upon to provide a definitive answer, short of referring a prospective declarant to the nearest consular post of the receiving country. Consuls may take statutory declarations in the forms required by their sending countries.[30]

All too often, particularly when dealing with statutory declarations for production in Canada, notaries merely witness the execution of the declaration and then complete the 'jurat' as it stands.

If required to take a statutory declaration for production in a present or former Commonwealth jurisdiction, on balance, the best approach by a notary to take is not to delete any part of the wording on the prescribed form as presented, but to add or have the following wording added above the place denoted for the declarant's signature:

> I also declare under penalty of perjury under the laws of the United States of America that the foregoing is true and correct.

A statutory declaration is not sworn or affirmed, but is merely 'declared'. There is no reason why an American notary cannot receive a declaration in the same manner as an oath or affirmation is received. The declarant must sign the statutory declaration and then make his or her verbal declaration to the notary in the following form:

> I solemnly and sincerely declare that this is my true name and handwriting and the contents of this, my statutory declaration, are true and correct.

The 'jurat' is then completed by the notary in the usual manner and the notary's journal is written up in the ordinary course.

---

30 See Chapter 1, 9 and n 29.

CHAPTER 5

Interpreters and Translators

To set the scene:

- in 2007:

    ○ 20 percent of the total United States population aged five years and over (approximately 55.4 million people) reported that they spoke a language other than English at home;[1] and

    ○ about eight percent of the entire population (approximately 24.5 million people) spoke English 'less than very well';[2]

- English is the official language or one of the official languages in only 47 countries of the world;[3]

- of America's top 15 trading partners, the official language of 11 of the countries is a language other than English;[4] and

- U.S. State Department Authentications Office rules require all documents in a foreign language which are submitted for authentication to be accompanied with a certified [notarized] English translation.[5]

---

1   Of those languages, the ten languages most frequently spoken were Spanish, Chinese, Tagalog, French (including patois, Cajun and Creole), Vietnamese, German, Korean, Russian, Italian and Portuguese.

   Shin, Hyon B and Robert A Kominski, *Language Use in the United States:2007*, American Community Survey Reports, ACZ-12, U.S. Census Bureau, Washington, DC (issued April 2010)

2   Ibid.

   'People speaking at a level below the "very well" category are thought to need English assistance in some situations'.

3   Those countries include 21 small Caribbean and Pacific Island states. United Kingdom and Australian self-governing dependencies and external territories are not included in the calculation. The official languages of each of the world's countries may be found in Appendix 6.

4   *U.S. Census Bureau Foreign Trade Statistics.*

   America's top trading partners (Total Trade-Goods) are Canada, China, Mexico, Japan, Germany, United Kingdom, South Korea, France, Taiwan, Brazil, India, Netherlands, Venezuela, Singapore and Saudi Arabia.

   <www.census.gov/foreign-trade/statistics/highlights/topcurman/html>.

5   See <www.state.gov/m/a/auth/c16920.html>.

The need for skilled interpreting and translating

Against that background, the importance of interpreting and translation in the process of notarizing documents for production abroad may readily be understood. So too, the need for notaries to appreciate and acquaint themselves with the skills possessed by trained interpreters and translators as well as with the need to properly document how, when, where and why interpreting or translation services were provided.

If asked, most people would incorrectly say that interpreting and translating are but two sides of the same coin; the interpreter translating orally from one language to another and the translator interpreting written text between two languages. In fact, the difference between interpreting and translating is substantial, as is the difference in the skills required for each of them. The tendency to lump interpreting and translating together in daily parlance as 'translating' does not help mark the difference between the two skills in the public mind.

It is fair to say that there is no such thing as a perfect translation or a perfect interpretation. Something is always 'lost in translation', but a good interpreter or translator can usually ensure that the part which is lost is of little matter to the person or reader to which it is principally directed.

Fluency and literacy are not enough

If a non-English-speaking person or someone who has difficulty with the language seeks the intervention of a notary, then unless the notary is fluent and literate in a language known by the person, in most cases it will be necessary to call on the services of an interpreter and, if necessary, the services of a translator.[6]

Obviously, it is not always necessary to use a professional interpreter or translator to assist with a notarization. But when translations or interpreting must be accurate and technically sound, there is simply no substitute for an experienced and knowledgeable professional.

It should not be thought that merely because a person is fluent in English and one or more other languages that he or she automatically has the ability to act as an interpreter or to prepare translations of documents, particularly legal documents. In trying to save time and money, many notaries allow young people who speak English and another language to act as interpreters for parents, grandparents or other relatives. It is inappropriate to do so. How and why it is thought that a child or a teenager is able to properly interpret or translate legal concepts from English to another language, when they manifestly do not themselves understand the concepts, remains a mystery.

---

6   Remarkably, in Arizona, California and Hawaii notaries are forbidden to do so. See below, 55 and 56.

What translators do

Professional translators almost always translate from foreign or 'source' languages into their native or 'target' languages. They must be able to write well and express themselves clearly and with precision in their target languages. Their principal skills are to understand both the culture and language of the text being translated and, through the use of reference materials and (technical) dictionaries, translate the text into the target language.

What interpreters do

On the other hand, interpreters must be able to translate in both directions at the same time, without the advantage of dictionaries or other reference materials. High quality interpretation is extremely difficult. Good interpreters must not only understand the idiom of both languages involved in the interpretation, but must be able to clearly and concisely express thoughts in both languages.

'Sight' translation is a hybrid activity commonly undertaken by an interpreter when he or she reads a document written in one language and orally translates it into another during the course of the interpretation.

The function of an interpreter is to put the person requiring interpretation services into a position which is as close as linguistically possible to an English speaker of similar background and education in the same legal or social setting. To achieve that aim, the interpreter must not add or omit anything, must interpret completely and accurately and must give proper consideration to the person's level and quality of language.[7]

> [Interpreting] ... obviously is not a single two-way street between two languages. Rather, it is a busy intersection at which at least five thoroughfares meet – the two languages with all their eccentricities, the cultures of the two speech communities and the speech situation in which the statement was uttered.[8]

Interpreters' oaths

It is usual to have an interpreter (professional or not) swear an appropriate oath or make an affirmation before commencing the interpretation. The following oath (or affirmation) may be made by an interpreter who is to assist by interpreting conversations between a notary and a prospective document signer.

> 'I solemnly swear (affirm) that I well understand both the English language and the [other] language and that to the best of my skill and ability I will well and truly interpret from the English language into the [other] language and vice-versa, all matters and things which I am required to interpret in relation to the notarization of a document for [name of signer].

---

7   *Interpreters in the Judicial System – A Handbook for Ohio Judges* published by the Supreme Court of Ohio Judicial & Court Services Division Interpreter Services Program (2008), 33.

8   P Farb, *Word Play – What Happens When People Talk* (1974), 199. (Quoted with approval by the Supreme Court of Minnesota in *State v Mitjans* (1987) 408 NW 2d, 824).

The notarial certificate should reflect the fact that an interpreter's services were used. For example, a short form acknowledgment might read:

> This instrument was acknowledged before me through the sworn (affirmed) interpretation of [name of interpreter] on [date] by [name of person].

The following oath (or affirmation) may be made by interpreter whose services are provided to interpret the contents of an affidavit in English to another language spoken by the affiant, and to interpret the oath to be taken by the affiant.[9]

> I solemnly swear (affirm) that I well understand both the English language and the [other] language and that to the best of my skill and ability I will well and truly interpret the contents of this affidavit to [Affiant's name] who is the affiant named in it and that I will well and truly interpret the oath (affirmation) to be administered to [Affiant's name] and that I will make true and fair explanations in the [other] language of all matters and things which I shall be required to explain in relation to the making of the affidavit.

When an interpreter has been used to interpret the oath or affirmation and the contents of an affidavit, the jurat for the affidavit should reflect the fact. The following is an example of a jurat:

> Subscribed to and sworn by [Affiant's name] at [place] this [date] through the interpretation of [Interpreter's name], she having first sworn that to the best of her skill and ability, she would well and truly interpret to [Affiant's name] the contents of this affidavit and the oath/affirmation to be administered.

Deaf and hard-of-hearing signers

The most effective way of communicating with deaf and hard-of-hearing persons will vary from case to case. It will depend upon a variety of factors such as the degree of hearing loss, the age at which the loss occurred, the person's education and the means of communication which the person commonly employs. Typically, communication is in writing or by speech reading (or 'lip reading' as it is commonly known) or by the use of sign language, particularly American Sign Language.[10]

If a deaf or hard of hearing person can read and write English and is able to respond to written questions or statements, notarization tends not to be too difficult. Problems can and do arise when English is a deaf person's second

---

9   The actual administration of the oath or affirmation may be varied to make it binding on the interpreter's conscience.

10 As only about 25 percent of speech is visible 'on the lips', profoundly deaf people usually understand only a relatively small amount of what is being said without recourse to other means of communication such as American Sign Language (ASL).

ASL is a fully developed, uniquely structured language. It is the primary language of the deaf community in the United States. Other countries have their own national equivalents of ASL. For example, in Australia, the sign language is known as 'Auslan'. While sharing common elements with ASL, Auslan differs significantly from ASL in structure, grammar, syntax and vocabulary.

language or where the person has limited proficiency in English. Local schools for deaf and hearing impaired persons are usually able to provide suitably qualified interpreters.

Translations

Translation is a serious matter not to be taken lightly, even if it is not always necessary to engage the services of a professional translator. Where it is essential that a translation be of first quality, then only a first quality professional translator will do.

Having once engaged a professional translator, the mistake people commonly make is to impose unrealistic time limits for the completion of the work. It takes about an hour to translate 250–300 words of a technical document, excluding checking, formatting and revisions. A 3,000 word legal or technical document should take about two days to complete. Translation services offering 'rush' or 'expedited' services often do so with the risk of a consequent reduction in quality.

Machine translations

Translation software is improving all the time. It is fast and often comes free with office or home computer programs. It can be a helpful tool if a person merely wishes to ascertain the gist of an incoming document in an unfamiliar language. The programs are not suitable for any serious or important translations or any translation for an official purpose.[11] This is not to decry the value of computers and computer assisted translations in the hands of experts, but computerized translation is now no closer to replacing translation by human translators than it has been at any time in the past.[12]

Dual language documents prepared abroad

Dual language documents prepared abroad are frequently sent to the United States for execution and subsequent notarization. Powers of attorney in favor of foreign patent and trademark attorneys head the list, followed by documents relating to the corporate governance of overseas subsidiaries of American corporations or foreign entities in which American corporations have interests.

When a document is cast in both English and another language, it is easy to see how a signer can, unconsciously, give equal credence to both versions or, where English is the signer's first or only language, can assume that he or she is really only signing the English version.

---

11 One of the first automatic translation machines was built by Professor Katsuo Ohno of Kyushu University in Japan. It was initially demonstrated in September 1960 at the Mitsubishi Electric Co. The machine was designed to translate English and German into Japanese. It contained 1,500 transistors and 18,000 diodes and was touted as being capable of translating 200 words.

Over the years, machine translation has had a number of prominent supporters. No less a person than President Bill Clinton said when predicting innovations in science and engineering in the 21st century that, 'Soon researchers will bring us devices that can translate foreign languages as fast as you can talk.' (William J. Clinton, *Address Before a Joint Session of the Congress on the State of the Union* (27 January 2000).

12 Mory Sofer, *The Translator's Handbook*, (Schrieber Publishing Inc., 2004), 81.

As a rule, if a dual language document is received from a non-English-speaking jurisdiction, the foreign language version is definitive. A person signing a dual language document should not take it for granted that it is the English version which is definitive or even that it is an accurate rendition of the foreign language counterpart.

Some of the most appalling translations of documents into English emanate from foreign countries. There is no hard evidence available to suggest that the translations are deliberately incorrect. The most likely explanation is that the translations have been prepared in good faith by foreign lawyers or accountants, whose knowledge of the English language and of American commercial customs and terminology is far more limited than the translators believe.

On the whole, English language versions of dual language powers of attorney prepared by the better European, Middle Eastern and Central and South American firms of patent and trademark attorneys are true and fair translations of their foreign language equivalents. Regrettably, English language versions of dual language documents emanating from other sources abroad are not always as accurate or reliable as they might be.

It is not a notary's function to comment on the quality of the English version of a dual language document, even if the notary is capable of doing so. Nor is a notary in any way responsible for the content of a document written in English or any other language. But, without crossing the line into the unauthorized practice of law, it is open to a notary to ask a prospective signer to consider whether or not a dual language document which is to be notarized should be first referred to a professional translator for checking.

Translating English language documents into foreign languages

Almost without exception, notarized English language documents must first be translated into the local language before being used for official purposes in a non-English-speaking destination.

In the ordinary course, the chances are that a professional American translator will prepare a true and fair translation of an English language document, the use of which in the destination country will not disadvantage the interests of the American individual or corporate entity concerned.

Allowing a translator abroad to undertake a translation of a notarized English document has its disadvantages and advantages. The principal disadvantage relates to the quality of the work. On the other hand, in a number of countries, the engagement of a local translator at a substantial fee can help grease the wheels.

There are of course many important exceptions. In Brazil, for example, all foreign language documents which are to be used for official purposes must be translated into Portuguese. Brazil has a cadre of sworn public translators whose qualifications are impeccable and whose fees are set by law.[13]

---

13 For further information see José Henrique Lamensdorf, *Almost Everything You Want to Know about Certified [sworn] Translators in Brazil*. <www.lamensdorf.com.br>.

Argentina, the Czech Republic, Denmark, France, Poland, Spain and Venezuela are countries which also have systems of sworn translators. Those translators can almost always be relied upon absolutely.[14]

Translating foreign language documents into English

Documents solely drawn in a foreign language are also frequently sent to the United States for execution and notarizing and subsequent legalization. In many cases, foreign language documents for use abroad are prepared within the United States.

In either circumstance, it may be necessary to retain a translator, not only to satisfy the requirements of the U.S. State Department Authentications Office, but also to assure document signers who are not literate in the particular language as to precisely what it is that they are signing and to leave them with a written record which they understand. As always, when choosing a translator, the emphasis should be on competency and not price.

U.S. State Department authentication guidelines

Federal regulations forbid the U.S. State Department from certifying a document 'when it has good reason to believe that the certification is desired for an unlawful or improper purpose'.[15]

It is therefore the duty of the State Department Authentication Officer to examine not only the document which the Department is asked to authenticate (e.g. the certification of a state or territory Secretary of State), but also the fundamental document to which previous seals or other certifications may have been affixed by other authorities (i.e. in the present context, the notarized document).[16] The Authentication Officer is also required to 'request such additional information as may be necessary to establish that the requested authentication will serve the interests of justice and is not contrary to public policy'.[17]

To comply with federal regulations, all notarized foreign language documents which are to be authenticated by the U.S. State Department Authentications

---

14 Typically, sworn translators hold special qualifications and are registered with the courts and/ or various public offices. Only state certified translators (sworn translators) are entitled to produce translations for official use. Sworn translators function within fairly rigorous regulatory frameworks and are liable in law for the quality and accuracy of their translations.

Unfortunately, not all countries in Europe and the Americas have unified systems for accrediting sworn translators. For example, in Belgium, a translator seeking accreditation in Brussels must pass an appropriate test and undergo a process which can take upwards of 18 months to complete. In smaller towns, it is sufficient for an applicant to merely write a letter to the local court.

15 *Code of Federal Regulations*, Title 22 : Foreign Relations §131.2 Refusal of Certification for Unlawful Purpose.

16 Ibid

17 Ibid.

§131.2(b) goes on to say that documents which have the effect of furthering or supporting the restrictive trade practices or boycotts fostered or imposed by foreign countries against countries friendly to the United States shall be considered contrary to public policy for the purposes of the regulations.

Office must be accompanied by a sworn notarized English language translation, thereby enabling the Authentications Officer to assess the nature and content of the foreign language documents.

It should be noted that, typically, state and territory procedures do not require the submission of English language translations in support of applications for authentication or the affixing of an apostille.

Translators' affidavits

Whenever a notarized English language document is destined for a non-English speaking country abroad and has been translated into or from a foreign language by an American translator, the translator should swear an appropriate affidavit of translation.[18]

The following is an example of a translator's affidavit which should be sworn or affirmed in the usual way.

I, **[AB]** of [address] swear/affirm and say as follows:

1.   I am literate in both the [*other*] language and the English language and am competent to make translations of documents from the English language to the [other] language.

2.   Annexed to this affidavit and marked 'A' is a [description of document] in the English language.

3.   I have prepared and true and fair [*other*] language translation of the document marked 'A' which is annexed to this affidavit and marked 'B'.

Sworn/affirmed etc.

A lack of state and territory guidelines

Despite the obvious importance of translation and interpretation as adjuncts to notarial practice generally, and the need for consistent guidelines for notaries to follow, only about one-third of U.S. jurisdictions have taken the trouble to address the issue at all;[19] and then without any uniformity or consistency between them.

In a number of cases, it is clear that in laying down rules, legislators and/or bureaucrats have simply overlooked the services that professional interpreters and translators are able to provide. In others, unnecessary restrictions have been imposed on notaries which make it difficult for them to carry out their duties for both domestic and international purposes. Perversely, in those jurisdictions, where there has been no attempt to provide guidelines, notaries are often better served than many of their counterparts elsewhere, by being able to apply a degree

---

18   Translators do not make oaths or affirmations as to their competence or their obligation to prepare a true and fair translation of a particular document before embarking on the task.

19   Alaska, Arizona, California, Connecticut, Florida, Georgia, Hawaii, Illinois, Indiana, Maine, Massachusetts, Michigan, Mississippi, Montana, North Dakota, Oregon, Wisconsin and Wyoming.

of common sense and by being free to seek out and use the services of interpreters and translators when there is need to do so.

Legislation in **Florida**, **Illinois** and **Indiana** and guidelines in **Wyoming** simply and sensibly provide that a notary must not take the acknowledgment of a person who does not speak or understand English, unless the nature and effect of the [presumably, English language] instrument to be notarized is translated into a language the person understands.[20]

Most of the other jurisdictions which have turned their attention to the interpreters and translators urge caution on notaries, when notarizing foreign language documents or dealing with signers who do not understand English or who have difficulties with the language.

However:

- In **Alaska**, notaries are instructed not to notarize a document if the notary and the signer cannot communicate directly without the assistance of a translator.[21]

- **Arizona** notaries may not notarize documents in foreign languages which they cannot read and which [presumably] they do not understand. The notary must be able to read enough of the language to describe the document in his or her journal to ensure that he or she is not attesting to information outside the scope of his or her authority.[22]

- In **California**, where almost half the population speaks English 'less than very well',[23] the legislation governing notaries is silent when it comes to the use of interpreters and translators. Strangely, the California *Notary Public Handbook* advises notaries in that state not to use an interpreter to communicate with a signer

  to either swear to or affirm the contents of an affidavit or to the acknowledge the execution of a document ... as vital information could be lost in the translation ... [and] .... the customer should be referred to a notary who speaks the customer's language.[24]

---

20 *Florida Statutes* § 117.107(6), *Illinois Compiled Statutes* Ch 5 §312/6-104(f) and *Indiana Code* §33-42-2-2[a](5) and *Wyoming Notaries Public Handbook*.

   The legislation does not however deal with the notary's obligations in relation to the taking of an acknowledgment of a person who does not speak or understand English where the acknowledgment relates to a document in a language the person understands but the notary does not.

21 Lt Governor's website – Notary Resources Frequently Asked Questions.

22 Arizona *Notary Public Reference Manual* (Rev July 2010, 19).

23 See n 2 above.

24 California *Notary Public Handbook* (2011), 18. One can only speculate as to the reasons for advice of that nature, given the number and quality of interpreters readily available in California. Hopefully, the reference to an 'interpreter' is a reference to an unqualified interpreter.

25 Ibid, 18.

- A **Hawaii** notary is instructed never to notarize a document that has been written in a foreign language unless he has a thorough understanding of the foreign language in which the document is written. Similarly:

  ... a notary should not notarize a document written in English if the parties to the document who appear before the notary speak a foreign language unfamiliar to the notary. In the latter instance, the notary should refer the parties to another notary who speaks the foreign language, or to the foreign consulate, or to an attorney.[26]

- A **Maine** notary should never sign a notarial certificate on a document the notary does not understand, but may do so if the document is first translated into English.[27]

- Legislation in **North Dakota** provides that;

  In the case of a document drafted in a language other than English ...[a notary may not notarize it if] ... the document is not accompanied by a permanently affixed and accurate written English translation.[28]

- An **Oregon** notary;

  ... who fluently reads and writes a ... [foreign] language may notarize the signature on a document written in that language ... When in doubt a notary can always refuse to notarize and refer the customer to a bilingual notary.[29]

Finding an interpreter or a translator

According to the U.S. Department of Labor, Bureau of Labor Statistics, in 2008 there were approximately 50,900 interpreters and translators holding down jobs in their fields within the United States. That number is projected to increase to about 62,200 by 2018.[30] The Bureau speculates that the actual number of interpreters and translators in work is probably significantly higher than the official figure, because of the number of part-timers who only work in the industry sporadically.[31]

Significant numbers of government, not-for-profit and private organizations are able to assist in locating and dealing with translators and interpreters. Most of them are accessible via the internet. One of the oldest and best regarded

---

26 *State of Hawaii Notary Public Manual* (Rev. 1986), 6.

27 Maine *Notary Public Handbook and Resource Guide*, 8.

28 *North Dakota Century Code* 44-06-13.1(1)(i). Failure to comply with this requirement is a disciplinary offence.

29 *State of Oregon Notary Public Guide*, 51.

30 Bureau of Labor Statistics, *Occupational Outlook Handbook, 2010–11, Interpreters and Translators* <www.bls.gov/OCO/OCO5175.htm>.

31 Ibid.

organizations is the American Translators Association (ATA) which is a national not-for-profit association established in 1959. The ATA presently has about 10,000 members throughout the United States.[32]

The National Association of Judiciary Interpreters and Translators[33] and the Registry of Interpreters for the Deaf[34] both have excellent websites which are easy to access and negotiate. The Northwest Translators and Interpreters Society maintains a comprehensive list of translator and interpreter organizations operating in the United States and a large number of countries abroad.[35]

---

32 See website, <www.atanet.org>.
33 See website, <www.najit.org>.
34 See website, <www.rid.org>.
35 Found at <www.notisnet.or/resources/links/orgs.html>.

CHAPTER 6

COPY CERTIFICATION

Certifying copies of documents of domestic or foreign origin is probably the most common service that notaries around the world are called upon to provide for international purposes.[1] Yet, remarkably, the power of American notaries to perform what is perceived internationally to be a simple, basic notarial service is often heavily circumscribed – to the point where sometimes the service cannot be provided at all, or an ersatz certification is prepared which may not be acceptable for use in the country in which it is to be produced.

Save for a general, but not identically formulated restriction on certifying copies of domestic vital records and other public documents, there is no policy consensus or legislative consistency between U.S. jurisdictions in relation to the power of American notaries to certify copy documents.[2] Nor is there any apparent logic to the limitations often placed on the copying and certification powers which are granted.

Copies of U.S. naturalization or citizenship papers

It is a federal offence punishable by up to 25 years imprisonment for any person, including a notary, who

> … without lawful authority, prints, photographs, makes or executes any print or impression in the likeness of a certificate of arrival, declaration of intention to become a citizen or certificate of naturalization or citizenship or any part thereof.[3]

The Department of Homeland Security, through U.S. Citizen and Immigration Services, may provide certified true copies of naturalization or citizenship papers if the requester's identity and status as a naturalized citizen can be confirmed by the USCIS office at which the request is processed.[4]

---

1   Documents which are copied and notarized include birth, marriage and death certificates, passports, divorce decrees, academic transcripts, diplomas, references, personal papers and commercial documents ranging from simple one page letters to financial statements and joint venture agreements comprising hundreds of pages. The list is endless.

2   For example, Massachusetts notaries are advised that they may certify copies of passports but Texas notaries are instructed not to do so.

3   18 USC §1426.

   The offence relates only to U.S. naturalization and citizenship papers. It is not a federal offence to copy or notarize a copy of a U.S. passport.

4   For further information, see USCIS website, <www.uscis.gov>.

Certifying photographs

Notaries are often requested to certify that a photograph of a person is a 'true likeness' or 'genuine photograph' of the person. For example, powers of attorney for production in parts of India must have photographs of the donors attached. As a rule, a photograph must be certified by the notary as being a true likeness of the donor.

'Photograph certification' is not a power granted to notaries by legislation anywhere in the United States, nor, generally speaking, is it an 'approved' practice. Direct certification of photographs is only possible in a few jurisdictions. In most states and territories, notaries are forced to provide the service obliquely.

National Notary Association President Milton Valera has rightly observed that:

> ... in a sense, notaries perform a photo-certification every time they compare a picture on an ID card against the physical appearance of a document signer. Photo-certification of facial appearance would impose no taxing new responsibilities on the notary and might be authorized by law as a valuable public service.[5]

In the early 1990s, the NNA negotiated an acceptable compromise with the National Board of Medical Examiners, which enabled notaries to notarize a United States Medical Licensing Examination identification form containing the applicant's photograph, without actually certifying the photograph as such.

The agreed certificate reads:

> I certify that on the date set forth below the individual named above did appear personally before me and that I did identify this applicant by:
>
> (a)   comparing his/her physical appearance with the photograph on the identifying document presented by the applicant with the photograph affixed hereto; and
>
> (b)   comparing the applicant's signature made in my presence on this form with the signature on his/her identifying document.[6]

If it is proposed to make use of a form of this nature, care should be taken to have it 'cleared' by the relevant state or territory notary authority. Where necessary, the form should be prepared by an attorney.

Another method might be for the client to state in the context of the document to which the photograph is attached, that the photograph attached to the document is his or her genuine photograph and true likeness. The overall notarization of the document would then capture and include the client's statement.[7]

---

5   Milton G. Valera, *New Technology and a Global Economy Demand That American Notaries Better Prepare for the Future*, 32 J Marshall L Rev, 935 at 955.

6   Ibid.

7   A similar means of certifying photographs is approved in Oregon. See discussion about certification of copy documents in Oregon at 70 and 71 below.

Notes concerning vital records and other public documents

1. Precisely which documents fall within legislative definitions of
   - vital records
   - official documents
   - public records
   - public documents
   - public recorded documents; and
   - publicly recordable documents

   (together referred to as '**Public Documents**') varies, often significantly, between the states and territories.[8]

2. In the balance of this chapter
   - when outlining the powers of notaries to certify copies of Public Documents, no attempt will be made to cover the field;[9] and
   - unless in legislation or pertinent notary materials specific mention is made of Public Documents emanating from places outside the state or territory under discussion, it will be assumed that references to Public Documents or classes of Public Documents in the legislation or materials are references only to the Public Documents of the particular state or territory.

Notaries with little or no power to directly certify copy documents

Notaries in Alaska, Connecticut, Illinois, Michigan, New Jersey, North Carolina, Ohio, Rhode Island, South Carolina, South Dakota, Tennessee and the Virgin Islands have no power to directly certify copy documents of any description for domestic or international purposes. Nebraska, New York and DC notaries are not authorized to certify copy documents for domestic purposes, but, as set out below, they are able to do so for international use.

Three states namely, California, Hawaii and Kentucky, have given such limited authority to their notaries to certify copies that notaries in those states might just as well be said to have no power to do so.[10]

---

8   For example, in Guam, college transcripts are specifically defined as being public records. (See answer to Question 10 of Notary Public FAQs published by the Office of the Attorney General of Guam).

   In Arizona, college transcripts do not fall within the definition of public 'records'. (See *Arizona Revised Statutes* §41-1350).

9   Those who need to know precisely which copies of Public Documents may be certified by notaries in a particular state or territory must undertake their own research or obtain appropriate professional advice.

10   In California, notaries may only certify:

   (a) copies of powers of attorney under Section 4307 of the *Probate Code*; and

   (b) copies of entries in their own journals if ordered by the Secretary of State or by a Court.

   Hawaii and Kentucky notaries may only certify copies of their own records and take and certify necessary copies of dishonored bills of exchange which they have protested.

Copy certification by document custodians

Except for notaries holding office in DC, Nebraska and New York, notaries in each of the jurisdictions mentioned above who are required to perform copy certifications for international use are forced to resort to the cumbersome and unsatisfactory procedure commonly known as 'Copy Certification by Document Custodian'. The procedure involves the person who has the permanent or temporary custody of the copy document appearing before a notary and swearing an affidavit to which the copy is attached, that the copy document is a true copy of the original.[11] The sworn certification is then notarized in the ordinary way.

In practice, many notaries who take the affidavits of document custodians have been known to endorse an 'Exhibit' note on any attachment to the affidavit to the effect that

> This is the copy document referred to/attached to the affidavit of [*Affiant*] sworn before me today.

It is also possible for notaries to sign and/or impress their seals on each page of the copy document for identification purposes and for the affiant to describe the copy document in the affidavit as

> the attached copy [*type of document- e.g. contract or deed of assignment*] comprising [　] pages, each of which bears an impression of the official seal [*and/or signature*] of [*name of notary*] Notary Public for purposes of identification.

A notary who wishes to use either of these methods of identifying copy documents should, of course, first obtain appropriate legal advice to ensure that the proposed method is not improper under applicable local law.

Apart from the obvious fact that the procedure falls well short of actual notarial certification, as is noted in the Alaska legislation, assisting a person to select a notarial certificate or even giving advice as to how a copy document may be certified may cause the notary to fall foul of the law against unauthorized practice of law.[12]

Most of the jurisdictions recognize that the methodology may not always be acceptable abroad.[13] Alaska goes so far as to recommend to persons looking to obtain certified copies of their documents via the certification by Document Custodian method that they ought first 'contact the appropriate consulate ... [of the receiving country] ... and verify that a copy certified by this method will be acceptable'.[14]

11　The jurisdictions which recommend the methodology tend to also prescribe or recommend forms for the purpose.

12　*Alaska Statutes* §44.50.061. Also see 'Frequently Asked Questions' on the Alaskan Lt Governor's website, <ltgov.alaska.gov/treadwill/notaries/authentications.html>.

13　For example, academic institutions and prospective government or private employers in Spain, Saudi Arabia and the United Arab Emirates will not accept notarized Certifications by Document Custodians in lieu of actual notarized copies of documents.

14　<ltgov.alaska.gov/treadwill/notaries/authentications.html>.

No official source in Alaska or in any of the other jurisdictions proffers any suggestions as to how a document custodian should proceed if the methodology proves to be unacceptable. In such cases, document custodians have no reasonable alternative but to arrange for notarizations by consular officers of receiving countries or by notaries holding office in a state or territory which allows its notaries to certify the particular copy documents.

It is a moot point as to whether or not the process entitles document custodians to swear affidavits relating to copies of vital records or other public documents in their possession, certified copies of which might otherwise be obtained from local authorities. The better view is that it does not. On the other hand, in the absence of specific legislative provisions to the contrary in a relevant jurisdiction, it is acceptable for document custodians to swear affidavits as to copies of 'out of state' vital records or other public documents.

American civil law notaries

Subject to meeting the various technical requirements and limitations relating to certifications generally which are imposed by their local laws, the civil law notaries of Alabama and Florida and all notaries in Louisiana and Puerto Rico are empowered to certify photographs and copies of documents which are to be produced abroad.[15]

DC, Nebraska and New York notaries

DC, Nebraska and New York notaries have no authority to certify copy documents for domestic purposes, save that DC notaries may provide copies of their notarial records to anyone who asks and who pays a $2 fee for the service.[16] As discussed in Chapter 3, uniquely among American notaries, DC, Nebraska and New York notaries are empowered to:

> ... perform such other acts, for use and effect beyond the jurisdiction of the District, as according to the law of any state or territory of the United States or any foreign government ... may be performed by notaries public.[17]

---

15 *Alabama Code* §36-20-50 and §36-20-51

Florida Statutes §118.10.3

Louisiana Revised Statutes Title 35

Laws of Puerto Rico §4-2048 and 2049.

Florida civil law notaries are not subject to the same limitations in relation to the making and certifying of copy documents as are Florida notaries generally.

16 *District of Columbia Code* §1-1210

17 Interestingly, while continuing to highlight the now virtually obsolete power to protest foreign bills of exchange, the *District of Columbia Notary Handbook* conspicuously fails to even mention the power granted by the DC Code §1-1210.

With that authority, notaries in those three jurisdictions are able to certify copy documents and photographs, for production abroad.[18] Even so, where officially certified copies of vital records and other public documents are available, they should be used in preference to notarized copies.

Notaries in Alabama, Indiana and Mississippi

Legislation in Alabama, Indiana and Mississippi does not specifically authorize notaries to certify copy documents or photographs.

However:

- in **Alabama**, notaries are authorized to:

    ... exercise such other powers ... [in addition to taking acknowledgments and proofs, administering oaths and executing protests] ... as, according to commercial usage or the laws of this state may belong to notaries public;[19]

- **Indiana** notaries may:

    do all acts that by common law and the custom of merchants, notaries are authorized to do;[20] and

- in **Mississippi**, a notary is able to:

    perform all duties ... [in addition to those specified in the Statute] ... required of notaries by commercial usage and also to make declarations and certify the truth thereof, under his seal of office, concerning all matters done by him by virtue of his office.[21]

While not as clear or as all embracing as the powers granted to DC, Nebraska and New York notaries, in the light of the longstanding United States common law practice and of the powers exercised by common law notaries elsewhere, the wording of the relevant legislation at very least probably entitles notaries from these three jurisdictions to certify copy documents for production outside the United States.[22]

---

18 The DC Notary Handbook also appears to be at odds with D.C. Code §1-1210 when it states (at 7), without citing authority that a DC notary does not have authority to certify a copy of a public record or a publicly recorded document. That is clearly so for domestic DC purposes. There is a respectable argument that may be mounted that DC notaries (and Nebraska and New York notaries) are indeed able to certify copies of public records or publicly recorded documents for production abroad unless there is specific legislative sanction relating to particular copy documents either within the United States or within the destination country.

19 *Alabama Code* §36-20-5.

20 *Indiana Code* §33-42-2-5.

21 *Mississippi Code* §25-33-11.

22 By virtue of the common law and long commercial usage, notaries in England, Australia and New Zealand and in virtually all other common law jurisdictions have the undisputed power and authority to certify copy documents and photographs for production outside their own countries.

Notary laws in Alabama and Indiana do not appear to limit the powers indirectly given to their notaries or the range of copy documents they may certify. However, the *Mississippi Administrative Code* provides that a notary who is not an employee of the issuing government agency may not certify or authenticate copies of any official (federal or state) government documents such as birth certificates, death certificates, passports and social security cards. Mississippi notaries may nonetheless notarize 'a signature on a document which has a copy of an official government document embedded or attached as an exhibit'.[23]

Certification of copy document by notaries within the Armed Services

Surprisingly, a lack of consistency in the copy certification rules also exists within the Armed Services.

- Other than for certain official military purposes, **army** personnel may not make certified copies of public records or publicly recorded documents, but may make certified copies of other documents where the originals are produced.[24]

- Authorized **navy** and **marine** personnel may

  [not] ... certify the authenticity of public, registered, or court records or documents, or issue certified copies of such documents or records

  but may make certified copies of other documents where the originals are produced.[25]

- **Air force** personnel, when acting as notaries, are instructed not to certify documents as true and accurate copies of original documents unless the originals have been created or maintained by notaries and other members of the legal office staff as part of their official responsibilities. They may however take appropriate affidavits from document custodians.[26]

- The **U.S. Coast Guard** does not appear to have a published policy in relation to copy certificates.

Where notaries are specifically empowered to certify copies

In the remaining 33 states and territories, notaries are specifically empowered to certify copy documents. While sharing many common features, the guidelines and statutes relating to copy certifications differ quite markedly between the jurisdictions, often causing extreme difficulties for clients who require copies of their documents to be notarized.

---

23 MISS ADMIN CODE Title 01, Part III, Cap14 §206(3).

24 *Army Regulation* 27-55 Legal Services Ch 4 §4-5.

25 *Manual of the Judge Advocate General* Chapter IX para 0908 (March 2004), Department of the Navy.

26 *Air Force Instructions* 51-504 (27 October 2003) para 21.

The following notes give an outline the position in each of the states and territories to which they relate and do not purport to be comprehensive.

- In **American Samoa**, notaries may not certify copies of documents which are vital records or public records or documents which are publicly recordable. The notary must personally copy or supervise the copying of any document and must use a photographic or electronic copying process.[27]

- **Arizona** notaries must certify that they personally made the photocopy of the particular original document. They may not certify copies of public records or documents which are publicly recordable.[28] *The Arizona Notary Public Reference Manual* (2011) cites marriage licences, birth and death certificates, divorce papers, court records and real estate deeds as examples of documents that are publicly recordable. The manual goes on to say that 'if the notary does not have access to a copy machine, the notary must not perform the copy certification'.[29]

- **Arkansas** notaries must either make or supervise the making of copies of original documents to be certified. They may not attest a copy of a vital record from Arkansas or any other state or territory of the United States or a vital record from any country of the world. Nor may they attest a copy of a public record if a copy may be made by the custodian of the public record.[30]

- A **Colorado** notary may only certify a copy of a document if the original document is exhibited to the notary together with a signed written request by the person requiring the certification which states that a certified copy or facsimile of the document cannot be obtained from the office of any clerk and recorder of public documents or custodian of documents in Colorado and the production of a facsimile or the preparation of a copy or the certification of a copy of the document does not violate any state or federal law.[31]

- In **Delaware** a notary is obliged to personally supervise the making of a photocopy of the original document. Notaries are not authorized to certify copies of official or public records.[32]

- **Florida** notaries, other than Florida civil law notaries, must either make or supervise the making of copies of original documents to be certified. They may not attest a copy of a vital record from Florida or any other state or territory of the United States or a vital record from any country of the world. Nor may they attest a copy of a public record if a copy is able to be made by the custodian of the public record.[33]

---

27 *American Samoa Code* §31.0307(4).

28 *Arizona Revised Statutes* §41-311(3).

29 Reference Manual, 24.

30 *Arkansas Code* §21-14-106(b).

31 *Colorado Revised Statutes* §12-55-120(1).

32 29 *Delaware Laws*, c 43 §4322(d).

33 *Florida Statutes* §117.05(12).

- A **Georgia** notary may make a certified copy of a document if the document presented for copying is an original document and is not a public record or a publicly recorded document, certified copies of which are available from an official source other than a notary and provided that the document is photocopied by the notary or under the notary's supervision.[34]

- Notaries in **Guam** may certify copy documents which are not copies of public records or publicly recordable documents.[35] In 'Frequently Asked Questions' on the Guam Attorney-General's website, it is noted that a College transcript is considered to be a public record and a copy may only be certified by the registrar of the College issuing the transcript.[36]

- **Idaho** notaries may 'certify that a copy of an original document is a true copy thereof, only if a certified copy of such original cannot be obtained from an official custodian of such document'. [37]

- **Iowa** legislation merely states that on certifying or attesting a copy of a document or other item, the notary must determine that the copy is a full, true and accurate transcription or reproduction of that which was copied.[38] Even though the *Pocketbook for Iowa Notaries Public* advises notaries to 'avoid certifying copies of public records such as birth/death certificates, court records and deeds,' strictly speaking, Iowa notaries are not forbidden to certify true copies of public records, provided the original is produced for copying. The Pocketbook comments that copies of documents filed at a public office cannot be certified by a notary, because the original is not available for copying.[39]

- The **Kansas** statute provides that in certifying or attesting a copy of a document or other item, the notary must determine that the copy is a full, true and accurate transcription or reproduction of that which was copied.[40] *The Kansas Notary Public Handbook* advises (at page 6) that a notary can certify a copy only if the notary personally has custody of the original document and makes the copy from the original. There does not seem to be any reason why Kansas notaries cannot make and certify copies of original vital records produced to them. They cannot however certify copies of publicly recorded documents, because the originals are filed at a public office. Whether or not birth, marriage and death certificates may be copied is uncertain, because on one view the original record is held at a public office.

---

34 *Georgia Code* §45-17-8(a)(6).
35 *Guam Code* §33104(3).
36 <www.guamattorneygeneral.com>.
37 *Idaho Code* §51-107(7).
38 *Iowa Code* §9E-9-4.
39 Pocketbook, 11.
40 *Kansas Statutes* §53-503(d).

- In **Maine**, the power to certify copy documents is not specifically granted to notaries as a discrete power. There are however various references in statutes to the certification of copies by notaries.[41] The Maine *Notary Public Handbook and Resource Guide* published by the Secretary of State assumes the power to certify copy documents and instructs notaries not to certify copies of birth certificates or other documents issued by government agencies.

- Notaries in **Maryland** are required 'to keep a fair register of all protests and other official acts done in the carrying out of the office of notary and must give a certified copy of any record in the notary's office to any person applying for the record on payment of the usual fees.'[42]

  Even though a notary cannot directly certify copies of Public Documents, there is a limited range of copies of private documents which may be certified. For example, where the notary has taken the acknowledgments of a party to a Deed of Assignment of Patent, a copy of that document must form part of the notary's 'fair register' and certified copies may be provided to interested persons.

- **Massachusetts** notaries must either make or supervise the making of copies of original documents which are to be certified. Copies to be certified may only be made using a photographic or electronic copying process.[43] The Governor's website confirms that a notary may certify a copy of a passport or a driver's license.[44]

  Elsewhere on the site, it is said that:

  > a notary should not certify a copy of a birth or death certificate since cities and towns have their own procedures for certifying birth and death certificates. Refer the person instead to the state Bureau of Vital Statistics or County Clerk's office in the county where the birth occurred. For foreign birth certificates, refer the person to the consulate of the country of origin.[45]

  Given the limited nature of the instructions and the apparent lack of legislative restrictions, Massachusetts notaries are probably able to certify copies of a wide range of government and private documents for production abroad.

- Notaries in **Minnesota** are entitled to certify copies of documents, electronic records or other items (personally photographed) other than Minnesota birth, death or marriage certificates. When doing so, a notary must determine that the proffered copy is a full, true and accurate transcription or reproduction of that which was copied.[46]

---

41 For example, when authorizing notaries to intervene in various marine matters, the legislation specifically allows Maine notaries to 'grant authenticated copies' (Me Rev Stat Ann title 4, c.19, §952).

42 *2010 Maryland Code*, State Government §18-107.

43 Revised Executive Order No. 455 (04-04) §§2 and 5(g).

44 <www.mass.gov> (FAQs).

45 Ibid.

46 *Minnesota Statutes* §358-42 and the Minnesota Secretary of State's Brochure, *You've Received your Notary Commission. What's Next?*

- In **Missouri**, a notary may only certify a facsimile of a document if he or she receives a written request (from the person requiring the document certification) stating that a certified copy or facsimile, preparation of a copy, or certification of a copy of the document does not violate any state or federal law. The legislation also makes it mandatory for Missouri notaries to keep copies of all documents they have certified as copies in their notarial protocols.[47]

  The Missouri Notary Public handbook makes the point that notaries must not 'certify copies of documents which state on the face of the document that they cannot be reproduced'. It also states that

  > Birth certificates, death certificates, marriage licences, divorce decrees and school documents (diplomas, transcripts) cannot be certified. Certified copies of these documents should be obtained from the issuing agency.[48]

- A **Montana** notary:

  > [may not certify a copy of] … a document issued by a public entity such as a birth, death or marriage certificate, unless the notary is employed by the entity issuing or holding the original version of that document.

  A notary may make and give a certified copy of any record kept or that originated in the notary public's place of employment.[49]

  The legislation suggests that notaries employed in legal offices, patent and trademark attorney offices, educational institutions and the like are able to certify copies of relatively wide ranges of documents kept at or originating from those offices or institutions. On the other hand, notaries employed in motor dealerships or libraries would only be able to certify a limited range of copies.

- In **New Hampshire**:

  > In certifying or attesting a copy of a document or other item, the notarial officer must determine that the proffered copy is a full, true and accurate representation of that which was copied.[50]

  The New Hampshire Notary Public and Justice of the Peace Manual advises that 'Examples of other items that could be copy certified include maps, diagrams, graphs etc.'[51] Notaries are not permitted to certify copies of vital records recorded or recordable instruments or apostille records.[52]

---

47 *Missouri Revised Statutes* §486.345.
48 *Missouri Notary Handbook* (updated May 2011), 31.
49 *Montana Code* §1-5-416(2)(c) and (g).
50 *New Hampshire Revised Statutes,* 4.56-B:2IV.
51 *New Hampshire Manual*, 31.
52 Ibid, 29 and 30.

- In **New Mexico**, notaries may not certify copies of documents which are vital records or public records or which are publicly recordable.[53] They may however certify copies of other documents provided that they personally copy or supervise the copying of the document 'using a photocopying or electronic copying process' and after comparing the document to the copy determining that the copy is accurate and complete.[54] A New Mexico notary may neither certify nor authenticate a photograph.[55]

- **Nevada** notaries are forbidden to 'certify photocopies of a certificate of birth, death or marriage or a divorce decree'[56] Otherwise, it seems that a Nevada notary may certify copies of any other documents whatsoever (save for U.S. naturalization and citizenship papers) provided that he or she personally photocopies the document presented and then certifies that the 'copy is a true and correct copy of the document that was presented'.[57]

- **North Dakota** notaries who certify or attest 'a copy of a record or an item that was copied shall determine that the copy is a full, true and accurate transcription or reproduction of the record of item.'[58] Notaries may not make or purport to make any certified copy of a vital record or recordable instrument or a public record containing an official seal.[59]

- In the **Northern Marianas**, a copy certification is 'a notarial act in which a notary certifies having made a photocopy of a document that is neither a public record or publicly recordable'.[60]

- The enumerated powers of **Oklahoma** notaries enable them to certify or attest copies of documents or other items provided that they determines that the proffered copy is a full and accurate transcript or reproduction of that which was copied.[61]

  In the case of official records, only the custodian of the official records may issue an official certified copy.[62]

- In **Oregon,** the *Notary Public Guide 2011* points out that

    notaries should not copy public records because certified copies are available from the agencies in charge of those records. It is illegal for example to certify copies of Oregon birth or death certificates.[63]

---

53 *New Mexico Statutes*, §4-12A-2D.
54 Ibid.
55 *New Mexico Statutes*, §4-12A-12.
56 *Nevada Revised Statutes*, §240-075(5).
57 *Nevada Revised Statutes*, §240.1655(2)(c).
58 *North Dakota Century Code*, §4.4-06.1-04.4.
59 *North Dakota Century Code*, §4.4-96.1-23.7.
60 *Attorney General Regulations* 1-105(3).
61 *Oklahoma Statutes*, §49-113.D.
62 Ibid.
63 *Oregon Notary Public Guide*, 2011, 31.

Some records such as the Oregon drivers license, U.S. passports and most professional licenses may be copied as 'copies of these documents cannot be obtained otherwise'.[64]

Photographs cannot be notarized because

> no photograph is a full and accurate reproduction and it does not have the elements of a document : a personal statement by the constituent and the constituent's signature.[65]

However, an Oregon notary may notarize a statement about a photograph (presumably by the client). After the notarial certificate is completed, the notary may use his or her official notary seal a second time so that it overlaps the photograph and the paper to which it is attached (being careful not to cover the face in the photograph). The procedure is described as 'a protection device which allows the receiving agency to know that the photograph is the one attached to the document at the time of notarization.'[66]

- In **Pennsylvania**, photocopies of documents issued by public entities (whether notarized or not), such as vital records and county documents will not be authenticated or have apostilles affixed to them by the Secretary of the Commonwealth's Authentication Unit.[67]

  Otherwise, it seems that Pennsylvania notaries are able to certify copies of virtually any documents produced to them for the purpose provided that in so doing they certify that a copy document 'is a true correct and complete copy of the original.'[68]

- **Texas** notaries are authorized to 'certify copies of documents not recordable in the public record'.[69] In addition to the usual vital records and documents such as 'Articles of Incorporation, certificates of formation or other business documents recorded with the Secretary of State or other state official', Texas notaries are instructed not to certify copies of passports, social security cards or military identification cards.[70]

---

64 Ibid, 40.

65 Ibid.

66 Ibid.

67 <www.portal.state.pa.us/portal/server.pt/community>.

68 *Notaries Public in Pennsylvania: A Position of Public Trust*, 18, 19 and 20. Available online at the Pennsylvania Department of State website <www.portal.state.pa.us>.

69 *Texas Business and Commercial Code* §406.016(5).

70 Given the terms of the legislative power to certify copies of documents, it is hard to see how the restriction on certifying copies of passports, social security cards or military identification cards is justified – particularly when there does not appear to be a restriction on certifying copies of driver's licenses, student ID cards and the like.

- In **Utah** the legislation authorizes a notary to certify that 'a photocopy is an accurate copy of a document that is neither a public record nor publicly recorded'.[71] The *2010 Notary Public Study Guide* does not discuss the extent of the power, nor do any of the official published materials for notaries appear to do so.[72] It seems that publicly recordable documents which have not actually been recorded may be certified, but photographs and transcriptions of documents may not.

- A **Vermont** notary may 'certify that a copy of a document is a true copy of another document'.[73] There is no prescribed form for the purpose. On its face, the power appears to be quite wide-ranging. In the *Short Guide for Vermont Notaries* published by the Vermont Secretary of State, the power is said to apply to any document of a personal nature, but does not apply to vital records such as birth, marriage, death or divorce records.[74] The *Short Guide* goes no further, but it would be surprising if the Vermont State Archives and Records Administrator would authenticate notarized copies of other Vermont public records, certified copies of which could be obtained from official sources.

- In **Virginia**, several legislative provisions relating to the certification of copy documents are (inadvertently) irrelevant or in conflict.

The *Virginia Notary Act* (the Act) defines 'Copy Certification' as meaning:

> ... a notarial act in which a notary (i) is presented with a document that is not a public record; (ii) copies or supervises the copying of the document using a photographic or electronic copying process; (iii) compares the document to the copy; and (iv) determines that the copy is accurate and complete.[75]

The expression 'Copy Certification' does not appear elsewhere in the Act or anywhere in the entire Code of Virginia.[76]

The Act goes on to provide that each notary is empowered:

> to certify that a copy of any document, other than a document in the custody of a court, is a true copy thereof' ('the Overarching Provision').[77]

---

71 *Utah Code*, §46-1-2(3).

72 The Study Guide may be found on the Lt. Governor's website, <www.notary.utah.gov>.

73 *Vermont Statutes*, Title 24 §445.

74 *Short Guide for Vermont Notaries*, 7.

75 *Code of Virginia*, §47.1-2.

76 A full search of the Code of Virginia may be made on the online database made available by the Virginia General Assembly at <leg1.state.va.us/ooo/src.htm>.

77 *Code of Virginia*, §47.1-12(iii). The Overarching Provision was re-enacted in March 2011 and contains an identical provision in the Act.

Virginia's *Notary Public Handbook* notes that

> Virginia Notaries are **not** authorized to certify true copies of birth, death or marriage certificates. Only the Division of Vital Records/Statistics may perform such a certification'.[78]

The handbook makes no comment about certification of copies of other public records. The Authentications Division of the Secretary of the Commonwealth's Office directs persons requiring copies of business documents, such as Certificates of Good Standing, to the State Corporation Commission.

Even though it can be cogently argued that the Overarching Provision entitles notaries to certify copies of any documents (other than documents in the custody of a court) including vital records and Public Documents of all description, the appropriate course for notaries to follow is to limit the range of copy documents they may certify in the manner suggested by the Secretary of the Commonwealth.

- A **Washington** notary must determine that the proffered copy of a document to be certified or attested is a full true and accurate transcription or reproduction of that which was copied.[79]

The limits of the copy certification power are far from clear. The only guidance for notaries may be found in 'Apostille Document Guidelines' published by the Corporations Division of the Washington Secretary of State's Department on its website. The guidelines consist of comments to the effect that copies of certain (enumerated) vital records 'do not need to be notarized' in order to have apostilles affixed to them.80 On balance, it is preferable for notaries in Washington not to certify copies of Public Documents but to leave the task to the public officials who ordinarily have custody of them.

- **West Virginia** notaries may certify a facsimile of a document on receipt of a signed written request stating that a certified copy or facsimile of the document cannot be obtained from the office of any recorder of Public Documents or custodian of documents in West Virginia and the production of a facsimile, preparation of a copy or certification of a copy of the document does not violate any state or federal law.[81] The legislation goes on to say that notaries in West Virginia must keep copies of all documents they have certified as copies together with other papers or copies relating to their notarial acts.[82] There is a prescribed form set out in the statute.

---

78 *A Handbook for Virginia Notaries Public* (2009), 4.
79 *Washington Revised Code,* §4.244.080(5).
80 <www.sos.wa.gov/corps/apostilles/ApostilleGuidelines.aspx>.
81 *West Virginia Code*, §296-5-104.
82 Ibid.

- In **Wisconsin**, it is an offence punishable by a fine of up to $10,000 or three years imprisonment or both for a notary to prepare or issue any paper or film which purports to be, or carries the appearance of, an original or a copy of a certified or uncertified vital record.[83] Vital records 'means certificates of birth, death, divorce or annulment, marriage documents and data related thereto.'[84]

No legislation directly relating to notaries and their powers and no materials published by the Wisconsin's Department of Financial Institutions (which has jurisdiction over appointing, educating and disciplining notaries) appears to forbid the certification by notaries of copies of Public Documents other than Vital Records. The Information Sheet published by the Wisconsin Secretary of State concerning Apostilles and Authentication Certificates implies that copies of Public Documents other than vital records may be certified by notaries as well as by public officers such as a Registrar of Deeds, School official, judge or a Certification Specialist of the Department of Financial Institutions.

In certifying or attesting a copy of a document or other item, a notary must determine that the preferred copy is a full, true and accurate transcription or reproduction of that which was copied.[85]

- **Wyoming** notaries may certify or attest to a copy of a document or other item which is not a copy of a vital record, public record or publicly recordable document. In certifying or attesting a copy, the notary must have the original document in his or her possession and must personally copy or supervise the copying of the document or other item using a photographic or electronic copying process.[86] A notary must not certify or authenticate a photograph.[87]

Certifying copies of copies

The general world-wide rule is that notaries ought not certify copies of copy documents where the originals are not or cannot be produced. Nonetheless, there are people who need to send notarized copies of documents abroad (typically copies of foreign vital records), but who for one reason or another are only able to produce transcriptions or other copies of the originals. Holocaust survivors, refugees, victims of natural disasters and their respective family members come to mind.

Sometimes, the copies are required to support applications to be made abroad for the issue of fresh or replacement documents. Often enough they are needed in relation to inheritance claims or to recover or obtain compensation for expropriated family real estate or other assets.

---

83 *Wisconsin Statutes*, §69.24.
84 *Wisconsin Statutes*, §69.01 (26).
85 *Wisconsin Statutes*, §706.07(2)(d).
86 *Wyoming Statutes*, §34-26-102(d).
87 *Wyoming Statutes*, §34-26-205(b).

In those circumstances, all that can be done is for a photocopy of the copy document to be made and for the custodian to swear an affidavit prepared by an attorney to which the copy is attached, to the effect that the (new) photocopy is a true and complete copy of the photocopied document, the original of which is lost, destroyed or otherwise unavailable. An explanation as to why the original document cannot be produced should be included in the affidavit. The affidavit should then be notarized in the ordinary course.[88]

Whether or not the procedure will be acceptable in the destination country is out of the notary's hands. In any event, it is a matter for the custodian of the copy document to make enquiries of the appropriate authorities abroad. It is not for the notary to make enquiries or provide any assurances to the custodian. The prudent course is for the notary to put a notation in his or her journal which is signed by the custodian that the 'certification' may or may not be acceptable abroad and that the notary has not given any advice or assurance in that regard.

Copy certification certificates

Almost all jurisdictions which allow copy certification prescribe the notarial certificates which are to be used for the purpose. Usually, certificates make provision for the insertion of a description of the copy document to which they relate.

To minimise the possibility of fraud, where possible the notary should sign and/or impress his or her seal on each page of the document which is to be certified. The copy should then be described in the notary's certificate as:

> the attached copy [description of document, e.g. contract, deed of assignment] comprising [ ] pages each of which bears an impression of my official seal [and/or] has been signed by me for purposes of identification.

In the case of a single page document, there is no reason why the notary's certificate cannot be endorsed on the back of the copy. The copy document can then be described as 'the copy document on the reverse of this certificate';

When certifying a copy of the particulars page and facing page of a passport, an appropriate description of the copy document is:

> the particulars page and facing page of [country] Passport number [number] issued to [name in full of passport holder] born on [date] at [place of birth].

If not endorsed on the back of the copy, the notary's certificate must be securely attached, in a tamper evident manner, to the copy document to which it relates.

---

88 Uniquely, Oregon notaries may certify a 'copy of a copy' provided that in the notary's certificate the wording 'a copy of a photocopy is used'. (*State of Oregon Notary Public Guide*, 2011, 40).

CHAPTER 7

POWERS OF ATTORNEY

Agency is among the world's oldest and most venerable legal concepts. As a written embodiment of agency, the power of attorney is, in turn, one of the world's oldest and most venerable legal documents.

Notarial intervention

Surviving protocols of early European notaries reveal that notarial intervention in the preparation and authentication of powers of attorney has always been a staple of notarial practice. For example, Angelo de Cartura was a notary who practiced in the Venetian colony of Crete in the 14th century. His protocol for the 12 months from May 1305 to May 1306 records the preparation of 574 notarial acts for the period, most which were commercial in nature. Sixty-eight of those acts were general or special powers of attorney prepared variously for domestic and international use.[1]

Three quarters of a millennium later, powers of attorney for both domestic and international use come before modern American notaries in ever increasing numbers. Those destined for use internationally are largely related to matters of trade and commerce, although the number of private transactions abroad in which American residents are involved each year is growing steadily.

Where a power of attorney is to be used within the United States, its execution and notarization follow a well trod path. A signatory in his or her own right or in a representative capacity appears before a notary who simply takes the signatory's acknowledgment and certifies it in the ordinary way on the instrument creating the power. Depending on local state or territory legislation, the instrument itself is either a deed or an instrument under hand; both forms being well known to American attorneys and notaries.

A power of attorney for use abroad is often a completely different kettle of fish. Having regard to the function and powers of their own notaries, there is an expectation in almost every civil law country that, where a foreign notary certifies the grant of a power of attorney in private form, the certification will go well beyond the parameters of a mere acknowledgment.

---

1   Alan M Stahl (ed), *The Documents of Angelo de Cartura and Donato Fontanella – Venetian Notaries in Fourteenth Century Crete* (Dumbarton Oaks, 1990).

For example, from the recipient's viewpoint, a notarial certificate appended to a simple power of attorney in private form for production in Bosnia, Croatia, Montenegro or Serbia in relation to an inheritance matter should include:

- the donor's full name and any former name if the donor was born in the destination country and has subsequently Americanized his or her name or changed it by marriage;

- the donor's date and place of birth;

- the donor's residential or professional address;

- particulars of the donor's identifying document or token, including its number;

- the donor's relationship to the deceased person in the destination country; and

- statements to the effect that:

  ○ the donor is of full age and has the capacity to enter into contracts and undertake obligations;

  ○ the power of attorney was executed in the presence of the notary on a specified date; and

  ○ the donor signed the power of attorney of his or her own free will.

Save for U.S. civil law notaries, in most cases American notaries are not authorized or entitled to prepare or complete notarial certificates in the forms typically required. In particular, they are not authorized to certify that a donor 'has the capacity to enter into contracts and undertake obligations'. Nor are they authorized to certify all the personal particulars which must be provided.

Generally speaking, the problem can be obviated if the power of attorney is executed in the presence of an attorney-at-law who prepares and provides an affidavit containing the requisite information about the donor. As well as taking the donor's acknowledgment, the notary also receives the attorney's affidavit which is then securely appended to the power of attorney.

To compound matters, powers of attorney in a number of countries and for certain purposes must be in authentic form in order to have efficacy. As a rule, powers of attorney for use in France, Germany, Italy, Portugal and Spain concerning the purchase and sale of real estate, the establishment and conduct of companies and inheritance matters all must be in authentic form.

Whereas it is accepted without question around the world that U.S. civil law notaries may prepare and complete documents in authentic form, as noted in Chapter 2, American notaries as a class are not entitled to do so. Therefore, inconvenient and frustrating as it may be, where it is essential that a power of attorney be in authentic form, there is often no practical alternative open to a donor but to by-pass notaries altogether and approach a consular officer of the destination country to provide notarial services pursuant to the powers vested in consuls by the *Vienna Convention on Consular Relations*.[2]

Powers of attorney for use in common law and mixed law jurisdictions

With few exceptions and subject to the occasional special formal requirement being met, the authorities in common law and mixed law jurisdictions usually have no difficulty in accepting ordinary American notarizations of powers of attorney emanating from the United States.

Where foreign law or practice requires certification of matters in relation to an aspect of a power of attorney or its execution beyond a certification which an American notary may lawfully provide, here again, a notarized certificate or affidavit by an American attorney-at-law dealing with the particular issues which is appended to the power of attorney will usually be sufficient for all purposes within the destination country.

Powers of attorney for use in Canada

Canada is a common law jurisdiction save for the province of Quebec which, for historical reasons, remains a (French) civil law outpost with regard to non-criminal matters.[3] Rules regulating the preparation, execution and content of powers of attorney vary from province to province. Legislation in all provinces, other than Quebec, contemplates forms reasonably similar to the forms which are familiar to most U.S. notaries and attorneys-at-law.

In Quebec, deeds including powers of attorney, which are prepared for use domestically are drawn up in authentic form by local notaries. In the French manner, the notaries retain the original documents in their protocols and issue certified copies which are completely probative for all purposes in Quebec.[4]

However, faced with the realities of inter-provincial commerce and the proximity and importance of the United States, Quebec's legislators have long since included provisions in the Civil Code to the effect that the form of a juridical act (i.e. a document creating or perfecting a legal obligation) may be governed by

---

2 Most of the major European and Central and South American countries maintain reasonably comprehensive consular networks within the United States. Career consular staff are usually well versed in the preparation and execution of powers of attorney in authentic form.

   See <www.state.gov/s/cpr/rls/dpl> and <www.state.gov/s/cpr/r/s/fco> for current particulars of foreign embassies and consulates in the United States.

3 *The Civil Code of Quebec* is a general public law of the province. Based on French antecedents, the Code is made up of ten books comprising over 3,000 sections. The Code is the backbone of Quebec's civil legal system. It is supplemented by legislation on specific subjects, for example *The Notaries Act* (R.S.Q. Chapter N-3).

   Criminal law in the whole of Canada including Quebec is under the exclusive jurisdiction of the federal government, however enforcement and prosecution and the administration of justice generally are within the jurisdiction of the individual provinces.

4 See Chapter 2, 24.

the law of the place where it is made.[5] Consequently, powers of attorney executed in the United States for production in Quebec may be prepared in normal 'American' forms and need not be in authentic form.

The Quebec Civil Code also provides that a power of attorney made outside Quebec by 'private writing' (i.e. a document not in authentic form) may be 'certified by a competent public officer … [e.g. a notary] … who has verified the identity and signature of the mandator'.[6]

All American notaries are therefore able to prove the execution of powers of attorney for use in Quebec by taking signers' acknowledgments and completing notarial certifications in the ordinary way.

The other Canadian provinces have their own rules relating to proof of execution of powers of attorney emanating from places outside Canada. Rules differ as between provinces, but importantly, throughout Canada, acknowledgments certified by American notaries in their standard state or territory forms are invariably accepted.

Powers of attorney for use in Latin America

Latin America comprises Mexico, the Dominican Republic and almost all of the Central and South American countries.[7] Each of them is a civil law jurisdiction. Within the confines of that tradition, each has its own formal requirements for powers of attorney to be used within its borders. Throughout the region, with a number of exceptions, instruments creating powers of attorney are required to be in authentic form.

Of all the Latin American countries, Mexico imposes the most rigorous requirements and standards for powers of attorney, wherever granted, for use in relation to commercial matters, inter-personal affairs and judicial proceedings.[8] Overwhelmingly, powers of attorney must be in authentic form, failing which they will be of no effect.

---

5   *Civil Code of Quebec*, s 3109.

    Among other things, the section provides that

        a juridical act is … [also] … valid … [for use in Quebec] … if it is made in the form prescribed by the law applicable to the content of the act, by the law of the place where the property which is the object of the act is situated when it is made or by the law of the domicile of one of the parties when the act is made.

6   *Civil Code of Quebec*, s 2823.

7   Cuba and Puerto Rico are usually considered to be part of Latin America, but for present purposes are excluded from the group.

    In Central America, Belize is an English-speaking common law jurisdiction. The 'Latin' countries of Central America are Costa Rica, El Salvador, Guatemala, Honduras, Nicaragua and Panama.

    In South America, Guyana is basically a common law jurisdiction, Suriname's legal system is based on Dutch law and French Guiana is one of France's Overseas Departments. The 'Latin' countries of South America are Argentina, Bolivia, Brazil, Chile, Colombia, Ecuador, Paraguay, Peru, Uruguay and Venezuela.

8   Throughout the significant part of the 20th century, Mexico's laws could only be categorized as being of 'extreme territorialism' – Jorge A Vargas *Enforcement of Judgments in Mexico*, 14 Northwestern Journal of International Law and Business (1993-1994), 396.

Without a practical approach such as that adopted in Quebec, and despite the NAFTA and the increasingly close links between Mexico and the United States, the strict requirements of the Mexican authorities are and will continue to be a severe headache for Americans having dealings in Mexico and therefore a continuing headache for the American notariat.

As American notaries (other than American civil law notaries) are unable to lawfully prepare or complete authentic form instruments, technically they have no role to play in relation to authentic form powers of attorney. As noted above, in most states and territories of the United States, powers of attorney in authentic form may only be executed and completed by consular officers of destination countries.

Unfortunately, anecdotal evidence suggests that this rule is all too often honored in the breach. Significant numbers of authentic form powers of attorney destined for Latin America are apparently completed by ordinary notaries (usually notaries who are also attorneys-at-law) whose signature and seals are subsequently authenticated by county, state and federal authorities without regard to the legal consequences which can flow from such actions.

The error is compounded by bureaucrats and others in many destination countries who will accept improper notarizations – either because they do not know or care or because the notarizations have been 'legalized' by the affixing of apostilles or by the chain of authentication. In the latter cases, it is wrongly thought that 'legalization' corrects any manifest errors in the preparation and execution of documents.

Two treaties relating to powers of attorney for Latin America

Two international treaties have muddied the waters in relation to powers of attorney for use in Latin American countries.

As a result of

- the entry into force in 1942 in the United States of the *Protocol on Uniformity of Powers of Attorney which are to be Utilized Abroad* [commonly known as the **Washington Protocol**] to which seven Central and South American countries are also party;[9] and

- the accession by 16 Latin American countries to the *1975 Inter-American Convention on the Legal Regime of Powers of Attorney to be Used Abroad* [commonly known as **the 1975 Inter-American Convention**] to which the United States **is not** a party[10]

notaries in the United States are frequently called upon to prepare or complete

---

9   The parties to the treaty are Bolivia, Brazil, Colombia, El Salvador, Mexico, Nicaragua, Panama and the United States.

   The treaty has not yet entered into force in Bolivia, Nicaragua or Panama, although often enough, patent and trademark attorneys in those countries seek notarial certificates for powers of attorney in forms which would be appropriate if the treaty were in force.

10 Argentina, Bolivia, Brazil, Chile, Costa Rica, Dominican Republic, Ecuador, El Salvador, Guatemala, Honduras, Mexico, Panama, Paraguay, Peru, Uruguay and Venezuela have all acceded to the treaty. Colombia and Nicaragua signed the adoption of the treaty on 30 January 1975, but neither country has yet acceded to it.

notarial certificates in the forms required by those treaties in relation to private form powers of attorney destined for Latin American countries.

Both treaties are founded upon notarial practice in civil law jurisdictions. They are directed toward ironing out minor procedural and certification differences between the contracting states with a view to developing an acceptable degree of uniformity in dealing with powers of attorney emanating from one contracting state for production and use in another.

The Washington Protocol

The Washington Protocol addresses three specific categories of powers of attorney:

- powers executed by or on behalf of natural persons;
- powers executed in the names of third parties or by delegates or substitutes; and
- powers executed in the names of juridical persons.

Article I of the *Washington Protocol* provides that:

1. If the power of attorney is executed by or on behalf of a **natural person** the ... [notary] ... shall certify from his own knowledge to the identity of the appearing party and to **his legal capacity to execute the instrument**.

2. If the power of attorney is executed **in the name of a third person** or **if it is delegated** or **if there is a substitution by the agent** the ... [notary] ... **in addition** to certifying in regard to the representative who executes the power of attorney, or delegates or makes a substitution, to the requirements mentioned in the foregoing paragraph, **shall also certify that such representative has in fact the authority to represent the person in whose name he appears and that this representation is legal** according to such authentic documents as for this purpose are exhibited to ... [the notary] ... and which ... [the notary] ... shall mention specifically, giving their dates, and their origin or source.

3. If the power of attorney is executed **in the name of a juridical person**, ... [the notary] ... **in addition** to the certification referred to in the foregoing paragraph, **shall certify** with respect to the juridical person in whose name the power is executed, **to its due organization, its home office, its present legal existence, and that the purposes for which the instrument is granted are within the scope or activities of the juridical person**; which declarations shall be based on the documents which for that purpose are presented to ... [the notary] ... such as the instrument of organization, bylaws, resolutions of the board of directors or other legal documents as shall substantiate the authority conferred. The ... [notary] ... shall specifically mention these documents giving their dates and their origin.[11] (*Emphasis added.*)

---

11 *Article 1, Washington Protocol.*

The name by which the treaty is commonly known, the fact that the United States is a party to it and the provisions of Article IX of the treaty have, for many years, led attorneys, notaries and others to (wrongly) believe that the *Washington Protocol* authorizes American notaries to provide the certifications set out in Article I in relation to non-authentic form powers of attorney executed and notarized in the United States for production in Mexico and the other contracting states.[12]

On its face, the *Washington Protocol* appears to grant U.S. notaries all the powers they would need in order to provide the certificates contemplated by the treaty. Article IX provides:

> In case of powers of attorney executed in any of the countries of the Pan American Union in accordance with the forgoing provisions, to be utilized in any other member country of the Union, notaries duly commissions [sic] as such under the laws of their respective countries shall be deemed to have authority to exercise functions and powers equivalent to those accorded to native notaries by the laws and regulations of (name of country).

Would that it were so – life would be so much easier for Americans doing business or having other dealings in Brazil, Colombia, El Salvador or Mexico. Sadly, despite the United States' active involvement in the drafting of the treaty and its ratification by President Roosevelt on April 3 1942, the *Washington Protocol* does not actually grant any of the requisite powers to most U.S. notaries.

The extent to which the provisions of an international treaty become part of a domestic legal system (if at all) is a serious and largely unresolved issue within government and academic legal circles around the world. The answer differs as between countries. As far as the United States is concerned, the position seems to be that treaties such as the *Washington Protocol* are not automatically self-executing, that is to say, they do not automatically become part of the domestic legal system particularly when they are inconsistent with current or later state or federal legislation.[13] In the present case, the terms of Article IX of the *Washington Protocol* are at odds with the powers vested in most American notaries by virtue of their state or territory legislation.

---

12 For example, see Alejandro Suarez-Mendez, *The Agent for Service of Process in Mexico*, 35 International Law News (Winter 2006), 1.

 Also see, Carol S Osmond, *Granting Powers of Attorney for use in Mexico and other Practical Aspects of Establishing a Mexican Business.*

 <www.oas.org/legal/english/osia/Carol_Osmond.doc>.

13 See generally, John H Jackson, *Status of Treaties in Domestic Legal Systems; a Policy Analysis,* 86 American Journal of International Law (1992), 310.

The U.S. State Department has put the status of the *Washington Protocol* beyond question for the time being at least. In response to enquiries from State Secretaries of State as Competent Authorities under the *Hague Apostille Convention,* the legal branch of the State Department has advised that:

> While certain provisions of the Protocol are intended to be directly enforceable, the Protocol is not intended to confer authorities upon U.S. State notaries beyond those which are conferred by state legal authorities governing notaries. Rather, notarial acts attesting to a person's legal authority performed in states or territories of the U.S. where notaries are given such authority are to be given full faith and credit in other countries that are parties to the Protocol.
>
> ...
>
> Given that the Protocol does not confer additional authorities to state notaries, the Department concurs with the U.S. State Competent Authorities' decision not to provide apostilles for notarial acts that go beyond the authorities granted to notaries within their states.[14]

That being so, only U.S. military notaries and notaries in Louisiana and Puerto Rico, civil law notaries in Alabama and Florida and possibly notaries in DC, Nebraska and New York have the power and authority to prepare and complete the notarial certificates intended by the *Washington Protocol* to be affixed to powers of attorney bound for Brazil, Colombia, El Salvador or Mexico.

The 1975 Inter-American Convention

As noted above, the United States **is not** a party to the *1975 Inter-American Convention.*[15] That does not prevent a good many notaries, lawyers and patent attorneys in those countries which are parties (which include the countries party to the *Washington Protocol*), acting as if the United States and therefore its notaries were subject to the Convention. Consequently, particularly in relation to intellectual property matters, they routinely prepare powers of attorney for U.S. recipients to execute and have notarized which are accompanied by pre-printed notarial certificates in the form required by the Convention.[16]

As it happens, the *1975 Inter-American Convention* is not only far less prescriptive in its certificate requirements than is the *Washington Protocol*, but it is far more flexible. Ironically, in practice, if not in theory, those notaries who are aware of and who avail themselves of that flexibility are often able to intervene in powers of attorney for production in the countries which are party to the *1975 Inter-American Convention.*

---

14 Found at *http://travel.State.gove/law/judicial/judicial_4319.html* (Legal and Public Policy Information).

15 That Convention is a convention of the Organization of American States which is an important international organization headquartered in Washington DC. The United States is a long-time member.

16 Far too many American notaries just blithely fill in the blanks in the proforma certificates, seemingly unaware that they are acting beyond their power and that they are making themselves liable for prosecution for the unauthorized practice of law.

Article 6 of the *1975 Inter-American Convention* provides that:

> In all powers of attorney ... [other than instruments in authentic form which are excluded by virtue of Article 2] ... the ... [notary] ... shall certify or attest to the following, if competent to do so:
>
> a. The identity of the principal as well as his statement as to his nationality, age, domicile and marital status;
>
> b. The authority of the principal to give a power of attorney on behalf of another natural person;
>
> c. The legal existence of the juridical person on whose behalf the power of attorney is given;
>
> d. The power of the principal to represent the juridical person and his authority to grant the power of attorney on its behalf.

However, Article 7 of the Convention provides that:

> Should there be no ... [notary] ... in the ... [relevant state or territory of the United States] ... in which the power of attorney is given who is competent to certify or attest to the items mentioned in Article 6, the following formalities shall be observed:
>
> a. The power of attorney shall include a sworn statement by the principal, or an affirmation that he will tell the truth, about the items specified in Article 6a.
>
> b. Legalized copies or other evidence with respect to the items specified in paragraphs b, c and d of the same article shall be appended to the power of attorney.
>
> c. The signature of the principal shall be authenticated.
>
> d. Such other requirements shall be observed as may be stipulated in the law under which the power of attorney is given.

Meeting the methodology requirements of Article 7 usually does not cause any difficulty for most American notaries. In consequence, even though the United States is not a party to the *1975 Inter-American Convention*, most notaries and patent and trademark attorneys in countries which are party to it will accept a power of attorney supported by a sworn/affirmed statement by an officer of a principal which is notarized in the ordinary course and which is appended to a power of attorney bearing a standard American acknowledgment.

CHAPTER 8

SHIPPING AND MARINE PROTESTS

Notaries in port cities have traditionally been active in the world of shipping and trade. Historically, in England and her colonies and throughout Europe, it fell to the notaries to prepare charter-parties,[1] bottomry bonds,[2] average agreements,[3] protests[4] and an array of other commercial documents in support of the explosion in trade which followed 16th century European colonial expansion.

These days, the focus of notarial intervention in shipping matters is directed more towards registering, chartering and purchasing merchant ships and seagoing pleasure craft. Nonetheless, entering notes of protest and extending protests remain on the agenda for a good many notaries holding office in seaport cities in all countries, including the United States.

Registering ships abroad

American notaries employed within the shipping and allied industries are often called upon to notarize the execution of agreements and copies of documents relating to chartering, purchasing or registering ships abroad.[5]

---

1   A charter-party is a contract by which an entire ship or a principal part of it is let to a merchant for the carriage of goods by sea to one or more ports.

2   A bottomry bond was a contract similar to a mortgage of a ship, whereby the owner of a ship borrowed money to enable him to carry on a voyage and pledged the keel or bottom of the ship as a security for repayment. It was an essential aspect of a bottomry bond that if the ship were lost at sea, the lender would lose all the money he advanced, but if the ship returned safely, the lender would not only receive his principal, but also the agreed premium or rate of interest, no matter by how much it exceeded the legal rate of interest.

3   Average agreements are instruments by which the consignees or owners of cargo, severally agree with the master on behalf of the ship owner to pay their respective proportions of general average losses and charges of a voyage and provide appropriate security in support. Once a consignee or owner of cargo signs an average agreement, he is able to receive his goods from the vessel without the goods being detained on board until payment in total of the general average and without waiting for any adjustments to the general average to be made.

4   The noun 'protest' is an old French/late middle English word, in current use, meaning a solemn affirmation of a fact, a written declaration by a notary (in relation to the presentation of a bill of exchange and the refusal of acceptance or payment) or a written declaration by a ship's master. (See entry for 'protest' in *The New Shorter Oxford English Dictionary*).

5   In 2009, the world's commercial fleet comprised approximately 75,000 vessels, of which approximately 48,000 exceeded 500 GT in size.
    Equasis Statistics, *The World Merchant Fleet in 2009* Table 2.1. <www.equasis.org>.

Flagging and registration procedures for ships on the *Norwegian International Ship Register* ('the NIS') are typical of the procedures prescribed by many, if not most, of the world's shipping nations and provide a good example for present purposes. Notaries play an important part in the flagging and registration process. Particularly having regard to the amount of money involved and to the consequences of carelessness or negligence on the notary's part, documents relating to the registration of ships must be dealt with by a notary with more than usual care.

Norway will register 'self-propelled passenger and cargo ships and hovercraft as well as drilling platforms and other movable installations' in the NIS. The *NIS Act* and the regulations made under it prescribe the documentation required for ships coming into the NIS from foreign registers to ensure that the register contains all relevant information about a vessel's specifications and ownership and the encumbrances to which it is subject.

In addition to documents such as a certificate of name and a tonnage certificate, applicants for registration must produce, as applicable:

- a bill of sale, where there is a concurrent change of ownership of the vessel upon registration;

- a builder's certificate and delivery protocol, where the vessel to be registered is newly built and delivered; and

- a certificate of ownership from the vessel's existing register where there will be no concurrent change of ownership upon registration,

all of which must be notarized and legalized.

If the ship is owned by a non-Norwegian entity, full particulars of partners, directors, shareholders, share capital and the like must also be provided and confirmed by an appropriate notarial act. Notarial intervention is also required in relation to mortgages which are to be registered.[6]

Marine protests

There are more than 300 shipping ports in the United States handling immense quantities of intrastate, interstate and overseas cargo. The noting of marine protests in relation to actual or suspected damage to vessels or their cargo and occasionally the noting of protests in relation to demurrage,[7] or other matters

---

6   The registration of ships in the NIS and in other shipping registers can be quite complex. Care should be taken by any notary involved in the process to be completely familiar with the minutiae of the requirements relating to the relevant notarial acts before accepting instructions.

7   'Demurrage' is a term referring to the period where the charterer of a ship remains in possession of the ship after normal lay time (i.e. the period usually allowed to load and unload cargo). It also refers to extra charges the charterer pays the ship owner for the extra use of the ship.

which may have an impact on the costs or profitability of a voyage are services provided by notaries holding office in the vicinities of those ports.[8]

Entering a note of protest

Entering a note of protest is a time honored formality utilized by ships' masters sailing under virtually all flags where, following incidents at sea or unusually bad weather, cargo or ships themselves have been damaged and the masters wish to record that the damage was not caused by their own negligence or misconduct or that of their officers or crew. An allied purpose is to set the groundwork for bringing or defending a claim under any relevant marine insurance policies.

Having regard to the nature of the jurisdiction generally and to the practical difficulties often experienced in bringing witnesses before them, English and American admiralty courts have traditionally been less rigid than other courts in the evidence they are prepared to admit. Most superior courts would give short shrift to a document such as a marine protest, but in the Courts of Admiralty, marine protests are usually considered to be compelling, but not conclusive, evidence of the facts they contain.

> The Court of Admiralty credits the protest, in general, from the assumption or belief that owning to its recency, it will be truthful, fair, and impartial in its representations, inasmuch as there cannot have been sufficient time for fabricating evidence ... and it is this recency which makes it valuable when that instrument is transported into the Admiralty Court, whether as evidence *per se*, or as a test of and in comparison with other evidence bearing a subsequent date which has been imported into the suit.[9]

As the great British admiralty judge, Dr. Stephen Lushington once observed,

> In all cases the protest ought to be brought in and if it were not, there would be no difficulty in forming a conclusion as to the reason why it was kept back.[10]

Until recent times, a ship's master, armed with his log, would present himself before a notary and request the notary to prepare and enter a note of protest in relation to an incident which had occurred at sea. Nowadays, notes of protest tend to be prepared by ships' masters in standard forms devised by shipowners or shipping agents rather than by notaries. The practice has its advantages for notaries and there is no reason why a notary should insist on personally preparing a note of protest rather than accepting a note prepared by a ship's master.

---

8   Notaries holding office in all American external territories and in virtually all of the littoral states, either have specific or sufficient powers to enter and certify copies of notes of protest and extended instruments of protest.

   A protest may also be noted before a consular official of the country under whose flag the ship is registered. Most consular officials carrying out their duties in the United States will refer the noting of protests to local notaries.

9   Unknown contributor, *On the Evidence Receivable in the Court of Admiralty*, 19 Law Mag Quart Rev Juris no 1853 at 67 and 68.

10 *10 Monthly Law Magazine*, 225. Quoted in *19 Law Mag Quart Rev Juris no 57* at 68.

Regardless who actually prepares a note of protest, if possible, copies of relevant pages of the ship's log should be appended to the note and should be certified by the master as being true and correct copies of those pages of the ship's log of which they purport to be copies.

A note of protest obtains its efficacy from the master's attendance before a notary and from the formal recording by the notary of the making of the note and the entry of the particulars of the note in the notary's register.

The rule is that a note of protest must be entered as soon as is reasonably practicable after a ship puts into port and preferably within 24 hours of docking. If the note is not prepared and entered within that period, then it must also include a short statement explaining the delay. Failure to enter a note of protest has traditionally acted as a bar to any subsequent attempt to prepare and utilize an extended protest in relation to the relevant events.

A note of protest is, at once, an outline statement by a ship's master of matters of concern to him supported by entries in the ship's log, and a formal notice of the master's intention to arrange for the preparation of an extended instrument of protest concerning those matters should that course become necessary at some time in the future.[11]

The preparation of a note of protest and arranging to have it entered by a notary is normally a task for a ship's master. Where the master has died or been injured at sea or is otherwise indisposed, then the task falls to the next ranking officer and then so on, down the line.[12]

Contents of a note of protest

Even though it may actually be prepared and executed in a form which is similar to a notarial act in public form, unlike a notarial protest for non-payment or non-acceptance of a bill of exchange which is the notary's personal protest arising out of facts known to the notary, a marine note of protest is the master's personal protest and the notary bears no responsibility for the accuracy of its contents.

It has been argued that, despite the fact that in preparing a note of protest, the notary is not certifying the truth of the events being recorded or their consequences, the notary should nonetheless check that the master's statements are consistent with the relevant entries in the ship's log and that they are not otherwise inherently contradictory.[13] This approach puts far too great an onus on the notary. If it were correct, it would change the notarial function in relation to marine protests from one of recording and archiving to one of investigation and verification verging on the judicial.

---

11 In practice, extended instruments of protest are only rarely prepared, but when they are, more often than not, they will be prepared by a notary or an attorney in a port other than the port in which the note of protest was entered.

12 In extreme circumstances, the particulars for inclusion in a note of protest or for that matter in an extended instrument of protest could be obtained from crewmen, passengers, shipping agents or forwarding agents. In the most extreme circumstance, details of relevant incidents may be provided by the notary himself from enquiries he has made. (A G Dunford, *The General Notary* (1999) at 94.)

13 Ibid, 93 and 94.

There is no specific form for a note of protest, but there are certain minima which a note should always contain. In addition to a brief statement of the circumstances giving rise to its preparation, a note must also contain particulars of the master, the vessel, the voyage and where appropriate, the cargo and a formal statement to the effect that the master enters or notes his protest.

As mentioned above, copies of the relevant pages of the ship's log certified by the master as being true copies should be appended to the note. The note itself must be signed by the master in the presence of the notary who ought also mark the appended copies of the pages of the ship's log.

The following is an example of a note of protest :

No. _____ of 20__

United States of America   )

State of................................)

County of............................)

City of.................................)

ON THIS   day of   20__, personally appeared at the office of **NP** Notary Public, holding office in [city] [State] in the United States of America, **AB** Master mariner and master of the vessel [vessel's name] ('**the Vessel**') of [tonnage] tonnes or thereabouts registered in the Port of [name of port] sailing from [port where voyage commenced] to [port of destination] laden with [type of cargo] now moored at [place of mooring] on [date of mooring] who fearing damage to the Vessel or her cargo from [brief statement of circumstances] **ENTERS THIS PROTEST** against all persons concerned for all damages, costs, charges and expenses arising from the circumstances described above **AND ANNEXES** copies of pages [   ] to [   ], both inclusive, of the ship's log which he certifies are true and correct copies of those pages.

(Signature of **AB**)

....

Master

(Notary's Signature)

....

Notary Public

My Commission expires ...

Seal

Immediately after the execution of a note of protest, particulars of the note are entered into the notary's register and a reference number is allocated. The notary then prepares two certified copies of the note and any annexures to it. One copy is for the master and the other is for the shipping agent who receives it on behalf of the shipowner.[14]

The original note is filed in the notary's protocol. If and when properly requested by or on behalf of the shipowner, the notary is able to issue further certified copies from time to time.

The following is an example of a notarially certified copy of an entry or note of a marine protest:

United States of America   )

State of..............................)

County of...........................)

City of................................)

I, NP Notary Public, **CERTIFY** that the annexed copy document marked 'A' which is initialled by me and bears an impression of my official Seal for purposes of identification, is a true and correct copy of the Note of Protest of **AB** the master of the vessel [*name of vessel*] dated [*date*] and the annexures to it, as registered in my office after the Master first identified himself to me by the production of his [*identifying document(s)*]

IN WITNESS of which I have subscribed my name and affixed my seal of office this _____ day of _____ Two thousand and _____

(Notary's Signature)

....

Notary Public

My Commission expires ...

Seal

Extended protests

Occasionally, masters, shipowners or marine insurance underwriters may require a protest to be extended, that is, set out with greater particularity and more solemnity than is the case with a note of protest. From an evidentiary viewpoint, it is important that the extended instrument of protest be prepared as soon as possible after the entry of the note of protest, but in any event, within a reasonable time after the vessel arrives at her port of destination.

---

14 Even if the notary is an employee of the shipping agent, the notary's register is the notary's property and a copy of the note must be given to the shipping agent or the shipping agent's representative.

When an extended instrument of protest is prepared, it is usual for those officers and crew members who have personal knowledge of the events to be recorded to appear before the notary together with the master and for them to all jointly and severally execute the instrument and formally make declarations or swear on oath as to the truth of the several matters and things contained in or appended to the extended protest.

By its nature, the preparation of an extended instrument of protest is a time consuming matter which should be undertaken by an attorney in the same manner and with the same level of care and attention to detail as if it were an affidavit to be filed in a superior court proceeding. Its purpose is to be used as evidence in proceedings arising out of or relating to the facts set out in it. Common law practice is to have the facts set out in the instrument verified by a declaration on oath appended to or forming part of the instrument.

An extended instrument of protest is traditionally prepared as a public form act. In the absence of specific legislative limitations placed on notaries in particular states or territories, there is no reason why a notary cannot complete an extended instrument of protest in public form.

As with a note of protest, particulars of an extended instrument of protest should be entered into the notary's register and a reference number should be allocated. Certified copies should be given to each of the appearers and to the shipping agent. If anyone else, such as the consigner of cargo seeks to obtain a certified copy of the instrument, the notary should only provide a copy with the consent of the shipowner.

The following is an example of the formal parts of an extended instrument of protest:

No. _____ of 20__

United States of America   )

State of..............................)

County of............................)

City of.................................)

ON THE____ day of _____ 20__ in the City of [   ] in the State of [   ] in the United States of America **BEFORE ME, NP** Notary Public, holding office in the City of [   ] **PERSONALLY APPEARED AB**, Master Mariner ('**the Master**') master of the vessel [*name of vessel*] ('**the Vessel**') who identified himself to me by the production of his [*identifying document(s)*] and noted a protest in my office upon arrival of the Vessel from [*port where the voyage commenced*] laden with a cargo of [*type of cargo*] against damage to the Vessel or her cargo from [*brief statement of circumstances*]

ON this____ day of _____ 20__ the Master again appeared before me at
[   ] this time together with the Vessel's first officer, **FO** (**the First Officer**)
and the Vessel's chief engineer, **CE** (**the Chief Engineer**) who both identified
themselves to me by the production of their respective [*identifying documents*] and
required me to extend the note of protest previously entered.

THE MASTER, the First Officer and the Chief Engineer (together called '**the
Appearers**') severally, declared on oath before me as follows, namely:

> [*Insert a detailed statement of the principal events of the voyage on which the
> Master intends to rely in support of the Protest. The statement must be based
> upon entries in the Vessel's log and on information supplied to the Notary by
> the Appears*]

FOR THAT REASON the Appearers did severally **DECLARE ON OATH AND
PROTEST**, and at the request of the Appearers, **BY THIS NOTARIAL ACT I
ALSO PUBLICY PROTEST** against all of the facts, incidents and occurrences
set out above and against each and every one of the persons concerned, so that all
loss, damage, costs and expenses which have arisen or which may arise by reason
of the matters set out above, may be borne by the appropriate persons whether due
to average or otherwise consequent upon the dangers and perils of navigation and
not by reason of the insufficiency of the Vessel, her tackle, outfit or rigging or the
negligence, misconduct or want of skill of the Appears or of any of the Vessel's crew.

ACCORDINGLY I have signed and sealed this notarial act to be of use and benefit
to all persons concerned as they may require from time to time.

IN WITNESS of which I have subscribed my name and affixed my seal of office
this____ day of _____ Two thousand and _____

(Notary's Signature)

....

Notary Public

My Commission expires ...

Seal

WE, **AB**, **FO** and **CE** being respectively the Master, the First Officer and the
Chief Engineer of the vessel [*name of vessel*] ('**the Vessel**') do jointly and severally
declare on oath as follows:

1.   At all material times we were on board the Vessel when the events of
the voyage described in the above Extended Ship Protest took place
and we make this Declaration from personal knowledge.

2,   The content of the declarations made by us in support of the above
Protest are true.

AND WE MAKE this declaration on oath believing it to be true and correct and in the knowledge that persons making false declarations are liable to the penalties of perjury.

SWORN by **AB, FO** and **CE**   )

severally at _____)

this _____ day of _____)

20__   )

Before me:

(Notary's Signature)

....

Notary Public

My Commission expires ...

Seal

CHAPTER 9

Signer Competency

It is axiomatic that no affidavit or declaration can properly be made and no deed or instrument under hand can be validly executed if the person seeking to do so lacks sufficient mental competency[1].

The distinction between comprehension and competency

At the outset, the distinction must be made between a signer's comprehension of the terms of the document he or she is about to sign and the signer's competency to sign it. In practice the distinction between comprehension and competency can sometimes be a little blurred. It is not always easy, particularly for younger or less experienced notaries to tell the difference. Nonetheless, there is a difference and it is an important one.

'**Comprehension**' is the act, fact or faculty of understanding, especially of writing or speech.[2]

'**Competency**' or '**capacity**' means the mental ability to understand problems and make decisions.[3]

A person may well have normal mental or intellectual ability (i.e. competency), but may not fully or properly comprehend (i.e. understand) the terms and conditions of a legal document. Equally, a person may be suffering from a mental illness or a degree of intellectual impairment, but may still understand the nature and effect of a legal document he or she is being asked to sign. In the United States, no state or territory directly or indirectly imposes an obligation on notaries to screen signers for actual comprehension.[4] Nor is there any common law duty for notaries to do so.[5]

---

1   In most common law jurisdictions outside the United States, the term 'capacity' is used when referring to a person's inherent mental or intellectual power or legal competency.

2   See entry for 'comprehension' in *The New Shorter Oxford Dictionary* (1993).

3   Entries for 'competency' and 'capacity' in *Black's Law Dictionary* (9th ed), 2009.

4   Arizona's *Notary Public Reference Manual* directs notaries in that state to ensure that a signer comprehends the underlying transaction. In the context, the direction almost certainly refers to 'competency' rather than 'comprehension'.

5   For a comprehensive discussion on the subject see Klint L Bruno and Michael L Closen, *Notaries Public and Document Signer Comprehension : a Dangerous Mirage in the Desert of Notarial Law and Practice*, 44 South Dakota Law Review (1999), 494.

In civil law jurisdictions, particularly in relation to real estate transactions, notaries are required to be satisfied that parties to the transaction have full capacity to enter into contracts and undertake obligations and that they well and truly understand the terms of the transaction and of the notarial act which they will sign together with the notary. Indeed, before executing a notarial act in authentic form, a European notary will read the entire document over to the parties (or their attorneys-in-fact) and will then explain the legal position to ensure that they do understand the transaction.

In America, a significant majority of states and territories make it clear, either in legislation or in notary materials, that a notary should refuse to notarize the signature of a person whose demeanor causes the notary to have compelling concerns about whether the person knows or understands the consequences of the transaction requiring the notarial act. [6] There is no doubt that in those jurisdictions, where both materials and legislation are silent, the common law would support any notary who declined to notarize a document due to a perceived lack of signer competency.

Signer Competency generally

Fortunately, in the majority of cases, the question of competency is not something of concern – partly because in the absence of evidence to the contrary, all adults are presumed to be competent, and partly because it is usually patent from indicia such as discussions which take place when an appointment is made, the manner in which a document is approached, handled and signed, and a person's general demeanor, that the person indeed is competent.

There will always be a limited number of occasions when the matter of a signer's competency is not clear cut. Obviously, when the slightest suspicion of lack of competency arises, a notary cannot properly provide any notarial services until being completely satisfied that a problem does not exist.

Regrettably, there is no single 'off-the-shelf' medical or legal test for competency. The level of competency required of a person to enter into contracts and undertake obligations largely depends on the individual's ability to understand the nature and consequences of his or her actions in relation to a particular transaction. A good rule of thumb is, the more important or complex the transaction and the greater the amount involved, the greater the level of understanding required.[7]

---

6   Alaska, American Samoa, Arizona, Colorado, Connecticut, Delaware, Florida, Georgia, Guam, Hawaii, Illinois, Indiana, Iowa, Kansas, Maine, Massachusetts, Minnesota, Mississippi, Montana, New Mexico, North Carolina, Oregon, Rhode Island, South Carolina, South Dakota, Texas, Vermont, West Virginia and Wisconsin.

7   Roger West, *Dementia Awareness for Lawyers*, (A paper presented at a seminar conducted in October 2001 by the Continuing Legal Education Department of the Faculty of Law, University of New South Wales).

The problem is compounded by the fact that, although lack of competency is generally tied to mental, physical or intellectual impairment or disability, the assessment of which fall into the medical domain, the question of competency is a legal construct which ultimately falls to the courts to determine.

Testamentary capacity

The law has long regarded the making of a will as being the act of an individual which requires the highest level of competency. The classic statements of law concerning competency relate to testamentary capacity, and it is from those statements that the guiding principles relating to competency generally have emerged.

The exposition of principles by Cockburn CJ in *Banks v Goodfellow*[8] remains the leading judicial statement in the common law world concerning testamentary capacity. His Honor said:

> It is essential ... that a testator shall understand the nature of the act and its effects; shall understand the extent of the property of which he is disposing; shall be able to comprehend and appreciate the claims to which he ought to give effect and, with a view to the latter object, that no disorder of the mind shall poison his affections, pervert his sense of right, or prevent the exercise of his natural faculties – that no insane delusion shall influence his will in disposing of his property and bring about a disposal which, if the mind had been sound, would not have been made.

> Here, then, we have the measure of the degree of mental power which should be insisted on. If the human instincts and affections, or the moral sense, become perverted by mental disease; if insane suspicion or aversion take the place of natural affection; if reason and judgement are lost, and the mind becomes a prey to insane delusions calculated to interfere with and disturb its functions and to lead to a testamentary disposition due only to their baneful influence – in such a case it is obvious that the condition of the testamentary power fails and that a will made under such circumstances ought not to stand.

His Honor later commented about a testator having only a partial unsoundness of mind and said:

> ... a degree or form of unsoundness which neither disturbs the exercise of the faculties necessary for such an act (i.e. disposing of property), nor is capable of influencing the result, ought not take away the power of making a will or place a person so circumstanced is a less advantageous position than others with regard to their right ...[9]

---

8   (1870) LR 5QB 549 at 565.

9   Ibid, 566.

When considering the level of competency required by two of three joint proprietors of land in Tasmania to execute deeds reversing a joint tenancy, in *Gibbons v Wright* the High Court of Australia found that:

> The law does not prescribe any fixed standard of sanity as requisite for the validity of all transactions. It requires in relation to each particular matter or piece of business transacted, that each party shall have such a soundness of mind as to be capable of understanding the general nature of what he is doing by his participation.[10]

The court went on to find that the level of competency required by the law in relation to an instrument is relative to the particular transaction being effected by means of the instrument, and may be described as the capacity to 'understand the nature of the transaction when it is explained'.

As alluded to above, lack of competency can be brought about by mental illness, physical disability, intellectual disability or a combination of them. In dealing with physically or intellectually disabled people or those suffering from mental illness, a notary should not assume that physical or intellectual disability or mental illness automatically equates to lack of competency.

Instead, time should be spent and effort made to determine whether or not the person requiring notarial services does in fact have a sufficient level of competency to 'understand the general nature of what he is doing by his participation' and to 'understand the nature of [the] transaction when it is explained'.[11]

Mental illness

When discussing competency, terms such as 'dementia' 'mental illness' and 'intellectual disability' are commonly bandied about by the notariat and by the legal profession. This, all too often without any real appreciation of their meanings or of the differences between them, and more importantly, without knowing how to communicate properly and deal with people in order to determine their level of competency.

It is therefore appropriate to take a short excursus into matters medical and then briefly to consider a number of techniques that may be of assistance to notaries interviewing persons who appear to have an intellectual impairment or to be suffering from dementia or mental illness.[12]

---

10 (1954) 91 CLR 423 (Dixon CJ, Kitto and Taylor JJ.)

11 If it turns out that, say, an intellectually impaired person, does have sufficient competency to execute a document such as a power of attorney, there is no reason why, in the notary's journal it cannot be stated that although the donor suffers from a degree of intellectual impairment, the notary is satisfied that the donor had sufficient capacity to properly execute the power of attorney concerned.

12 I am indebted to Dr Leon Fennessy MB BS DPM FRANZCP, for his contribution to the preparation of this part of the chapter.

'Mental illness' is a generic term covering a number of disorders of the mind which typically, but not always, result in diminished competency in those affected. It is important to distinguish between mental illness and intellectual disability, although occasionally, at a superficial level, the distinction may be difficult to see or recognize. [13] With proper medication, many mental illnesses can be treated and kept under control so that mentally ill persons may not in fact suffer any significant diminution in competency.

Dementia

The condition known as 'dementia' has become more common among the increasing number of elderly in Western society. Dementia is not itself a disease. Rather, it is a descriptive term for the loss of the ability to think, remember, and reason that arises out of a number of diseases or physical conditions which tend to affect older persons and which, to a greater or lesser degree, prevent sufferers from functioning normally on a day-to-day basis. Some of the better known causes of dementia are Alzheimer's disease,[14] Huntington's disease,[15] Parkinson's disease,[16] and serious substance abuse, particularly alcohol abuse.

Regardless of the specific cause, dementia generally exhibits a common progression. Typically it begins benignly, often over a period of years. Initially, there is a loss of memory, especially short-term memory. Subsequently, the person may become lost while driving or walking in places once known extremely well. Questions and answers are quickly forgotten. Significant personality changes may take place. As intellectual functions deteriorate, the sufferer typically has difficulty in naming objects and understanding concepts. The person finds it difficult to concentrate or follow a conversation. Motor skills steadily become lost.

Other symptoms may include robust denial of the problem and increasing periods of depression, anxiety and demoralization. Often, sufferers exhibit emotional incontinence and respond inappropriately to social situations in which they find themselves. For example at a funeral, a person in an advanced stage of dementia might start laughing uncontrollably.

Certainly, in the early stages of dementia, a person could well have sufficient competency to execute a range of documents, including a power of attorney. But again to state the obvious, a notary must proceed with extreme caution once there is even the slightest suspicion that a person wishing to take an oath or execute a document has a problem that could bear upon his or her competency.

---

13 'Intellectual disability' and 'mental retardation' are two names for exactly the same thing. 'Intellectual disability' is the expression which is generally used throughout the English speaking world and which is now gaining currency within the United States as the preferred term. In 2007, the American Association on Mental Retardation changed its name to the American Association on Intellectual and Developmental Disabilities.

14 A progressive degenerative brain disease usually striking after age 65.

15 An inherited degenerative brain disease.

16 A progressive disorder of the central nervous system.

Schizophrenia

Schizophrenia apparently affects approximately one percent of the population and is one of the most seriously disabling of the mental illnesses. It tends to have an onset before the age of 45 years. Popular belief notwithstanding, people suffering from schizophrenia do not have dual or split personalities.

Schizophrenics typically suffer from hallucination (i.e. seeing or hearing things that are not real) or delusions (i.e. false beliefs which are not borne out by the facts or by objective evidence), and usually have poor reasoning ability and loss of memory. More often than not, schizophrenics suffer from lack of judgment. They typically exhibit inappropriate emotional responses to external events.

The affective disorders

The most common mental illnesses are the so-called 'affective' or 'mood' disorders which are believed to affect about eight percent of the population, at least to some degree. 'Bipolar' disorder is where a person swings between extreme high moods and extreme low moods. 'Unipolar' disorder is where a person suffers from persistent severe depression and manic phases. Persons suffering from bipolar disorder will often be delusional, impulsive and erratic. Typically, they will be short tempered and argumentative and will have grandiose ideas coupled with extremely poor judgment.

Persons suffering from depression, whether because of unipolar disorder or in the depressive phase of bipolar disorder, usually exhibit a loss of interest in daily activities and have an inability to concentrate. Typically they also suffer from feelings of despondency or sadness and feelings of guilt and hopelessness.

Although there are a number of other mental illnesses which, in their active phases, can and do effect competence from a legal viewpoint, the affective disorders and schizophrenia tend to be the most obvious of the more common disorders, if not treated.

Clearly, a notary is not expected to be a psychiatrist. But when faced with someone who obviously is exhibiting symptoms which are consistent with one or other of the more common forms of mental illness, the notary must take steps to be satisfied that the person indeed is sufficiently competent to attend to the tasks in hand.

When in doubt, the first step is to seek advice from an expert in the area, with a view to ascertaining whether or not the person is suffering from a mental illness and if so, whether the person's competency is affected and to what degree. Even though the question of competency is a legal issue, the assessment of competency is primarily a matter for the clinical judgment of an appropriately qualified medical practitioner.

Whenever expert advice is sought and provided, it should always be in writing. Particularly where the advice is in favor of a person's competency, a careful notary will have the expert provide the advice in writing or in appropriate cases, by a sworn statement. It should go without saying that if, for whatever reason, a person, or those apparently helping the person, decline to allow a medical opinion to be provided, the notary should in turn eschew any further involvement with the transaction.

Intellectual disability

It is said that about one percent of the American population has an intellectual disability. Of those persons, about three quarters have a mild disability, with the remainder suffering moderate to profound disablement.[17] Intellectual disability in relation to a person over the age of five years is the concurrent existence of:

- significant sub-average general intellectual functioning, and

- significant deficits in adaptive behavior

each of which became manifest before the age of 18 years.[18]

All too commonly, community attitudes towards the intellectually disabled are based on negative stereotypes which affect the manner in which disabled people are treated. Anecdotal evidence indicates, for example, that some lawyers and judicial officers have difficulty in accepting that persons with 'low IQ' are able to give reliable evidence.[19]

There are several techniques appropriate for communicating with intellectually disabled persons, which can also be of assistance when dealing with persons apparently suffering from mental illness. They include the following:

- language used should be simple, direct, free of abstract concepts and unnecessary information, paced to allow understanding (but not so slow as to be patronizing), clear (but not loud) and mindful of the tendency of people with an intellectual disability to take words literally;

- questions should be non-leading, short and free of multiple concepts and multiple negatives;

- all questions and information should be directed to the person and not to the person's carer or service provider;

- reassurance and encouragement of the client often is necessary to overcome the client's inexperience and fear of legal decision making, and

- most importantly, the client's understanding cannot be assumed merely because he or she does not ask questions, and the client should be periodically asked to explain matters in his or her own words.[20]

---

17 Generally see the American Association on Intellectual and Developmental Disability (AAIDD) website, <www.aamr.org>.

18 According to the AIDD, a significantly below average intelligence is an IQ of about 70 or less. Significant deficits in adaptive behaviour involve difficulties with everyday life and personal skills when compared with other persons of the same age and culture, e.g. the ability to dress or bath without help or to express thoughts clearly.

19 Reported in *People with an Intellectual Disability and the Criminal Justice System.*(New South Wales Law Reform Commission Discussion Paper 35, October 1994), Ch 3 at para 3.12.

20 Ibid, at para 3.29.

CHAPTER 10

AUTHENTICATING NOTARIZATIONS

In the United States, as in most other countries, notarizations, vital records, documents emanating from courts or officials connected with the courts and other public documents of domestic origin enjoy a special status.[1] Having been prepared by government or by trustworthy institutions or officials appointed or approved by government, public documents are generally considered to have the highest possible evidentiary value. As a rule, they are accepted as being *prima facie* genuine and are admitted in evidence by local courts without proof of the signatures or seals which they bear.

Legalization

For reasons ranging from a lack of familiarity with other countries' legal systems to fears of forgery and knavery, proof of the authenticity of foreign public documents has long been required by officialdom in most jurisdictions as a pre-condition to the use or efficacy of those documents within their territories. To meet that need, sooner or later most countries came to adopt the practice of consular authentication or 'legalization' of foreign public documents.

Contrary to popular belief within the consular services and bureaucracies of a significant number of countries, to say nothing of the belief of many bankers, patent attorneys, lawyers and members of the public, 'legalization' does not in any way certify the truth or accuracy of information contained in a document, nor does it enhance the value of the document or its contents.

Legalization is merely:

> The formality by which the diplomatic or consular agents of the country in which the document has to be produced, certify the authenticity of the signature, the capacity in which the person signing the document has acted and, where appropriate, the identity of the seal or stamp which it bears.[2]

---

1   The definition of 'public document' differs from jurisdiction to jurisdiction and from time to time. Presently, the most common definition in general use around the world is that found in Article 1 of the Hague Conference on Private International Law *Convention of October 5, 1961 Abolishing the Requirement for Legalization for Foreign Public Documents. (**The Apostille Convention**)*

The English language version of the Apostille Convention is found in Appendix 3 below. The definition of 'public documents' set out in the *Apostille Convention* appears later in this chapter.

2   Article 2, *The Apostille Convention.*

The earliest legislative reference to a requirement for consular authentication of documents to be produced outside their countries of origin appears to be in the French *Marine Ordinance of August 1681*, which provided that:

> No Instruments written in Foreign Countries where there are ... [French] ... Consuls shall be of any Value, if they are not made Authentick (sic) by them.[3]

By virtue of a treaty of commerce signed on 6 February 1778, it was also France which first granted the right to consular representation to the United States.[4]

Within a relatively short time, the new republic concluded commercial treaties with other European nations which guaranteed the right to consuls.[5] By the beginning of the 19th century, American consular officers were found in posts around the world and were routinely legalizing documents such as powers of attorney which were to be produced within the territory of the United States.

The following certificate of authenticity in relation to a power of attorney was prepared in 1805 by Augustin Madan, who was the first United States' consul in South America.

> I Augustin Madan, Consul of the United States of America Do hereby certify that the annexed Power of Attorney confered by the deceased James Buffington on his mate Artemas Harrington and signed by the notary public of the port Don Jos. Manual Sabogat and testified by other two notaries Don Manuel Garcia and Don Andres Martinez to whose signatures and to this said Public instrument due faith and Credit is given Judicially, and extrajudicially. In testimony whereof I subscribed my name and affixed the seal of my office at this port of Laguaria August seventeenth, year of our Lord one thousand eight hundred and five.[6]

Until the early 19th century, it probably would not have been too difficult for a consul to personally satisfy himself as to the identity and status of the notary or other public official whose signature and seal were to be authenticated. One can imagine that in many European posts and certainly in most Caribbean and South American port towns, consuls and notaries were acquainted socially at least. However, as the number of notaries and public officials swelled to meet the needs of burgeoning cities and international trade, maintaining contact would have become increasingly difficult. In large cities such as London and Paris, it would have become nigh on impossible for consuls to know or even recognize all the city's notaries and senior public officials.

---

3   Section X, Article XXIII. *The Ordinance of Lewis* [sic] *XIV King of France and Navarre Given at Fontainebleau in the month of August 1861. Concerning the Marine.* 'The Consuls of the French Nations in Foreign Countries' (Translated from French by Alexander Justice and appearing in his *General Treatise of the Dominion of the Sea and a Compleat Body of the Sea Laws,* (2nd ed, London. Between 1707 and 1724, 274,).

4   William Palfrey was America's first formally designated consul. He was appointed in 1780 but did not take up his post as his ship was lost at sea on the voyage to France. The position was taken up by Thomas Barclay Chester Lloyd Jones. (*The Consular Service of the United States – its history and activities,* University of Pennsylvania, 1906, 2).

5   Ibid.

6   From the author's personal collection of early notarial instruments and related documents.

Therefore, from about the mid-19th century onwards, most countries began to prove the authenticity of foreign notarial acts and other public documents by using the services of their consuls abroad, not as a direct interface with notaries and public officials actually known to them, but as the final link in a process which became known as the 'chain of authentication'.

The chain of authentication

The chain of authentication involves a series of verifications by acceptable people or bodies endorsed on the subject document, where each successive person or body in the chain is either familiar with or is able to satisfactorily identify the immediately preceding verifier or signatory.

The process culminates in the signature and official stamp or seal of an official, usually a consular officer of the country where the document is to be produced, which either do not require formal proof or may be readily provable in the courts or institutions of that country.

Over time, the final link, namely the signature and stamp or seal of a consular officer or other recognized official became known as 'legalization' and still occasionally, in the United States, as 'consularization'.[7]

Despite the adoption in 1961 of an international convention abolishing chain legalization as between the Contracting States, to which 102 countries including the United States are now party (see below), proving the authenticity of foreign public documents by the chain of authentication is still required by about half of the world's sovereign states.[8]

The length of the chain varies. In some countries it only comprises two links including legalization by a consulate of the destination country.[9] On the other hand, in the United States, the chain can be quite lengthy. Typically, in relation to a notarization it involves:

1. the certification of the notary's signature and seal by the county clerk of the county in which the notary is registered;

2. the certification of the county clerk's certificate by the Secretary of State's office of the state in which the county is located;

---

7   With hindsight, it may have been preferable for the expression 'consularisation' to have caught on. 'Legalization' is an inappropriate shorthand to describe the final part of the authentication process. It is an evocative word, the use of which elevates the process to which it relates from being an important but, nonetheless, mundane administrative task, to an activity of great solemnity and significance, at least in the minds of a good many of those involved in the process.

8   Those countries include Brazil, China, Indonesia; the countries of the Arab League (other than Oman), almost all the South East Asian countries and significant parts of Africa (See Appendix 6).

9   For example, in Australia, the Department of Foreign Affairs and Trade (DFAT) office in a notary's home state or territory will authenticate the notary's signature and seal on a document. The document bearing the DFAT stamp is then legalized by the relevant consulate.

3. the authentication of the State Secretary of State's certificate by the Authentications Unit of the U.S. Department of State in Washington DC; and

4. the legalization of the U.S. Department of State's authentication by a consular officer of the destination country.

At each step of the way, the notarized document must be sent or delivered to the relevant office by or on behalf of the person requiring the legalization and must be returned to or picked up by the lodging party. It is not unknown for the entire process to take upwards of six or seven weeks.

Occasionally, additional procedures are required in destination countries. For example, on arrival in Chile, a legalized notarization must be presented at the 'Legalization' section of the Consular Department of the Ministry of Foreign Affairs in Santiago (which is only open from 9.00 a.m. to noon each weekday) to have the consul's signature certified.

The *Apostille Convention*

In 1955, the Council of Europe requested the Hague Conference on Private International Law to give consideration to the drafting of a convention which would alleviate the problems associated with legalization and at the same time, retain the effect of what was considered to be an indispensable legal formality in proving documents crossing national borders. [10]

The reference ultimately resulted in the adoption of the **Hague Convention of October 5, 1961 Abolishing the Requirement of Legalization for Foreign Public Documents** (*'the Apostille Convention'*) at the Ninth Session of the Hague Conference.[11]

The purpose of the *Apostille Convention* was to replace legalization of foreign public documents as between the Contracting States with a universally recognized, simple, dated, numbered and regulated certificate in a prescribed

---

10 The Hague Conference on Private International Law is an inter-governmental organization, the first session of which was convened in 1893 by the Netherlands government on the initiative of T M C Asser (who, in 1911, was awarded the Nobel Peace Prize). Its purpose is to work for the progressive unification of the rules of private international law. (*Statute of the Hague Conference*, Article 1).

11 The governments of 18 member states sent delegations to the Ninth Session.

A five member Observer Delegation from the United States attended the Session and took an active part in the deliberations. The U.S. delegates were Messrs. Philip W Amram (Washington DC), Joseph C Barrett (Arkansas), James C Dezendorf (Oregon), Kurt H Nadelmann (Massachusetts) and Willis L M Rees (New York).

It is noteworthy that, 'The discussion provoked by the United States Observers ... [was] ... to the advantage of the Hague Conference', and they 'were made to feel ... that their active participation in the work of the conference ... [was] ... welcome and desired.'

(Kurt H Nadelmann, *The Hague Conference on Private International Law Ninth Session*, American Journal of Comparative Law, Vol 9, Issue 4 (Autumn 1960), 583).

form which would be placed on a public document to be produced within the territory of a Contracting State, by a so-called 'Competent Authority' in another Contracting State from which the document emanated.[12]

The Convention established a regime whereby the only formality which is required in the Contracting States to certify the authenticity of the signature and capacity in which a person signing a public document has acted (and where appropriate, the identity of the seal or stamp on the document), is the addition of a prescribed certificate to be known as an 'apostille'.[13]

That requirement is subject to two riders. The first is that where, in specific cases, as between two or more Contracting States, legalization of particular documents is not otherwise required, there is no need to have apostilles affixed to the documents concerned.[14] The second is that the Convention only overrides the provisions of a treaty, convention, or agreement between two or more contracting states relating to the certification of signatures, seals or stamps on public documents if those provisions are more rigorous than the formality of the affixing of an apostille.[15]

---

12 A full list of the Contracting States and their various overseas departments, dependencies and territories which are subject to the *Apostille Convention* as at 31 December 2011 is set out in Appendix 4.

13 *Apostille Convention,* Article 3.

'Apostille' (pronounced 'apostee') was originally an early 16th century French word, which meant a short recommendation or recommendatory note written by an influential person on the margin of a petition or at the foot of a letter. (J Ch Tarver, *The Royal Phraseological English-French, French-English Dictionary*, 3rd ed London, 1858).

The form of the apostille is set out in an annex to the Convention.

14 Ibid.

For example, Australia and New Zealand are both parties to the Convention. Before it became a party, New Zealand did not require Australian public documents to be legalized or otherwise authenticated before production within its territory. Therefore, even though the Convention now applies to New Zealand, apostilles need not be affixed to Australian public documents to be produced there and vice versa.

In addition to the *Apostille Convention*, there are presently a number of other conventions on foot in Europe involving differing numbers of contracting states, which exempt certain classes of documents from the requirements for legalization within the territories of the various contracting states. Those conventions deal with matters such as the abolition of legalization of documents executed by diplomatic agents or consular officers (London 7 June 1968) and international co-operation in administrative assistance to refugees (Basel 3 September 1985). As between the contracting states, apostilles need not be affixed to those documents subject to any relevant convention(s) which would otherwise be considered to be 'public documents' for the purposes of the *Apostille Convention*.

15 *Apostille Convention,* Article 8.

This Article appears to be a 'belts and braces' provision which seeks to make it absolutely clear that the Convention is a simplification mechanism designed to replace more complex procedures. It is hard to imagine the provisions of a treaty between two countries which set up mechanisms for the legalization of public documents where the formalities of legalization were simpler (i.e. less rigorous) than the affixing of an apostille.

U.S. accession to the *Apostille Convention*

The United States has been a Member State of the Hague Conference since 15 October 1964.[16] It acceded to the *Apostille Convention* on 24 August 1980 and the Convention entered into force for the whole of the United States and its territories on 15 October 1981.

U.S. Competent Authorities

In accordance with the Convention's requirements, on becoming party to the *Apostille Convention,* the United States designated a number of authorities competent to affix apostilles to U.S. public documents destined for production in other 'convention' countries, namely:

- **The U.S. Department of State Authentications Office** to affix apostilles to

  ◦ documents issued by federal agencies; and

  ◦ notarizations by military notaries;

- **The U.S. Department of State, Bureau of Consular Affairs** (Passport Services, Vital Records Section) to affix apostilles to

  ◦ consular reports of births, deaths and marriages of U.S. citizens abroad; and

  ◦ certificates of births and deaths originally issued by the Panama Canal Zone Government between 1904 and 1979;

- **Clerks and deputy clerks of the U.S. Federal Courts** to affix apostilles issued by those courts;[17] and

- **Authorities in each state and territory and the District of Columbia** (typically the State Secretary of State) to affix apostilles to notarizations and other public documents emanating from those jurisdictions.

For obvious practical reasons, the group of Competent Authorities in large part mirrors the group of state and federal authorities involved in authenticating notarizations and other public documents for the purposes of 'chain' legalization.[18]

---

16 There is a difference between 'Members' of the Hague Conference and parties to particular Hague Conventions. It is not necessary for a party to a convention to be a Member state.

17 Although not specifically stated, the intention was that apostilles would be affixed to documents issued by a particular federal court by the clerk or deputy clerk of that court.

   The U.S. Department of Justice may authenticate the seal of the federal court and the U.S. Department of State Authentications Office will affix an apostille to the Justice Department's authentication.

18 Particulars of the designated Competent Authorities which authenticate notarizations may be found in Appendix 5.

'Apostillize' and 'apostillization'

Even though consular legalization as such has been abolished as between the Contracting States, the affixing of an apostille to a public document is nonetheless still generally known colloquially as 'legalization'.

In recent times, there has been an attempt by the Permanent Bureau of the Hague Conference to introduce the word 'apostillize' as a verb and the word 'apostillization' as a noun in relation to the affixing of an apostille. Despite their quaint blend of French and English, use of those words is beginning to gain some currency, at least in Europe.

'Public documents' for the purposes of the *Apostille Convention*

Having regard to then generally accepted notions as to which documents were 'public documents' for the purpose of legalizing them by a chain of authentication, the framers of the *Apostille Convention* decided that the following documents should be deemed to be 'public documents' for the purposes of the Convention, namely:

- documents emanating from an authority or an official connected with the courts or tribunals of the state, including those emanating from a public prosecutor, a clerk of court or a process server (*huissier de justice*);

- administrative documents;

- **notarial acts**; and

- official certificates which are placed on documents signed by persons in their private capacity such as official certificates recording the registration of a document or the fact that it was in existence on a certain date and official and **notarial authentications of signatures**.[19]
  (*emphasis added*).

Notarizations as public documents

In his Explanatory Report on the Convention, the Convention's rapporteur, Professor Yvon Loussouarn, did not offer a reason why in addition to 'notarial acts', 'notarial authentications of signatures' were deemed to be 'public documents'.[20]

It may be that the framers of the Convention had American notaries in mind when inserting the provision. Even if they did not, the provision enables apostilles to be affixed to notarized documents in order to authenticate the signatures and seals of American notaries who do not, as a rule, prepare notarial acts in the sense that term is understood elsewhere in the world.[21] If the provision did not exist, American notarizations might well have been excluded from the operation of the *Apostille Convention*.

---

19 *Apostille Convention*, Article 1.
20 HCCH Publications 1961.
21 See Chapter 2.

The form of an apostille

The annex to the *Apostille Convention* prescribes a model certificate which is specified as being 'in the form of a square with sides at least 9 centimetres long'.

Most Contracting States utilize certificates which follow the model in both size and style. However, a number of American states and territories have developed apostilles which are full page size. The Convention itself does not make apostilles of that nature illegal or inappropriate. It is a matter for each state or territory to decide upon the type and style of apostille to be used.

Affixing an apostille

Regrettably, the *Apostille Convention* does not stipulate a method of affixing apostilles to public documents. In 2003, a Special Commission of the Hague Conference noted the wide variety of means utilized by different states for affixing apostilles as follows:

> These means may include 'rubber stamp', glue, (multi-coloured) ribbons, wax seals, impressed seals, self-adhesive stickers etc. ... [When the apostille is attached to the public document as a separate document, referred to in the treaty as an 'allonge'] ... these means may include glue, grommets, staples etc.[22]

After having described the different methodologies, the Special Commission decided to leave the matter in the hands of the individual countries after commenting that all the means set out above were acceptable under the Convention.[23]

In a letter sent to the National Association of Secretaries of State on 9 July 2004, the U.S. Department of State wrote, among other things:

> ... as a practical matter, many foreign courts expect to see Apostilles attached with a fair degree of formality. To the extent that pre-printed Apostille allonges are used, it is essential that you consider using special anti-fraud watermarked paper, stick-on gold seals, and/or wet signatures, and that you **employ a staple or grommet system that is fraud-resistant** (*emphasis added*). All Apostilles and allonges should be permanently affixed to the public document by the state issuing authority and not by the customer.[24]

The 2003 Hague Conference Special Commission unquestionably erred in its decision. It should have stipulated that any means of affixing an apostille in a manner which enables it to be readily detached from the public document to which it relates is unacceptable practice which would entitle a receiving state to refuse acceptance.

---

22 2003 Special Commission Conclusion No. 16.

23 Ibid.

24 Department of State letter regarding electronic records and formality of apostille (July 9, 2004). <www.state.gov/s1/2004/78075.htm>.

The Hague Conference Special Commission of 2009 was not prepared to formally reverse the 2003 decision, but made it clear that;

> without excluding any specific means of affixing an Apostille ... [The Special Commission encouraged] the use of methods that would evidence any tampering with the method of affixation.[25]

The success of the *Apostille Convention*

Since its entry into force half a century ago, the success of the *Apostille Convention* has been remarkable. It is the most widely ratified and used of all the Hague Conventions. In 2010, over 10 million apostilles were issued in (then)100 countries around the world.[26] In the same year, when surveying foreign direct investment regulation across 87 economies, the World Bank acknowledged the positive impact of the *Apostille Convention* on the ability of foreign investors to start up businesses in those countries which were party to the Convention.[27]

At the Third Regional Meeting of the e-APP for Europe project held in Paris on 4–5 October 2011 (which co-incided with the commemoration of the 50th Anniversary of the adoption of the *Apostille Convention)*, the participants noted

> the invaluable and ongoing contribution of the Apostille Convention to the international circulation of public documents and the important advantages it brings to individuals and businesses in the course of their cross-border movements and activities.[28]

The electronic Apostille Program

The introduction of the electronic Apostille Program (e-APP), an initiative of the Hague Conference and the National Notary Association, is the most important recent innovation relating to the future of the apostille. The program has two independent components

• the electronic register (the e-Register); and

• the electronic apostille (the e-Apostille)

which may be implemented together or individually.[29]

Officially launched in April 2006, the e-APP has not yet reached the ambitious goals originally set for it, but the move toward implementation is gradually gathering momentum in the United States and elsewhere in the world.[30]

---

25 Conclusion and Recommendation No. 91 of the 2009 Special Commission.

26 Response of the Hague Conference Permanent Bureau of 10 May 2011 to the European Commission Green Paper, Less bureaucracy for citizens : promoting free movement of public documents and recognition of the effects of civil status records (Released 14 December 2010) <www.hcch.net>.

27 The World Bank Group *Investing Across Borders* 2010 (Washington DC).

28 Conclusion & Recommendation No 1 of the Meeting.

29 Details of both components may be found on the e-APP website <www.e-app.info>.

    The site provides information about both components as well as a memorandum on some of the technical aspects underlying the suggested model for the issuing of e-Apostilles.

30 See <www.e-app.info>. The Hague Conference and the NNA publish an implementation charge which is updated periodically and which may be found on the Hague Conference e-APP website.

This is particularly so in relation to the introduction of e-Registers. The technology is inexpensive and simple. Inputting data into an e-Register is neither difficult nor time consuming. The implementation of an e-Register associated with a simple website established and controlled by the issuing Competent Authority affords recipients of documents bearing apostilles to readily search the register to confirm whether or not an apostille is genuine.

As at October 2011, approximately 60 Competent Authorities in 12 countries had implemented one or both of the e-APP components in all or part of their territories. In the United States, eight states, led by Rhode Island (in February 2007), have put e-Registers in place.[31]

It is expected that by 2015, the majority of American jurisdictions will be on board. How long it will take for electronic apostilles to become a norm is still a matter for speculation.

Reminding people of the need to authenticate notarizations

It should not be assumed simply because a country has acceded to the *Apostille Convention* and has announced its accession and subsequently the entry into force of the Convention in its official government media, that all its public servants, lawyers, bank officials, public institutions and authorities, let alone the public generally, will immediately be familiar with the apostille system or even be aware that it has replaced consular legalization of public documents emanating from other Convention countries.

It also should not be assumed that all lawyers, bank staff, public officials and others in the United States or abroad have even heard of 'legalization' in any form or if they have, that they understand the difference between consular legalization and authentication by the affixing of an apostille or that they appreciate that for the foreseeable future, the two systems will both operate in tandem depending upon the origin or destination of documents.

Pointing out to a document signer that a notarization must be properly authenticated before it can be used in a destination country does not constitute the unauthorized practice of law by a notary. Nor does explaining to the signer how and where to have a notarized document legalized.

As many notaries will attest, problems can and do arise where a person seeking to have a document notarized for production abroad has been told by a government official, a lawyer, a bank officer or often enough, a helpful relative in the destination country which has become subject to the *Apostille Convention* that after being notarized, the notarization must be legalized by the country's consular officials before it can be used.

Most people will accept being told by a notary, albeit, sometimes a little reluctantly, that the affixing of an apostille has replaced consular legalization in a particular case for a particular country. But there is always a small and usually

---

31 California, Colorado, Kansas, North Carolina, Rhode Island, Texas, Washington, West Virginia.

voluble minority who know better or believe what they have been (wrongly) told by someone in the destination country and who, frequently hysterically, insist on consular legalization. A notary can only direct people to the need for authentication.

Under those circumstances, most consular officers will do the right thing and refuse to legalize notarizations which have been proffered to them for the purpose. Others resolve the problem by agreeing to put a consular stamp on a document which bears an apostille – an incorrect but completely understandable response to the intense pressure members of the public can often bring to bear.

Authenticating notarizations by military notaries

Notarizations by military notaries have apostilles affixed to them or are authenticated for chain legalization purposes by the U.S. Department of State Authentications office. In addition to meeting the office's usual authentication requirements, persons submitting military notarizations must also advise the Authentications Office in writing that the notarization has been performed by a military notary pursuant to 10 USC 1044a.[32]

Notes on practical aspects of authenticating notarizations

- **World authentication requirements**

    An outline of world authentication requirements for notarizations to be produced outside the United States (as at 31 December 2011) is found at **Appendix 6** below.

- **Contact details for federal, state and territory authorities**

    Appendix 5 provides contact details for the federal, state and territory authorities responsible for affixing apostilles to notarizations and other public documents or for authenticating them for chain of authentication 'legalization'.

    Administrative requirements, procedures and fees vary considerably between the authorities. Current information relating to authentications and apostilles is available from the relevant authorities and/or from their websites.

- **Hague Apostille Convention countries**

    A list of Contracting States and their territories and dependencies which are subject to the *Apostille Convention* (as at 31 December 2011) is found at **Appendix 4**.

    The number of States Party to the Convention is increasing. Up-to-date information about the *Apostille Convention* and the states which are party to it may be found at the Apostille Section of the Hague Conference website, <www.hcch.net>.

---

32 *Army Regulation,* 27-55 Notarial Services, 17 November 2003 para 4-6.

- **Consular legalization fees and administrative requirements**

  Most consular websites carry details of fees and administrative requirements for the provision of legalization services.

  Legalization fees charged by consulates vary from a few dollars to several hundred dollars. There is no overall prescribed fee and there is no consistency or logic in the level of fees.

  Care should be taken to check whether there is any need to provide one or more (simple) photocopies of documents submitted for legalization.

  The consulates of a number of non-English speaking countries also insist upon receiving (sworn) translations into their own language of any English language public documents which are to be legalized and any underlying English language documents which have been notarized

- **Contact particulars for foreign diplomatic and consular posts**

  Particulars of foreign diplomatic and consular posts accredited to the United States from time to time may be found at the U.S. Department of State websites, <www.state.gov/s/cpr/rls/dpl/> and <www.state.gov/s/cpr/r/s/fco>.

- **Important Reminder**

  Where an apostille is or ought to be affixed in the United States for a notarization for production in another 'Hague Convention' country, it is improper and in breach of the *Apostille Convention* to have the document 'legalized' by a consular officer of the receiving country.

OFAC sanctions

Although not directly relevant to notarizations and legalizations as such, there is however one important matter which can impinge directly upon certain transactions which may involve notarized documents.

The office of Foreign Assets Control (OFAC) of the U.S. Department of the Treasury

> administers and enforces economic and trade sanctions based on U.S. foreign policy and national security goals, against targeted foreign countries and regimes, terrorists, international narcotics traffickers, those engaged in activities related to the proliferation of weapons of mass destruction and other threats to the national security, foreign policy or economy of the United States.[33]

Persons or entities engaged in international transactions must constantly remain vigilant to ensure that their activities do not breach U.S. economic and trade sanctions. An outline of current OFAC programs may be found at **Appendix 2**.

---

33 <www.treasury.gov/about/organizational-structure/offices/Pages/Office-of/-Foreign-Assets-Control.aspx>.

APPENDIX 1

An Introduction to the Civil Law

A short introduction to the civil law, which is more widely distributed throughout the world than is the common law and in many ways, is far more influential.

AN INTRODUCTION TO THE CIVIL LAW

A legal tradition ... is a set of deeply rooted, historically conditioned attitudes about the nature of law, about the role of law in the society and the polity, about the proper organization of a legal system, and about the way law is or should be made, applied, studied, perfected and taught.[1]

The civil law tradition

Named after the *jus civile* of the Roman Empire, upon which it is based, the civil law is one of the world's great legal traditions.

Its hallmarks include:

* the obvious influence of Roman law and canon law at its very foundation:

* a fundamental classification of law into private law and public law:

* a clear separation of powers enabling legislators to make laws and preventing judges (who are merely career public servants) from doing so:

* the compilation of and reliance upon, notionally, all encompassing legal codes as the primary sources of law:

* recourse to legal scholars instead of judges to interpret the legal codes:

* the mandating of inquisitorial rather than adversarial court procedures; and

* the entrenchment of a notariat vested with *publica fides* (public faith) which exercises a central role in relation to real estate transactions, inheritance and succession and the formation and conduct of business entities.

Civil law is the principal legal system in most of Europe, all of Central and South America and significant parts of Asia and Africa. In North America, pockets of the civil law continue to flourish in Louisiana, Puerto Rico and Quebec.[2] Modern private and public international law are largely the product of lawyers and academics raised and trained in the civil law tradition.[3]

---

1   John Henry Merryman and Rogelio Perez-Perdomo, *The Civil Law Tradition* (Stamford University Press, 3rd ed 2007), 2.

2   The International Union of Notaries, which is a non-government organization founded in 1948 to co-ordinate and represent the interests of the civil law notariat, presently has some 80 member notariats, mostly drawn from the world's civil law jurisdictions. Membership is steadily expanding.

3   For example, the *Hague Conference on Private International Law* was convened in 1893 by the Netherlands government. Since 1945 it has adopted 39 international conventions across a wide spectrum, including family law, trade and financial law, administrative and judicial co-operation and international litigation.

As at 31 December 2011, there were 71 states and one Regional Economic Union which were full members of the Hague Conference. The United States has been a member since 15 October 1954. Of the member states, 53 are civil law jurisdictions.

As it has evolved over the years, the civil law is far from monolithic. In the same way as the laws of the states and territories of the United States differ significantly in many respects, but are nonetheless part of a distinct and cohesive legal tradition, so it is with the civil law. Each of the civil law jurisdictions is demonstrably 'civil law' in nature, but each has developed its own variations on a theme.

The early period

The civil law tradition began its development in Europe from about the 12th century, based upon Roman law as codified in the *Corpus Juris Civilis* (the Body of Civil Law) prepared in Constantinople between 529 and 565 by order of the Emperor Justinian.[4]

In the early 12th century, the first universities began to appear in Mediterranean Europe. The outstanding center for the teaching of law was established in the Italian city of Bologna in 1116. By the mid-12th century, there were approximately 10,000 law students in Bologna coming from all over Europe.[5] Its jurists (legal experts) and those of other mediaeval European universities have become known as 'glossators' (writers of 'glosses').[6]

The glossators revived the *Corpus Juris Civilis* and adapted the Roman system of law as revealed by it to the interpersonal and commercial requirements of post-medieval Mediterranean Europe. Their interpolations and legal advice were embodied in *summae* (short legal treatises) which ultimately developed into complete statements of law on discrete legal subjects.[7]

---

4   The *Codex Justinianeus* as it is sometimes called, comprises four parts or 'books' namely:

    (1)   the *Digesta*, a collection of scattered laws, imperial edicts and decisions of the Roman Senate;

    (2)   the *Codex Constitutiones,* the opinions of learned Roman jurists;

    (3)   the *Institutiones*, an elementary text book for students; and

    (4)   the *Novellae Constitutiones*, a collection of Justinian's new ordinances published between 534 and 565.

5   Barry Nicholas, *An Introduction to Roman Law*, (Clarendon Press, 1962), 46.

6   Derived from the medieval latin *'glossa'* meaning an explanation of a difficult word, a 'gloss' is a comment or explanation or interpretation or paraphrase. A 'glossator' is a commentator, especially on texts of civil and canon law. (*The New Shorter Oxford English Dictionary* (1993)).

7   The leading glossator of the 13th century was the University of Bologna jurist, Accursius, whose *glossa ordinaria* (assembly of glosses) totalled almost 100,000 individual commentaries on aspects of the *Corpus Juris Civilis*, was written over 40 years from about 1220 to about 1260.

The *Siete Partidas*

In the late 13th century, Alfonso X, King of Castille, Leon and Galicia (1257 – 1284)[8] conceived and oversaw the preparation of a comprehensive code of law for Spain, known as *Codigo de Las Siete Partidas* (the Code of the Seven Parts of the Law).[9]

Inspired by a deeply religious view of the world, the *Siete Partidas* was based upon Roman law as interpreted by the glossators and as brought to Spain by legal scholars trained by them or at Spanish universities which had introduced their methodology.

Considered to be Spain's most important contribution to the development of the civil law, the *Siete Partidas* comprised 182 articles setting out a total of 2,802 laws.[10] It remained the basis of Spanish law until 1889 when it was replaced by the *Codigo Civil* (the Civil Code) which took its inspiration from the *Code Napoleon* and which is still in force in Spain. It also was the legal system imposed by the Spanish on their colonies in the Americas. In consequence, the *Siete Partidas* is the foundation of the legal system of most of modern Central and South America.

The codification mindset

The 'codification' mindset continued in Europe throughout the renaissance and post-renaissance periods and during the years leading up to the emergence of the European nation state. European jurisprudence saw codification as a means of ensuring that the law was readily known and understood and readily accessible to all. The *Corpus Juris Civilis* and through it, the system of Roman law, was the obvious starting point for the codification process.

---

8   Alfonso X is one of the 23 lawmakers depicted in marble relief portraits over the gallery doors of the House of Representatives chamber of the United States Capitol. The 23 were chosen in recognition of their contributions to the basic philosophical and legal principles upon which American law is founded.

    They are, in order from the right of the Speaker's chair, George Mason, Robert Pothier, Jean Baptiste Colbert, Edward I, Alfonso X, Gregory IX, Saint Louis, Justinian I, Tribonian, Lycurgus, Hammurabi, Moses, Solon, Papinian, Gaius, Maimonides, Suleiman, Innocent III, Simon de Montfort, Hugo Grotius, Sir William Blackstone, Napoleon I and Thomas Jefferson.

9   The Code was originally called *Livrio de las legies* (Book of Laws). It was given its present name in the 14th century.

10 The first letter of the title of each of the Books forms an acrostic of the King's name. The *Siete Partidas* are:

   (1)   A servicio de Dios ... (For the service of God ...)

   (2)   La fe catholica ... (The Catholic Faith ...)

   (3)   Fizo Nuestro Sennor Dios ... (Our Lord God did ...)

   (4)   Onras sennalados ... (Special Rites ...)

   (5)   Nascen entre los ommes ... (Among men there arise ...)

   (6)   Sesudamente dixeron ... (The ancient wise men sagely said ...)

   (7)   Olvidanca et atreuimiento ... (Forgetfulness and boldness ...)

   ('*Siete Partidas*' at http://en.wikipedia.org)

In *'Principal Features and Methods of Codification'*,[11] Professor Jean Louis Bergel observed that:

> [The] greatest codifications responded to important political, social or technical changes, usually occurring after revolutions or following a country's accession to independence. New political, philosophical and religious ideologies were then put forth and implemented by the new authorities.[12]

The French and German civil codes and their influence

Unquestionably, the two most influential of the modern civil codes, are the French code and the German code. The impetus for the former was the French Revolution of 1789 and for the latter, the founding of the modern German State.

Both the French and the German codes have been amended, modified and supplemented over the years, but their underlying philosophies and methodologies have remained remarkably consistent.

The Code Civil of France

The *Code Civil des Francais*, now called the *Code Civil* was Napoleon's brainchild. He believed it to be his greatest achievement. Indeed, while in exile on St. Helena, Napoleon said:

> My true glory is not that I have won forty battles. Waterloo will blow away the memory of those victories. What nothing can blow away, what will live eternally, is my Civil Code.[13]

Napoleon commissioned the drafting of his comprehensive code of French law in 1800. The task took four years. On completion, the code comprised 2,281 Articles in three Books, namely:

- **Book I,**

Articles 1 – 6:	General principles of law and their application.
Articles 7 – 515:	Civil rights, status of persons, marriage, divorce and paternity.

- **Book II,**

Articles 516 – 570:	Real and personal property, ownership and rights relating to property.

- **Book III,**

Articles 711 – 2281	Rights of succession, contracts and obligations.

The code did not deal with criminal law, commercial law or civil procedure. Those matters were the subject of later codes.

---

11 48 Lousiana Law Review (1987-1988), 1073.

12 Ibid, 1077.

13 Quoted by Bergel, above, 1078 and 1079.

The *Code Civil* was compulsorily introduced into France's colonies and into those countries such as Belgium and Luxembourg which at material times were under French rule. It also inspired the Dutch civil code, various Italian civil codes, the Romanian code, the Portuguese code, the Spanish *Codigo Civil*, the Brazilian code, the Chilean code and the codes of Argentina, Uruguay and Venezuela. In Quebec, the *Code Civil* was the principal model for the *Quebec Civil Code* of 1866. The *Louisiana Civil Codes* of 1808, 1825 and 1870 were all primarily born of the French code.

The BGB

Germany's code, the *Burgerliches Gesetzbuch* (the BGB), is the work of a special commission of German legal scholars set up in 1873. After a lengthy gestation, the code took effect on 1 January 1900.

The BGB comprises five books, namely:

- **Book I**   General principles, natural and juristic persons, things, classifications of legal acts and prescriptive periods.

- **Book II**   The law of obligations, contracts and the law of delict (torts).

- **Book III**   Real and personal property and securities.

- **Book IV**   Family law, including marriage.

- **Book V**   Succession, wills, settlements and inheritance.

The BGB went on to significantly influence the private law of Switzerland, Greece, Japan, the former USSR and Scandinavia. In turn, the Swiss civil code, the *Schweizeriche Zivilgesetzbuch* (the ZGB), which conceptually is closer to the common law than many civil law jurists care to admit, has won significant plaudits internationally. Modern legislators within the civil law jurisdictions often look to the ZGB for inspiration. For example, in 1926, the then new Turkish republic adopted the ZGB, almost holus-bolus, as the new Turkish civil code.

The future of the civil law tradition

What then of the future? It is trite to say that the world is just a global village and that as a result, the distinctions between the great legal traditions are blurring as they converge to develop cohesive responses to the problems besetting the village.

The fact is that the interaction between legal traditions and in particular between the civil and common law traditions must necessarily have an impact one on the other and each of them is changing as a result.

What impact will those changes have on civil law? For the answer, it is appropriate to turn again to Professors Merryman and Perez-Perdoma.

> Do changes in the civil law tradition indicate its decline? Certainly not ... change is a sign of continued life ... [It] would be inaccurate to assume that the civil law tradition is losing its vitality. On the contrary, it may be more alive than ever.[14]

---

14 Merryman and Perez-Perdoma, above, 159-160.

APPENDIX 2

OFAC Economic and Trade Sanctions Programs

An overview of the Office of Foreign Assets Control (OFAC) of the U.S. Department of the Treasury economic and trade sanctions programs against targeted

- foreign countries and regimes;
- terrorists;
- international narcotics traffickers;
- persons and entities engaged in activities relating to the proliferation of weapons of mass destruction; and
- other threats to the national security, foreign policy or economy of the United States.

As at 31 December 2011

The Office of Foreign Assets Control

The Office of Foreign Assets Control (OFAC) of the U.S. Department of the Treasury administers and enforces U.S. economic and trade sanctions programs against targeted

- foreign countries and regimes;
- terrorists;
- international narcotics traffickers;
- persons and entities engaged in activities relating to the proliferation of weapons of mass destruction; and
- other threats to the national security, foreign policy or economy of the United States.

OFAC's authority

OFAC acts under

- Presidential national emergency powers; and
- authority granted by specific legislation

to impose controls on transactions and freeze assets under U.S. jurisdiction.

Who must comply with OFAC regulations?

All

- U.S. citizens and permanent resident aliens (regardless of their location);
- persons and entities within the United States; and
- U.S. incorporated entities and their foreign branches

must comply with OFAC Regulations.

In the case of certain programs, such as those relating to Cuba and North Korea, all foreign subsidiaries owned or controlled by U.S. companies must also comply with the relevant OFAC Regulations.

Certain programs also require compliance by foreign persons in possession of goods of U.S. origin.

Prohibited transactions

OFAC regulations proscribe certain trade or financial transactions and other dealings unless:

- expressly authorized by OFAC on a case-by-case basis; or
- expressly exempted by statute.

Because each program is based on different foreign policy and national security goals, prohibitions may vary between programs.

Exceptions to the prohibitions

OFAC Regulations often make provision for general licenses authorizing the performance of certain categories of transactions.

OFAC also issues specific licenses on a case-by-case basis under certain limited situations and conditions.

Guidance on how to request a specific license may be found on the OFAC website.

Penalties for violation of OFAC regulations

Penalties for violations can be substantial.

Depending on the program

- criminal penalties for wilful violations can include fines ranging from $50,000 to $10,000,000 and imprisonment from 10 to 30 years; and
- civil penalties range from $250,000 or twice the amount of each underlying transaction to a maximum of $1,075,000 for each violation.

Current sanctions programs

Current comprehensive sanctions programs target:

- Burma (Myanmar);
- Cuba;
- Iran; and
- Sudan.

Non-comprehensive programs target:

- Belarus;
- Côte d'Ivoire;
- Democratic Republic of the Congo;
- Iraq;
- Liberia (Former regime of Charles Taylor);
- Persons undermining the sovereignty of Lebanon or its democratic processes and institutions;
- North Korea;
- Sierra Leone;
- Syria; and
- Zimbabwe.

Programs also target:

- foreign narcotics traffickers;

- foreign terrorists; and

- proliferators of weapons of mass destruction.

The SDN list

In addition to the program set out above, OFAC publishes a list of **Specially Designated Nationals and Blocked Persons** (**the SDN list**) (presently exceeding 500 pages) which includes names of companies and individuals who are connected with the sanctions targets and are located throughout the world.

A number of named individuals and entities are known to move from country to country and may end up in locations where they would be least expected.

All U.S. persons are prohibited from dealing with SDNs wherever they are located from time to time and all SDN assets are 'blocked'.

The OFAC website

The OFAC website is an invaluable resource. Its 'Frequently Asked Questions' page is comprehensive and thorough.

The website also provides:

- full particulars of current and past sanctions programs;

- guidance information;

- legislation and executive orders;

- risk matrices for:

  o financial institutions;

  o the charitable sector; and

  o the securities sector;

- federal register notices;

- particulars of Specially Designated Nationals and Blocked Persons; and

- answers to technology questions.

OFAC has published the following important note on its website

OFAC has undertaken an initiative to post on its website answers to questions of general applicability frequently asked by the public. The initiative is intended to be part of OFAC's commitment to regulatory transparency and customer service. OFAC is continuing to prepare answers to additional questions that are often asked and additional questions and answers will be posted periodically. Comments are welcome via the 'E-mail OFAC' link on OFAC's homepage.

It should be noted however that OFAC is unable to treat any information submitted concerning FAQs as confidential or proprietary to the submitter and no information submitted concerning FAQs will be treated as such.

The questions and answers highlight key issues and topics relating to economic sanctions and the procedures and practices of OFAC. They are intended only as general information to assist persons subject to United States jurisdiction to comply with legal requirements and to facilitate an understanding of the scope and purposes of sanctions programs.

It is very important to note that U.S. businesses, individuals and others subject to OFAC jurisdiction must comply with the full legal requirements of OFAC's programs which are set out in the applicable statutes, Executive Orders, and implementing regulations found in Title 31 Chapter V of the *Code of Federal Regulations* and in Federal Register documents that update the regulations.

The reader is further cautioned that specific facts may alter an analysis and, because each program reflects unique foreign policy and national security contexts, a particular answer will not always be applicable to all programs or at all times.

For further assistance, call OFAC's Compliance Programs Division at 202/622-2490 or OFAC'S Licensing Division at 202/622-2480 or write to the Office of Foreign Assets Control, U.S. Department of the Treasury, 1500 Pennsylvania Avenue, NW, Washington, DC 20220.

APPENDIX 3

The Hague Apostille Convention

Convention of October 5, 1961 Abolishing the Requirement
of Legalization for Foreign Public Documents.

(English language version)

Published with the permission of the Hague Conference Secretariat.

CONVENTION ABOLISHING THE REQUIREMENT
OF LEGALIZATION FOR FOREIGN PUBLIC DOCUMENTS

The Hague, October 5, 1961

(The Convention entered into force for the United States on 15 October 1981)

The States signatory to the present Convention,

Desiring to abolish the requirement of diplomatic or consular legalization for foreign public documents,

Have resolved to conclude a Convention to this effect and have agreed upon the following provisions:

ARTICLE 1

The present Convention shall apply to public documents which have been executed in the territory of one Contracting State and which have to be produced in the territory of another Contacting State.

For the purpose of the present Convention, the following are deemed to be public documents:

(a)   documents emanating from an authority or an official connected with the courts or tribunals of the State, including those emanating from a public prosecutor, a clerk of a court or a process server (*'huissier de justice'*);

(b)   administrative documents;

(c)   notarial acts;

(d)   official certificates which are placed on documents signed by person in their private capacity, such as official certificates recording the registration of a document or the fact that it was in existence on a certain date and official notarial authentications of signatures.

However, the present Convention shall not apply:

(a)   to documents executed by diplomatic or consular agents;

(b)   to administrative documents dealing directly with commercial or customs operations.

ARTICLE 2

Each Contracting State shall exempt from legislation documents to which the present Convention applies and which have to be produced in its territory. For the purposes of the present Convention, legalization means only the formality by which the diplomatic or consular agents of the country in which the document has to be produced, certify the authenticity of the signature, the capacity in which

132

the person signing the document has acted and, where appropriate, the identity of the seal or stamp which it bears.

ARTICLE 3

The only formality that may be required in order to certify the authenticity of the signature, the capacity in which the person signing the document has acted and, where appropriate, the identity of the seal or stamp which it bears, is the addition of the certificate described in Article 4, issued by the competent authority of the State from which the document emanates.

However, the formality mentioned in the preceding paragraph cannot be required when either the laws, regulations or practice in force in the State where the document is produced or an agreement between two or more Contracting States have abolished or simplified it, or exempted the document itself from legalization.

ARTICLE 4

The certificate referred to in the first paragraph of Article 3 shall be placed on the document itself or on an 'allonge'; it shall be in the form of the model annexed to the present Convention.

It may, however, be drawn up in the official language of the authority which issues it. The standard terms appearing therein may be in a second language also. The title 'Apostille (Convention de La Haye du 5 octobre 1961)' shall be in the French language.

ARTICLE 5

The certificate shall be issued at the request of the person who has signed the document or of any bearer.

When properly filled in, it will certify the authenticity of the signature, the capacity in which the person signing the document has acted and, where appropriate, the identity of the seal or stamp which the document bears.

The signature, seal and stamp on the certificate are exempt from all certification.

ARTICLE 6

Each Contracting State shall designate by reference to their official function, the authorities who are competent to issue the certificate referred to in the first paragraph of Article 3.

It shall give notice of such designation to the Ministry of Foreign Affairs of the Netherlands at the time it deposits its instrument of ratification or of accession or its declaration of extension. It shall also give notice of any change in the designated authorities.

ARTICLE 7

Each of the authorities designated in accordance with Article 6 shall keep a register or card index in which it shall record the certificates issued, specifying:

(a)   the number and date of the certificate,

(b)   the name of the person signing the public document and the capacity in which he has acted, or in the case of unsigned documents, the name of the authority which has affixed the seal or stamp.

At the request of any interested person, the authority which has issued the certificate shall verify whether the particulars in the certificate correspond with those in the register or card index.

ARTICLE 8

When a treaty, convention or agreement between two or more Contracting States contains provisions which subject the certification of a signature, seal or stamp to certain formalities , the present Convention will only override such provisions if those formalities are more rigorous than the formality referred to in Articles 3 and 4.

ARTICLE 9

Each Contracting State shall take the necessary steps to prevent the performance of legalizations by its diplomatic or consular agents in cases where the present Convention provides for exemption.

ARTICLE 10

The present Convention shall be open for signature by the States represented at Ninth session of the Hague Conference on Private International Law and Iceland, Ireland, Liechtenstein and Turkey.

It shall be ratified, and the instruments of ratification shall be deposited with the Ministry of Foreign Affairs of the Netherlands.

ARTICLE 11

The present Convention shall enter into force on the sixtieth day after the deposit of the third instrument of ratification referred to in the second paragraph of Article 10.

The Convention shall enter into force for each signatory State which ratifies subsequently on the sixtieth day after the deposit of its instrument of ratification.

ARTICLE 12

Any State not referred to in Article 10 may accede to the present Convention after it has entered into force in accordance with the first paragraph of Article 11. The instrument of accession shall be deposited with the Ministry of Foreign Affairs of the Netherlands.

Such accession shall have effect only as regards the relations between the acceding State and those Contracting States which have not raised an objection to its accession in the six months after receipt of the notification referred to in sub-paragraph *(d)* of Article 15. Any such objection shall be notified to the Ministry of Foreign Affairs of the Netherlands.

The Convention shall enter into force between the acceding State and the States which have raised no objection to its accession on the sixtieth day after the expiry of the period of six months mentioned in the preceding paragraph.

ARTICLE 13

Any State may, at the time of signature, ratification or accession, declare that the present Convention shall extend to all the territories for the international relations of which it is responsible, or to one or more of them. Such a declaration shall take effect on the date of entry into force of the Convention for the State concerned.

At any time thereafter, such extensions shall be notified to the Ministry of Foreign Affairs of the Netherlands.

When the declaration of extension is made by a State which has signed and ratified, the Convention shall enter into force for the territories concerned in accordance with Article 11. When the declaration of extension is made by a State which has acceded, the Convention shall enter into force for the territories concerned in accordance with Article 12.

ARTICLE 14

The present Convention shall remain in force for five years from the date of its entry into force in accordance with the first paragraph of Article 11, even for States which have ratified it or acceded to it subsequently.

It there has been no denunciation, the Convention shall be renewed tacitly every five years.

Any denunciation shall be notified to the Minister of Foreign Affairs of the Netherlands at least six months before the end of the five year period.

It may be limited to certain of the territories to which the Convention applies.

The denunciation will only have effect as regards the State which has notified it.

The Convention shall remain in force for the other Contracting States.

ARTICLE 15

The Ministry of Foreign Affairs of the Netherlands shall give notice to the States referred to in Article 10, and to the States which have acceded in accordance with Article 12, of the following:

(a)   the notification referred to in the second paragraph of Article 6;

(b)   the signatures and ratifications referred to in Article 10;

(c)   the date on which the present Convention enters into force in accordance with the first paragraph of Article 11;

(d)   the accessions and objections referred to in Article 12 and the date on which such accessions take effect;

(e)   the extensions referred to in Article 13 and the date on which they take effect;

(f)   the denunciations referred to in the third paragraph of Article 14.

In witness whereof the undersigned, being duly authorised thereto, have signed the present Convention.

Done at The Hague the 5th October 1961, in French and in English, the French text prevailing in case of divergence between the two texts, in a single copy which shall be deposited in the archives of the Government of the Netherlands, and of which a certified copy shall be sent, through the diplomatic channel, to each of the States represented at the Ninth session of the Hague Conference on Private International Law and also to Iceland, Ireland, Liechtenstein and Turkey.

ANNEX TO THE CONVENTION

Model of certificate

The certificate will be in the form of a square with sides at least 9 centimetres long.

APOSTILLE
(Convention de La Haye Du 5 Octobre 1961)

1. Country:
   This public document
2. has been signed by
3. acting in the capacity of
4. bears the seal/stamp of

                              Certified

5. at   6. the
7. by
8. N°
9. Seal/Stamp   10. Signature:

APPENDIX 4

STATES PARTY TO THE HAGUE APOSTILLE CONVENTION

A list of countries and their territories, dependencies and autonomous regions which are subject to the Hague Apostille Convention.

As at 31 December 2011

The number of States Party to The Convention is increasing. Up to date information about the Apostille Convention and the States which are party to it may be found on the Hague Conference website <www.hcch.net>.

Countries and their dependencies, territories and autonomous regions which are subject to the *Hague Apostille Convention*.

As at 31 December 2011

Albania

American Samoa
(USA territory to which the Convention has been extended)

Andorra

Angola
(Portuguese territory to which the Convention has been extended)

Anguilla
(UK territory to which the Convention has been extended)

Antigua and Barbuda

Argentina

Armenia

Aruba
(A constituent country of the Netherlands to which the Convention applies)

Australia

Austria

Azerbaijan

Azores
(Autonomous region of Portugal)

Bahamas

Barbados

Belarus

Belgium

Belize

Bermuda
(UK territory to which the Convention has been extended)

Bonaire
(A special municipality of the Netherlands to which the Convention applies)

Bosnia & Herzegovina

Botswana

British Antarctic Territory
(UK territory to which the Convention has been extended)

British Virgin Islands
(UK territory to which the Convention has been extended)

Brunei Darussalam

Bulgaria

Cape Verde

Cayman Islands
(UK territory to which the Convention has been extended)

Christmas Island
(Australian territory to which the Convention has been extended)

Cocos Island
(Australian territory to which the Convention has been extended)

Colombia

Comoros *

Cook Islands

Costa Rica

Croatia

Curacao
(A constituent country of the Netherlands to which the Convention applies)

Cyprus

Czech Republic

Denmark

Djibouti *

Dominica

Dominican Republic

Ecuador

El Salvador

Estonia

Falkland Islands
(UK territory to which the Convention has been extended)

Fiji

Finland

France

French Guiana
(French overseas department)

French Polynesia
(French territory to which the Convention has been extended)

French Southern and Antarctic Lands
(French territory to which the Convention has been extended)

Georgia

Germany

Gibraltar
(UK territory to which the Convention has been extended)

Greece

Grenada

Guadeloupe
(French overseas department)

Guam
(USA territory to which the Convention has been extended)

Guernsey
(UK territory to which the Convention has been extended)

Guyana*
(Formerly British Guyana)

Honduras

Hong Kong

Hungary

Iceland

India

Ireland

Isle of Man
(UK territory to which the Convention has been extended)

Israel

Italy

Japan

Jersey
(UK territory to which the Convention has been extended)

Kazakhstan

Kiribati *

Kyrgyzstan

Latvia

Lesotho
(Formerly Basutoland)

Liberia

Liechtenstein

Lithuania

Luxembourg

Macau

Macedonia
(Former Yugoslav Republic)

Madeira
(Autonomous region of Portugal)

Malawi

Malta

Marshall Islands

Martinique
(French overseas department)

Mauritius

Mayotte
(French territorial collectivity)

Mexico

Moldova

Monaco

Mongolia

Montenegro

Montserrat
(UK territory to which the Convention has been extended)

Mozambique*

Namibia

Netherlands

New Caledonia
(French territory to which the Convention has been extended)

New Zealand

Niue

Norfolk Island
(Australian territory to which the Convention has been extended)

Northern Mariana Islands
(Cth associated with USA to which the Convention applies)

Norway

Panama

Peru

Pitcairn Islands

(UK territory to which the Convention has been extended)

Poland

Portugal

Puerto Rico

(Cth associated with USA to which the Convention applies)

Republic of Korea

(South Korea)

Reunion

(French overseas department)

Romania

Russian Federation

St. Helena

(UK territory to which the Convention has been extended)

St. Kitts and Nevis

(Formerly Saint Christopher and Nevis)

St. Lucia

St. Pierre and Miquelon

(French territory to which the Convention has been extended)

St. Vincent and The Grenadines

(Formerly St. Vincent)

Saba

(A special municipality of the the Netherlands to which the Convention applies)

Samoa

San Marino

Sao Tome and Principe

Serbia

Seychelles

Sint Eustatius

(A special municipality of the Netherlands to which the Convention applies)

Sint Maarten

(A constituent country of the Netherlands to which the Convention applies)

Slovakia

Slovenia

Solomon Islands*

South Africa

South Georgia & South Sandwich Islands

(UK territory to which the Convention has been extended)

Spain

Suriname

Swaziland

Sweden

Switzerland

Tonga

Trinidad and Tobago

Turkey

Turks and Caicos Islands

(UK territory to which the Convention has been extended)

Tuvalu*

(Formerly Ellice Islands)

Ukraine

United Kingdom

United States of America

Vanuatu

Venezuela

Virgin Islands of the United States

(USA territory to which the Convention has been extended)

Wallis and Futuna

(French territory to which the Convention has been extended)

Zimbabwe *

(Formerly South Rhodesia)

---

* Denotes a country which is now independent, but was formerly a dependent territory to which the Convention was extended. This country has not yet made a formal declaration as to the continuation in force of the Convention.

Notes:

1. **Denmark** has declared that the Convention does not yet apply for Greenland and the Faroe Islands, which are self-governing Danish overseas administrative divisions.

2. **Kosovo** declared its independence from Serbia on 17 February 2008. Kosovo has not made a formal declaration as to the continuance in force of the Convention. For the time being, Kosovo should be treated as being subject to the Convention and apostilles should be affixed to notarizations to be produced there.

3. **Oman** acceded to the Convention on 12 May 2011. In the ordinary course, the Convention will enter into force for Oman on 30 January 2012.

4. **New Zealand** has declared that the Convention does not apply for Tokelau, which is a self administered New Zealand territory.

5. **Uzbekistan** acceded to the Convention on 25 July 2011. In the ordinary course, the Convention will enter into force in Uzbekistan on 15 April 2012.

APPENDIX 5

FEDERAL, STATE AND TERRITORY AUTHENTICATION AUTHORITIES

Contact particulars of the federal, state and territory authorities responsible for authenticating notarizations emanating from the United States for production in jurisdictions abroad.

As at 31 December 2011

NOTES

- This appendix is only directed toward the authentication of notarizations emanating from the United States for production in jurisdictions abroad.

- Information about obtaining apostilles or authentication certificates for chain legalization purposes may be obtained from the various Authorities and their websites.

- Websites also provide information concerning the authentication of public documents other than notarizations.

- **Before submitting documents by mail or attending at offices for 'walk in' counter services, it is essential to check with the appropriate Authority to confirm fees, opening hours and other administrative requirements.**

FEDERAL AUTHORITY

U.S. DEPARTMENT OF STATE

The Department of State Authentications Office is responsible for

- affixing apostilles to notarizations by **military notaries**; and
- issuing authentication certificates under the seal of the U.S. Department of State for 'chain' legalizations for notarizations which originate from the states and territories and which have already been certified under the official seal of the relevant state or territory authority.

Mail

U.S. Department of State
Authentications office
518 23rd Street, NW SA-1
Columbia Plaza
WASHINGTON, DC 20520

Counter Service:

Authentications Office
Columbia Plaza Store Front
518 23rd Street NW
WASHINGTON, DC 20520

Status Enquiries:

Tel: (202) 663-1848
Fax: (202) 663-3636
TDD: (202) 663-3468
Website: http://www.state.gov/m/a/auth/

STATE AND TERRITORY AUTHORITIES

The following state and territory authorities are responsible for

- affixing apostilles; and

- issuing authentication certificates for 'chain' legalization purposes

for notarizations carried out within their jurisdictions set out below.

ALABAMA

Mail:

Office of the Secretary of State
Authentication Division
100 North Union Street
Suite 770
MONTGOMERY, AL 36130
Tel: (334) 242-5325
Fax: (334) 353-8269
Website: http://www.sos.state.al.us/AdminServices/Authentications.aspx

ALASKA

Mail:

Office of the Lieutenant Governor
Authentications Department
240 Main Street
Room 301
JUNEAU, AK 99801
Tel: (907) 465-3509
Fax: (907) 465-5400
Website: http://www.ltgov.alaska.gov/notary/authentications.php

ARIZONA

Mail:

Office of the Secretary of State
Business Services, Notary Division
1700 W Washington Street
7th Floor
PHOENIX, AZ 85007-2888

Counter Service:

Office of the Secretary of State
Business Services, Notary Division
Capitol Executive Tower
1700 W. Washington Street
1st Floor, Room 103
PHOENIX, AZ 85007-2888
Tel: (602) 542-6187
Website: http://www.azsos.gov/notary/Apostille.htm

ARKANSAS

Mail:

Office of Secretary of State
Business & Commercial Services
State Capitol,
LITTLE ROCK, AR 72201
Tel: (501) 682-3409
Website: http://www.sos.arkansas.gov/BCS/Pages/apostilleCertification.aspx

CALIFORNIA

Mail:

Office of the Secretary of State
Business Programs Division
Notary Public Section
P O BOX 942877
SACRAMENTO, CA 94277-0001

Counter Service:

Office of the Secretary of State
Business Programs Division
Notary Public Section
1500 11th Street
2nd Floor
SACRAMENTO, CA 95814
Tel: (916) 653-3595

Mail & Counter Service:

California Secretary of State's Office
300 South Spring Street
Room 12513
LOS ANGELES , CA 90013
Website: http://www.sos.ca.gov/business/notary/authentication.htm

COLORADO

Mail & Counter Service:

Colorado Secretary of State
1700 Broadway
Suite 200
DENVER, CO 80290
Tel: (303) 894-2200
Fax: (303) 869-4864
Website: http://www.sos.state.co.us/pubs/BusinessAndLicensing/orderForms.html

CONNECTICUT

Mail:

Authentications & Apostilles
Connecticut Secretary of State
P O BOX 150470
HARTFORD, CT 06115-0470

Counter Service:

Authentications & Apostilles
Connecticut Secretary of State
30 Trinity Street
HARTFORD, CT 06106
Tel: (860) 509-6100
Website: http://www.ct.gov/sots

DELAWARE

Mail & Counter Service:

Office of the Secretary of State
Division of Corporations
John G. Townsend Building
401 Federal Street
Suite 4
DOVER, DE 19901
Tel: (302) 739-3073
Website: http://www.corp.delaware.gov/apost_info.shtml

DISTRICT OF COLUMBIA

Mail & Counter Service:

Office of the Secretary, DC
Office of Notary Commissions & Authentications
441 4th Street NW
Room 810S
WASHINGTON, DC 20001
Tel: (202) 727-3117
Fax: (202) 727-8457
Website: http://www.os.dc.gov/os/site/default.asp

FLORIDA

Mail:

Department of State
Division of Corporations
Apostille Certification
P O BOX 6800
TALLAHASSEE, FL 32314-6800

Courier:

Department of State
Division of Corporations
Clifton Building, Apostille Section
2661 Executive Center Circle
TALLAHASSEE, FL 32301
Tel: (850) 245-6945
Fax: (850) 245-6014
Website: http://www.notaries.dos.state.fl.us/notproc7.html

GEORGIA

Mail & Counter Service:

Georgia Superior Court Clerks' Cooperative Authority
Notary Division
1875 Century Boulevard
Suite 100
ATLANTA, GA 30345
Tel: (404) 327-6023
Website: http://www.gsccca.org/Projects/apost.asp

HAWAII

Mail:

Office of the Lieutenant Governor
State Capitol
5th Floor
HONOLULU, Hawaii 96813
Tel: (808) 586-0255
Website: http://www.hawaii.gov/ltgov/office/apostilles

IDAHO

Mail:

Office of Secretary of State
Notary Department
PO Box 83720
BOISE ID 83720-0080

Counter Service:

Office of Secretary of State
Notary Department
450 N 4th Street
BOISE ID 83702
Tel: (208) 332-2810
Website: http://www.sos.idaho.gov/notary/apostill.htm.htm

ILLINOIS

Mail:

Office of the Secretary of State
Notaries Public Division
Department of Index
111 E. Monroe
SPRINGFIELD, IL 62756
Tel: (217) 782-7017
Fax: (217) 524-0930
Website: http://www.cyberdriveillinois.com/departments/index/divisions.html

INDIANA

Mail & Counter Service:

Indiana Secretary of State
Authentication Department
302 W Washington Street
Room E-018
INDIANAPOLIS, IN 46204
Tel: (317) 232-2677
Website: http://www.in.gov/sos/business/apostille/

IOWA

Mail:

Secretary of State
First Floor, Lucas Building
321 E 12th Street
DES MOINES, IA 50319
Tel: (515) 281-5204
Website: http://www.sos.state.ia.us

KANSAS

Mail & Counter Service:

Office of Secretary of State
Notary Clerk
Memorial Hall, 1st Floor
120 SW 10th Avenue
TOPEKA, KS 66612-1594
Tel: (785) 296-4564
Website: http://www.sos.ks.gov/business/notary_public/certifications.html

KENTUCKY

Mail:

Office of Secretary of State
Authentications and Apostilles
P O BOX 718
FRANKFORT, KY 40602-0718

Counter Service:

Office of Secretary of State
State Capitol
700 Capitol Avenue
Suite 158
FRANKFORT, KY 40601
Tel: (502) 564-3490
Fax: (502) 5645687
Website: http://www.sos.ky.gov/adminservices/apostilles/default.htm

LOUISIANA

Mail:

Louisiana Secretary of State
Commissions Division
P O Box 94125
BATON ROUGE, LA 70804-9125

Counter Service:

Louisiana Secretary of State
Commissions Division
8585 Archives Avenue
BATON ROUGE, LA 70809
Tel: (225) 922-0330
Website: http://www.sos.louisiana.gov/tabid/134/Default.aspx

MAINE

Mail:

Secretary of State
Division of Corporations, UCC & Commissions
101 State House Station
AUGUSTA, ME 04333-0101

Courier:

Secretary of State
Division of Corporations, UCC & Commissions
111 Sewall Street
4th Floor
AUGUSTA, ME 04330
Tel: (207) 624-7752
Website: http:// www.maine.gov/sos/cec/notary/apostilles.html

MARYLAND

Mail & Counter Service:

Office of the Secretary of State
16 Francis Street
1st Floor
ANNAPOLIS, MD 21401
Tel: (410) 974-5521
Website: http://www.sos.state.md.us/Certifications/Certifications.aspx

MASSACHUSETTS

Mail:

Secretary of the Commonwealth
Public Records Division
Commissions Section
One Ashburton Place
Room 1719
BOSTON, MA 02108
Tel: (617) 727-2836
Website: http://www.sec.state.ma.us/pre

Secretary of the Commonwealth
Public Records Division
Commissions Section
436 Dwight Street
Room 102
SPRINGFIELD, MA 01103
Tel: (413) 784-1376
Website: http://www.sec.state.ma.us/wso

Secretary of the Commonwealth
Public Records Division
Commissions Section
218 South Main Street
Suite 206
FALL RIVER, MA 02721
Tel: (508) 646-1374
Website: http://www.sec.state.ma.us/wso

Counter Service:

Secretary of the Commonwealth
Public Records Division
Commissions Section
McCormack Building, Room 1719
One Ashburton Place
BOSTON, MA 02108
Tel: (617) 727-2836
Website: http://www.state.ma.us/sec/pre/precom/comidx.htm

MICHIGAN

Mail:

Department of State
Office of the Great Seal
7064 Crowner Drive
LANSING, MI 48918

Counter Service:

Office of the Great Seal
Richard H. Austin Building 1st Floor
430 W. Allegan Street
LANSING, MI
Capital Area SUPER!Center
3315 E. Michigan Ave.
LANSING, MI

Clinton Township SUPER!Center
37015 Gratiot Avenue
CLINTON TOWNSHIP, MI

Detroit New Center SUPER!Center
Cadillac Place Building, MI
3046 West Grand Boulevard, Suite L650
DOWNTOWN DETROIT, MI

Flint Area SUPER!Center
5512 Fenton Road
FLINT, MI

Grand Rapids SUPER!Center
Centerpoint Mall 6-B
3665 28th Street SE
GRAND RAPIDS, MI

Livonia Area SUPER!Center
17176 Farmington Road
LIVONIA, MI

Marquette County PLUS
U2025 U.S. 41 West
MARQUETTE, MI

Oakland County SUPER!Center
1608 N Perry Road
PONTIAC, MI
Tel: (1 888) 767-6424
Website: http://www.michigan.gov/sos

MINNESOTA

Mail & Counter Service:

Retirement Systems of Minnesota Building
Minnesota Secretary of State–Certification
60 Empire Drive
Suite 100
SAINT PAUL, MN 55103-2141
Tel: (1 877) 551-6767
Fax: (651) 215-1009
Website: http://www.sos.state.mn.us/index.aspx?page=984

MISSISSIPPI

Mail:

Secretary of State
Notary/Apostille/Authentication
P O Box 136
JACKSON, MS 39205-0136

Counter Service:

Secretary of State
Notary/Apostille/Authentication
700 North Street
JACKSON, MS 39202
Tel: (601) 359-1615
Website: http://www.sos.ms.gov/business_services_notaries6.aspx

MISSOURI

Mail:

Secretary of State's Office
Commission Division
600 West Main
Room 322
JEFFERSON CITY, MO 65101
Tel: (573) 751-2783
Fax: (573) 751-8199
Website: http://www.sos.mo.gov/business/commissions/certify.asp

MONTANA

Mail:

Secretary of State
Notary and Certification Services
P O Box 202801
1301 6th Avenue
HELENA, MT 59620-2801

Counter Service (Appointment required):

Office of Secretary of State
State Capitol Building
1301 E. 6th Avenue
HELENA, MT 59601
Tel: (406) 444-1877
Website: http://www.sos.mt.gov/Notary/Certifications/

NEBRASKA

Mail:

Secretary of State's Office
Business Services Division
Notary Section
P O Box 95104
LINCOLN, NE 68509

Counter Service :

Secretary of State's Office
Business Services Division
Notary Section
State Capitol Building, Suite 1301
1445 K Street
LINCOLN, NE 68508
Tel: (402) 471-2558
Website: http://www.sos.ne.gov/business/apostilles/index.html

NEVADA

Mail:

Secretary of State
101 North Carson Street
Suite 3
CARSON CITY, NV 89701
Tel: (775) 684-5708
Website: http://www.nvsos.gov/index.aspx?page=124

NEW HAMPSHIRE

Mail:

Office of Secretary of State
Apostilles & Certifications
107 North Main Street
CONCORD, NH 03301

Counter Service:

Office of Secretary of State
Apostilles & Certifications
Statehouse, Room 204
107 North Main Street
CONCORD, NH 03301
Tel: (603) 271-3242
Fax: (603) 271-6316
Website: http://www.sos.nh.gov/certific.htm

NEW JERSEY

Mail:

NJ Division of Revenue
Notary Unit
P O Box 452
TRENTON, NJ 08646

Counter Service:

NJ Division of Revenue
Notary Unit
33 West State Street
5th Floor
TRENTON, NJ 08608-1214
Website: http://www.nj.gov/treasury/revenue/dcr/programs/apostilles.shtml

NEW MEXICO

Mail & Counter Service:

Office of the Secretary of State
Operations Division
New Mexico State Capitol North
325 Don Gaspar
Suite 300
SANTA FE, NM 87501
Tel: (1 800) 477-3632
Website: http://www.sos.state.nm.us/sos-Apostille.html

NEW YORK

Mail:

New York Department of State
Division of Corporations, State Records,
and Uniform Commercial Code
99 Washington Avenue
6th Floor
ALBANY, NY 12231

Counter Service:

New York Department of State
Division of Corporations, State Records,
and Uniform Commercial Code
99 Washington Avenue
6th Floor
ALBANY, NY 12231
Tel: (212) 417-5747
Website: http://www.dos.ny.gov/corps/apostille.html

New York Department of State
Division of Licensing Services
123 William Street
19th Floor
NEW YORK, NY 10038
Tel: (212) 417-5747

NORTH CAROLINA

Mail:

Authentication Office
NC Secretary of State
P O Box 29622
RALEIGH, NC 27626-0622

Counter Service:

Authentication Office
NC Secretary of State
Old Revenue Building Complex
2 South Salisbury Street
RALEIGH, NC 27601-2903
Tel: (919) 807-2140
Website: http://www.secretary.state.nc.us/authen

NORTH DAKOTA

Mail:

Office of Secretary of State
State of North Dakota
600 E Boulevard Ave.
Dept 108; 1st Floor
BISMARCK, ND 58505-0500
Tel: (701) 328-2901
Website: http://www.state.gov/m/a/auth

OHIO

Mail:

Ohio Secretary of State
Client Service Center
180 E. Broad Street
Suite 103
COLUMBUS, OH 43215

Counter Service:

Ohio Secretary of State
Client Service Center
Continental Plaza
180 E. Broad Street
Suite 103
COLUMBUS, OH 43215
Tel: (877) 767-6446
Website: http://www.sos.state.oh.us/SOS/authentication.aspx

OKLAHOMA

Mail & Counter Service:

Office of Secretary of State
Certification Department
2300 N. Lincoln Boulevard
Room 101
OKLAHOMA CITY, OK 73105-4897
Tel: (405) 521-4211
Website: http://www.sos.ok.gov/business/apostilles.aspx

OREGON

Mail:

Office of Secretary of State
Corporations Division
255 Capitol Street NE
Suite 151
SALEM, OR 97310
Tel: (503) 986-2593
Fax: (503) 986-2300
Website: http://wwwfilinginoregon.com

PENNSYLVANIA

Mail & Counter Service:

Pennsylvania Department of State
Bureau of Commissions, Elections & Legislation
Room 210 North Office Building
HARRISBURG, PA 17120-0029
Tel: (717) 787-5280
Website:http://www.dos.state.pa.us

RHODE ISLAND

Mail:

State of Rhode Island and Providence Plantations
Office of the Secretary of State
Authentications
148 W River Street
PROVIDENCE, RI 02903

Counter Service:

Division of Business Services
Office of Secretary of State
148 West River Street
PROVIDENCE, RI 02904
Tel: (401) 222-1487
Fax: (401) 222-1309
Website: http://www.sos.ri.gov/business/apostilles/

SOUTH CAROLINA

Mail & Counter Service:

Authentications Office
SC Secretary of State's Office
1205 Pendleton Street
Suite 525
COLUMBIA, SC 29201
Tel: (803) 734-2512
Website: http://www.scsos.com/Notaries_and_Apostilles/Apostilles

SOUTH DAKOTA

Mail & Counter Service:

Office of Secretary of State
Notary Administrator
State Capitol Building
500 East Capitol Avenue
2nd Floor, Suite 204
PIERRE, SD 57501-5070
Tel: (605) 773-5007
Website: http://www.sdsos.gov

TENNESSEE

Mail:

State of Tennessee
Department of State
Division of Business Services
NTS Unit
312 Eighth Avenue North
6th Floor, William R. Snodgrass Tower
NASHVILLE, TN 37243

Counter Service:

State of Tennessee
Department of State
Division of Business Services
6th Floor, William R. Snodgrass Tower
312 Eighth Avenue North
NASHVILLE, TN
Tel: (615) 741-3699
Website: http://www.tn.gov/sos/forms/apos.pdf

TEXAS

Mail:

Secretary of State
Authentications Unit
P O Box 13550
AUSTIN, TX 78711-3550

Counter Service:

Secretary of State
Authentications Unit
1019 Brazos, B-13
Room B-05
AUSTIN, TX 78701
Tel : (512) 463-5705
Website: http://www.sos.state.tx.us/authinfo.shtml

UTAH

Mail & Counter Service:

Utah State Capitol
Authentications & Apostilles
350 N. State Street
Suite 220
SALT LAKE CITY, UT 84114
Tel: (801) 538-1041
Website: http://www.authentications.utah.gov/process.html

VERMONT

Mail & Counter Service:

Office of the Secretary of State
VT State Archives & Records Administration
1078 U.S. Route 2 – Middlesex
MONTPELIER, VT 05633-7701
Tel: (802) 828-3287
Website: http://www.sec.state.vt.us

VIRGINIA

Mail :

Secretary of the Commonwealth's Office
Authentication Division
1111 East Broad Street
1st Floor
RICHMOND, VA 23219

Counter Service:

Authentication Division
1111 East Broad Street
1st Floor
RICHMOND, VA 23219
Tel: (804) 692-2536
Website: http://www.commonwealth.virginia.gov/Authentications/
authentications.cfm

WASHINGTON

Mail:

Office of the Secretary of State
Corporations Division
Apostille & Certificate Program
P O Box 40228
OLYMPIA, WA 98504-0228
Tel: (360) 725-0344

Counter Service:

Office of the Secretary of State
Corporations Division
Apostille & Certificate Program
Dolliver Building
801 Capitol Way South
OLYMPIA, WA 98504
Tel: (360) 725-0344
Website: http://www.sos.wa.gov/corps/apostilles

WEST VIRGINIA

Counter Service:

Secretary of state
Building 1, Suite 157-K
1900 Kanawha Blvd East
CHARLESTON, WV 25305-0770
Tel: (304) 558-6000
Website: http://www.sos.wv.gov/business-licensing/authentications/Pages/
default.aspx

WISCONSIN

Mail & Counter Service:

Wisconsin Secretary of State
Certification Desk
30 W. Mifflin Street
10th Floor
MADISON, WI 53703
Tel: (608) 266-5503
Website: http://www.sos.state.wi.us/apostilles.htm

WYOMING

Mail:

Wyoming Secretary of State's Office
Authentication Services
State Capitol Building
200 West 24th Street
CHEYENNE, WY 82002-0020
Tel: (307) 777-5335
Fax: (307) 777-5339
Website:http://soswy.state.wy.us/AdminServices/AuthenticationOverview.aspx

AMERICAN SAMOA

Office of the Governor
A.P. Lutali Executive Office Building
PAGO PAGO, AS 96799
Tel: (011) 684-633-4116
Website: http://www.americansamoa.gov

GUAM

Office of the Governor
P O Box 2950
AGANA, GU 96910
Tel: (671) 475-9380
Website: http://www.governor.guam.gov

NORTHERN MARIANA ISLANDS

Attorney General
Juan A. Sablan Memorial Building
Capital Hill,
Caller Box 10007
SAIPAN MP 96950
Website: http://www.gov.mp

PUERTO RICO

Supreme Court of Puerto Rico
Office of Notarial Inspection
P O Box 190860
SAN JUAN, PR 00919-0860
Tel: (787) 763-8816
Website: http://www.lexjuris.com/lexnotaria.htm

U.S. VIRGIN ISLANDS

Office of the Lieutenant Governor
1131 King Street
Suite 101
Christiansted
ST CROIX, USVI 00802
Tel: (340) 774-2991
Website: http://www.ltg.gov.vi

APPENDIX 6

Outline of World Authentication Requirements for Notarizations

An outline of world requirements for the
authentication of notarizations to be produced outside
the United States and its territories.

As at 31 December 2011

NOTES

- **Apostilles have replaced consular legalization in Hague Convention Countries**

  The affixing of apostilles to notarizations and other public documents has completely replaced any need for consular legalization of those documents as between the United States and other countries which are party to the *Hague Apostille Convention* and throughout most of their territories, dependencies and autonomous regions.

- **Contact details for federal, state and territory authorities**

  Appendix 5 provides contact details for the federal, state and territory authorities responsible for affixing apostilles to notarizations and other public documents or for authenticating them for chain of authentication 'legalization'.

  Administrative requirements, procedures and fees vary considerably between the authorities. Current information relating to authentications and apostilles is available from the relevant authorities and/or from their websites.

- *Hague Apostille Convention* **countries**

  A list of Contracting States and their territories and dependencies which are subject to the *Apostille Convention*, as at 31 December 2011, is found at **Appendix 4**.

  The number of States Party to the Convention is increasing. Up-to-date information about the *Apostille Convention* and the states which are party to it may be found at the Apostille Section of the Hague Conference website <www.hcch.net>.

- **Consular legalization fees and administrative requirements**

  Most consular websites carry details of fees and administrative requirements for the provision of legalization services.

  Legalization fees charged by consulates vary from a few dollars to several hundred dollars. There is no overall prescribed fee and there is no consistency or logic in the level of fees.

  Care should be taken to check whether there is any need to provide one or more (simple) photocopies of documents submitted for legalization.

  The consulates of a number of non-English-speaking countries also insist upon receiving (sworn) translations into their own language of any English language public documents which are to be legalized and of any underlying English language documents which have been notarized.

- **Contact particulars for foreign diplomatic and consular posts**

  Particulars of foreign diplomatic and consular posts accredited to the United States from time to time may be found at the U.S. Department of State websites <www.state.gov/s/cpr/rls/dpl/> and <www.state.gov/s/cpr/rls/fco/>.

- **Important reminder**

  Where an apostille is or ought to be affixed in the United States on a notarization for production in another 'Hague Convention' country, it is improper and in breach of the *Apostille Convention* to have the document 'legalized' by a consular officer of the receiving country.

AFGHANISTAN

Official languages: Pashto and Dari

Legalization

American notarizations for production in the Islamic Republic of Afghanistan must first be legalized by its consular officers in the United States. Prior authentication of the notary's status, signature and seal by authorized U.S. state, territory, and/or federal officials is required for all notarizations which are submitted for legalization.

Legalization services for the United States and its territories are provided by:

The Consular Department
Embassy of Afghanistan

2341 Wyoming Ave NW
WASHINGTON, DC 20008
Tel: (202) 483-6410
Fax: (202) 483-6488
Website: www.embassyofafghanistan.org

Consulate General of Afghanistan

11040 Santa Monica Blvd
Suite 300
LOS ANGELES, CA 90025
Tel: (310) 473-6583
Fax: (310) 473-6775
Website: www.afghanconsulategeneral.org

Consulate General of Afghanistan

633 3rd Ave
Floor 27
NEW YORK, NY 10017
Tel: (212) 972-2276
Fax: (212) 972-2046
Website: www.afghanconsulate-ny.org

ALBANIA

Official language: Albanian

Legalization

The Republic of Albania is party to the *Hague Apostille Convention.*

American notarizations for production in Albania are therefore exempt from consular legalization. The only formality that may be required to certify the authenticity of the notary's status, signature and seal is the affixing of an apostille by the appropriate U.S. Competent Authority.

ALGERIA

Official language: Arabic

Legalization

American notarizations for production in the People's Democratic Republic of Algeria must first be legalized by its consular officers in the United States. Prior authentication of the notary's status, signature and seal by authorized U.S. state, territory and/or federal officials is required for all notarizations which are submitted for legalization.

Legalization services for the United States and its territories are provided by:

The Consular Section
Embassy of Algeria
2118 Kalorama Rd NW
WASHINGTON, DC 20008
Tel: (202) 265-2800
Fax: (202) 667-2174
Website: www.algeria-us.org

ANDORRA

Official language: Catalan

Legalization

The Principality of Andorra is party to the *Hague Apostille Convention.*

American notarizations for production in Andorra are therefore exempt from consular legalization. The only formality that may be required to certify the authenticity of the notary's status, signature and seal is the affixing of an apostille by the appropriate U.S. Competent Authority.

ANGOLA

Official language: Portuguese

Legalization

In 1969, Portugal extended the coverage of the *Hague Apostille Convention* to the Republic of Angola which, at the time, was a Portuguese colony. Since independence on 1 November 1975, Angola has not made a formal declaration as to the continuation in force of the Convention.

Documents for production in Angola to which apostilles have been affixed do not seem to be rejected. Therefore, for the time being, Angola should be treated as being subject to the Convention and the affixing of an apostille should be the only formality required to certify the authenticity of a notary's status, signature and seal.

ANGUILLA

Official language: English

Legalization

Anguilla is an overseas United Kingdom territory and the *Hague Apostille Convention* is in force there.

American notarizations for production in Anguilla are therefore exempt from consular legalization. The only formality that may be required to certify the authenticity of the notary's status, signature and seal is the affixing of an apostille by the appropriate U.S. Competent Authority.

ANTIGUA AND BARBUDA

Official language: English

Legalization

Antigua and Barbuda is party to the *Hague Apostille Convention*.

American notarizations for production in Antigua and Barbuda are therefore exempt from consular legalization. The only formality that may be required to certify the authenticity of the notary's status, signature and seal is the affixing of an apostille by the appropriate U.S. Competent Authority.

ARGENTINA

Official language: Spanish

Legalization

The Argentine Republic is party to the *Hague Apostille Convention*.

American notarizations for production in Argentina are therefore exempt from consular legalization. The only formality that may be required to certify the authenticity of the notary's status, signature and seal is the affixing of an apostille by the appropriate U.S. Competent Authority.

ARMENIA

Official language: Armenian

Legalization

The Republic of Armenia is party to the *Hague Apostille Convention*.

American notarizations for production in Armenia are therefore exempt from consular legalization. The only formality that may be required to certify the authenticity of the notary's status, signature and seal is the affixing of an apostille by the appropriate U.S. Competent Authority.

ARUBA

Official language: Dutch

Legalization

Aruba is a constituent country of the Kingdom of the Netherlands and the *Hague Apostille Convention* is in force there.

American notarizations for production in Aruba are therefore exempt from consular legalization. The only formality that may be required to certify the authenticity of the notary's status, signature and seal is the affixing of an apostille by the appropriate U.S. Competent Authority.

AUSTRALIA

Official language: English

Legalization

The Commonwealth of Australia is party to the *Hague Apostille Convention*.

American notarizations for production in Australia are therefore exempt from consular legalization. The only formality that may be required to certify the authenticity of the notary's status, signature and seal is the affixing of an apostille by the appropriate U.S. Competent Authority.

AUSTRIA

Official language: German

Legalization

The Republic of Austria is party to the *Hague Apostille Convention*.

American notarizations for production in Austria are therefore exempt from consular legalization. The only formality that may be required to certify the authenticity of the notary's status, signature and seal is the affixing of an apostille by the appropriate U.S. Competent Authority.

AZERBAIJAN

Official language: Azerbaijani

Legalization

The Republic of Azerbaijan is party to the *Hague Apostille Convention*.

American notarizations for production in Azerbaijan are therefore exempt from consular legalization. The only formality that may be required to certify the authenticity of the notary's status, signature and seal is the affixing of an apostille by the appropriate U.S. Competent Authority.

THE AZORES

Official language: Portuguese

Legalization

The Azores constitute a single autonomous region of Portugal and the *Hague Apostille Convention* is in force there.

American notarizations for production in The Azores are therefore exempt from consular legalization. The only formality that may be required to certify the authenticity of the notary's status, signature and seal is the affixing of an apostille by the appropriate U.S. Competent Authority.

THE BAHAMAS

Official language: English

Legalization

The Commonwealth of The Bahamas is party to the *Hague Apostille Convention*.

American notarizations for production in The Bahamas are therefore exempt from consular legalization. The only formality that may be required to certify the authenticity of the notary's status, signature and seal is the affixing of an apostille by the appropriate U.S. Competent Authority.

BAHRAIN

Official language: Arabic

English is the language of commerce.

Legalization

American notarizations for production in the Kingdom of Bahrain must first be legalized by its consular officers in the United States. Prior authentication of the notary's status, signature and seal by authorized U.S. state, territory and/or federal officials is required for all notarizations which are submitted for legalization.

Legalization services for the United States and its territories are provided by:

The Consular Section
Embassy of Bahrain

3502 International Drive NW
WASHINGTON, DC 20008
Tel: (202) 342-1111
Fax: (202) 362-2192
Website: www.bahrainembassy.org

BANGLADESH

Official language: English is used for legal and commercial purposes.

Legalization

American notarizations for production in the People's Republic of Bangladesh must first be legalized by its consular officers in the United States. Prior authentication of the notary's status, signature and seal by authorized U.S. state, territory and/or federal officials is required for all notarizations which are submitted for legalization.

Legalization services are provided by:

The Consular Section
Embassy of Bangladesh

3510 International Drive NW
WASHINGTON, DC 20008
Tel: (202) 244-0183
Fax: (202) 244-2771
Website: www.bdembassyusa.org

Jurisdiction throughout the United States and its territories.

Consulate General of Bangladesh

4201 Wilshire Blvd
Suite 605
LOS ANGELES, CA 90010
Tel: (323) 932-0100
Fax: (323) 932-9703
Website: www.bangladeshconsulatela.com

Jurisdiction throughout Arizona, California, Idaho, Nevada, Oregon, Utah, Washington and Wyoming.

Consulate General of Bangladesh

211 East 43rd St
Suite 502
NEW YORK, NY 10017
Tel: (212) 599-6767
Fax: (212) 682-9211
Website: www.bdcgny.org

Jurisdiction throughout Connecticut, Maine, Massachusetts, New Hampshire, New Jersey, New York, Rhode Island and Vermont.

BARBADOS

Official language: English

Legalization

Barbados is party to the *Hague Apostille Convention.*

American notarizations for production in Barbados are therefore exempt from consular legalization. The only formality that may be required to certify the authenticity of the notary's status, signature and seal is the affixing of an apostille by the appropriate U.S. Competent Authority.

BELARUS

Warning

The Republic of Belarus is subject to a U.S. Treasury Department Office of Foreign Assets Control sanctions program. Care must be taken to ensure that transactions with persons, entities or organizations in or relating to Belarus are not in violation of sanctions program regulations. (*See Appendix 2 for further information.*)

Official language: Belarusian

Legalization

Belarus is party to the *Hague Apostille Convention.*

American notarizations for production in Belarus are therefore exempt from consular legalization. The only formality that may be required to certify the authenticity of the notary's status, signature and seal is the affixing of an apostille by the appropriate U.S. Competent Authority.

BELGIUM

Official languages: French, Dutch and German

Legalization

The Kingdom of Belgium is party to the *Hague Apostille Convention.*

American notarizations for production in Belgium are therefore exempt from consular legalization. The only formality that may be required to certify the authenticity of the notary's status, signature and seal is the affixing of an apostille by the appropriate U.S. Competent Authority.

BELIZE

Official language: English

Legalization

Belize is party to the *Hague Apostille Convention*.

American notarizations for production in Belize are therefore exempt from consular legalization. The only formality that may be required to certify the authenticity of the notary's status, signature and seal is the affixing of an apostille by the appropriate U.S. Competent Authority.

BENIN

Official language: French

Legalization

American notarizations for production in the Republic of Benin must first be legalized by its consular officers in the United States. Prior authentication of the notary's status, signature and seal by authorized U.S. state, territory and/ or federal officials is required for all notarizations which are submitted for legalization.

Legalization services for the United States and its territories are provided by:

The Consular Section
Embassy of Benin

2124 Kalorama Rd NW
WASHINGTON, DC 20008
Tel: (202) 232-6656
Fax: (202) 265-1996
Website: www.beninembassy.us

BERMUDA

Official language: English

Legalization

Bermuda is a self-governing United Kingdom dependency and the *Hague Apostille Convention* is in force there.

American notarizations for production in Bermuda are therefore exempt from consular legalization. The only formality that may be required to certify the authenticity of the notary's status, signature and seal is the affixing of an apostille by the appropriate U.S. Competent Authority.

BHUTAN

Official languages: English, Dzongkha and Lhotsan

Legalization

The United States and the Kingdom of Bhutan have not yet established formal diplomatic relations. Bhutan's Permanent Mission to the United Nations has consular jurisdiction in the United States.

American notarizations for production in Bhutan must first be legalized by a consular officer at its Permanent Mission. Prior authentication of the notary's status, signature and seal by authorized U.S. state, territory and/or federal officials is required for all notarizations which are submitted for legalization.

Legalization services for the United States and its territories are provided by:

Consulate General of Bhutan
Permanent Mission to the United Nations

2 United Nations Plaza
27th Floor
NEW YORK, NY 10017
Tel: (212) 826-1919
Fax: (212) 826-2998

BOLIVIA

Official languages: Spanish, Aymara and Quenchua

Legalization

American notarizations for production in the Republic of Bolivia must first be legalized by its consular officers in the United States. Prior authentication of the notary's status, signature and seal by authorized U.S. state, territory and/ or federal officials is required for all notarizations which are submitted for legalization.

Legalization services are provided by:

The Consular Section
Embassy of Bolivia

4420 Connecticut Ave NW
Suite 2
WASHINGTON, DC 20008
Tel: (202) 232-4828
Fax: (202) 232-8017
Website: www.bolivia-usa.org

Jurisdiction throughout Delaware, Maryland, North Carolina, Washington DC, West Virginia, Virginia and Puerto Rico.

Honorary Consul of Bolivia

3413 Canacee Dr
MOBILE, AL 36693
Tel : (334) 666-6969
Fax: (334) 661-2873

Jurisdiction throughout Alabama.

Consulate General of Bolivia

3701 Wilshire Blvd
Suite 1065
LOS ANGELES, CA 90010
Tel: (213) 388-0475
Fax: (213) 384-6272

Jurisdiction throughout California, Hawaii and Nevada.

Consulate General of Bolivia

1101 Brickell Ave
North Tower
Suite 1103
MIAMI, FL 33131
Tel: (305) 670-0710
Fax: (305) 358-6305

Jurisdiction throughout Alabama, Florida and South Carolina.

Honorary Consul General of Bolivia

1401 Peachtree St NE
Suite 240
ATLANTA, GA 30309
Tel: (404) 522-0777
Fax: (404) 873-3335

Jurisdiction throughout Georgia and Tennessee.

Honorary Consul of Bolivia

1111 W Superior St
Suite 309
Melrose Park
CHICAGO, IL 60160
Tel: (708) 343-1234
Fax: (708) 343-4290

Jurisdiction throughout Illinois, Indiana, Iowa, Michigan, Minnesota and Wisconsin.

Honorary Consul General of Bolivia

85 Devonshire St
Suite 1000
BOSTON, MA 02109
Tel: (617) 742-1500
Fax: (617) 742-9130

Jurisdiction throughout Massachusetts.

Honorary Consul of Bolivia

18036 65th Ave N
MAPLE GROVE, MN 55311
Tel: (763) 424-0265
Fax: (763) 416-4684

Jurisdiction throughout Minnesota.

Consulate General of Bolivia

211 East 43rd St
Suite 702
NEW YORK, NY 10017
Tel: (212) 687-0530
Fax: (212) 687-0532

Jurisdiction throughout Connecticut, Maine, New Hampshire, New Jersey, New York, Pennsylvania, Rhode Island and Vermont.

Honorary Consul of Bolivia

210 Park Ave
Suite 1600
OKLAHOMA CITY, OK 73102
Tel: (405) 239-7900
Fax: (405) 235-5852

Jurisdiction throughout Oklahoma.

Honorary Consul of Bolivia

1409 Calle Lunchetti Union
SAN JUAN, PR 00907
Tel: (787) 722-5449
Fax: (787) 722-8457

Jurisdiction throughout Puerto Rico, Guam, Northern Marianas and U.S. Virgin Islands.

Honorary Consul of Bolivia

1881 Sylvan Ave
Suite 110
DALLAS, TX 75208
Tel: (214) 571-6131
Fax: (214) 651-9514

Jurisdiction throughout Texas.

Honorary Consul of Bolivia

16646 Clay Rd
Suite 200
HOUSTON, TX 77084
Tel: (281) 463-0017
Fax: (281) 463-0018
Website: www.web.wt.net/-coboltex

Jurisdiction throughout Arkansas, Kansas, Louisiana, Mississippi, Missouri, Nebraska, North Dakota, Oklahoma, South Dakota, Utah and Texas.

Honorary Consul of Bolivia

Park Ridge Building
15215 52nd Ave
Suite 100
SEATTLE, WA 98188
Tel: (206) 244-6696
Fax: (206) 243-3795

Jurisdiction throughout Alaska, Idaho, Montana, Oregon, Washington and Wyoming.

BONAIRE

Official language: Dutch

Legalization

Bonaire is a special municipality of the Kingdom of the Netherlands and the *Hague Apostille Convention* is in force there.

American notarizations for production in Bonaire are therefore exempt from consular legalization. The only formality that may be required to certify the authenticity of the notary's status, signature and seal is the affixing of an apostille by the appropriate U.S. Competent Authority.

BOSNIA AND HERZEGOVINA

Official languages: Serbian and Croatian

Legalization

Bosnia and Herzegovina is party to the *Hague Apostille Convention*.

American notarizations for production in Bosnia and Herzegovina are therefore exempt from consular legalization. The only formality that may be required to certify the authenticity of the notary's status, signature and seal is the affixing of an apostille by the appropriate U.S. Competent Authority.

BOTSWANA

Official languages: English and Setswana

Legalization

The Republic of Botswana is party to the *Hague Apostille Convention*.

American notarizations for production in Botswana are therefore exempt from consular legalization. The only formality that may be required to certify the authenticity of the notary's status, signature and seal is the affixing of an apostille by the appropriate U.S. Competent Authority.

BRAZIL

Official language: Portuguese

Legalization

American notarizations for production in the Federative Republic of Brazil must first be legalized by its consular officers in the United States. Prior authentication of the notary's status, signature and seal by authorized U.S. state, territory and/ or federal officials is required for all notarizations which are submitted for legalization.

Legalization services are provided by:

The Consular Section
Embassy of Brazil

3006 Massachusetts Ave NW
WASHINGTON, DC 20008
Tel: (202) 238-2805
Fax: (202) 238-2827
Website: www.brasilemb.org

Jurisdiction throughout Maryland, Ohio, Virginia, Washington DC and West Virginia.

Consulate General of Brazil

8484 Wilshire Blvd
Suites 711-730
LOS ANGELES, CA 90211
Tel: (323) 651-2664
Fax: (323) 651-1274
Website: www.brazilian-consulate.org

Jurisdiction throughout Arizona, Hawaii, Idaho, Montana, Nevada, Utah, Wyoming and the California counties of Imperial, Kern, Los Angeles, Orange Riverside, San Bernadino, San Diego, San Luis Obispo, Santa Barbara and Ventura.

Consulate General of Brazil

300 Montgomery St
Suite 300
SAN FRANCISCO, CA 94104
Tel: (415) 981-8170
Fax: (415) 981-4625
Website: www.brazilsf.org

Jurisdiction throughout Alaska, Oregon, Washington and the California counties of Alameda, Alpine, Amador, Butte, Calaveras, Colusa, Contra Costa, Del Norte, El Dorado, Fresno, Glenn, Humboldt, Inyo, Kings, Lake, Lassen, Ladedra, Martin, Mariposa, Mendocino, Merced, Modoc, Mono, Monterey, Napa, Nevada, Placer, Plumas, Sacramento, San Benedito, San Francisco, San Joaquin, San Mateo, Santa Clara, Santa Cruz, Shasta, Sierra, Siskyou, Solano, Sonoma, Stanislau, Sutter, Tehama, Trinity, Tulare, Tuolunme, Yolo and Yuma.

Consulate General of Brazil

80 SW 8th St
Suite 2600
MIAMI, FL 33133
Tel: (305) 285-6200
Fax: (305) 285-6229
Website: www.brazilmiami.org

Jurisdiction throughout Alabama, Florida, Georgia, Mississippi, North Carolina, South Carolina, Tennessee and U.S. external territories.

Consulate General of Brazil

401 N Michigan Ave
Suite 1850
CHICAGO, IL 60611
Tel: (312) 464-0244
Fax: (312) 464-0299

Jurisdiction throughout Illinois, Indiana, Iowa, Michigan, Minnesota, Missouri, Nebraska. North Dakota, South Dakota and Wisconsin.

Consulate General of Brazil

20 Park Plaza
Suite 810
BOSTON, MA 02116
Tel: (617) 542-4000
Fax: (617) 542-4318
Website: www.boston.itamaraty.gov.br/pt-br

Jurisdiction throughout Maine, Massachusetts, New Hampshire, Rhode Island and Vermont.

Consulate General of Brazil

1185 Avenue of the Americas
Floor 21
NEW YORK, NY 10036
Tel: (212) 827-0976
Fax: (212) 827-0225
Website: www.novayork.itamaraty.gov.br/pt-br

Jurisdiction throughout Connecticut, Delaware, New Jersey, New York and Pennsylvania.

Consulate General of Brazil

1233 W Loop S
Suite 1150
HOUSTON, TX 77027
Tel: (713) 961-3063
Fax: (713) 961-3070
Website: www.brazilhouston.org

Jurisdiction throughout Arkansas, Colorado, Kansas, Louisiana, New Mexico, Oklahoma and Texas.

BRITISH ANTARCTIC TERRITORY

Official language: English

Legalization

From the perspective of the United Kingdom, the British Antarctic Territory is one of its external territories and the *Hague Apostille Convention* is in force there. American notarizations for production in the British Antarctic Territory are therefore exempt from consular legalization. The only formality that may be required to certify the authenticity of the notary's status, signature and seal is the affixing of an apostille by the appropriate U.S. Competent Authority.

As far as the United States is concerned, the legal status of Antarctica remains in suspense under its *Antarctic Treaty of 1959* and the U.S. does not recognize the United Kingdom's claim to any part of Antarctica. Fortunately, in practice, the legalization of American notarizations for production in the British Antarctic Territory is not a significant problem.

BRITISH VIRGIN ISLANDS

Official language: English

Legalization

The British Virgin Islands constitute a single self-governing dependent territory of the United Kingdom and the *Hague Apostille Convention* is in force there.

American notarizations for production in British Virgin Islands are therefore exempt from consular legalization. The only formality that may be required to certify the authenticity of the notary's status, signature and seal is the affixing of an apostille by the appropriate U.S. Competent Authority.

BRUNEI

Official languages: English and Malay

Legalization

Brunei Darussalam is party to the *Hague Apostille Convention*.

American notarizations for production in Brunei are therefore exempt from consular legalization. The only formality that may be required to certify the authenticity of the notary's status, signature and seal is the affixing of an apostille by the appropriate U.S. Competent Authority.

BULGARIA

Official language: Bulgarian

Legalization

The Republic of Bulgaria is party to the *Hague Apostille Convention*.

American notarizations for production in Bulgaria are therefore exempt from consular legalization. The only formality that may be required to certify the authenticity of the notary's status, signature and seal is the affixing of an apostille by the appropriate U.S. Competent Authority.

BURKINA FASO

Official language: French

Legalization

American notarizations for production in Burkina Faso must first be legalized by its consular officers in the United States. Prior authentication of the notary's status, signature and seal by authorized U.S. state, territory and/or federal officials is required for all notarizations which are submitted for legalization.

Legalization services for the United States and its territories are provided by:

The Consular Section
Embassy of Burkina Faso

2340 Massachusetts Ave NW
WASHINGTON, DC 20008
Tel: (202) 332-5577
Fax: (202) 667-1882
Website: www.burkinaembassy-usa.org

BURMA

See Myanmar

BURUNDI

Official languages: French and Kirundi

Legalization

American notarizations for production in the Republic of Burundi must first be legalized by its consular officers in the United States. Prior authentication of the notary's status, signature and seal by authorized U.S. state, territory and/or federal officials is required for all notarizations which are submitted for legalization.

Legalization services for the United States and its territories are provided by:

The Consular Section
Embassy of Burundi

2233 Wisconsin Ave NW
Suite 212
WASHINGTON, DC 20007
Tel: (202) 342-2574
Fax: (202) 342-2578
Website: www.burundiembassy-usa.org

CAMBODIA

Official language: Khmer

Legalization

American notarizations for production in the Kingdom of Cambodia must first be legalized by its consular officers in the United States. Prior authentication of the notary's status, signature and seal by authorized U.S. state, territory and/or federal officials is required for all notarizations which are submitted for legalization.

Legalization services for the United States and its territories are provided by:

The Consular Section
Royal Embassy of Cambodia

4530 16th St NW
WASHINGTON, DC 20011
Tel: (202) 726-7742
Fax: (202) 726-8381
Website: www.embassyofcambodia.org

CAMEROON

Official languages: English and French

Legalization

American notarizations for production in the Republic of Cameroon must first be legalized by its consular officers in the United States. Prior authentication of the notary's status, signature and seal by authorized U.S. state, territory and/or federal officials is required for all notarizations which are submitted for legalization.

Legalization services for the United States and its territories are provided by:

The Consular Service
Embassy of the Republic of Cameroon

1700 Wisconsin Ave NW
WASHINGTON, DC 20007
Tel: (202) 265-8790
Fax: (202) 387-3826
Website: www.ambacam-usa.org

CANADA

Official languages: English and French

Legalization

In the absence of allegations to the contrary in a particular case, notarized documents emanating from any jurisdiction which are to be produced in Canada are presumed to be authentic. Prior authentication of a notary's status, signature and seal is not required.

CAPE VERDE

Official language: Portuguese

Legalization

Cape Verde is party to the *Hague Apostille Convention*.

American notarizations for production in Cape Verde are therefore exempt from consular legalization. The only formality that may be required to certify the authenticity of the notary's status, signature and seal is the affixing of an apostille by the appropriate U.S. Competent Authority.

CAYMAN ISLANDS

Official language: English

Legalization

The Cayman Islands constitute a self-governing United Kingdom dependency and the *Hague Apostille Convention* is in force there.

American notarizations for production in the Cayman Islands are therefore exempt from consular legalization. The only formality that may be required to certify the authenticity of the notary's status, signature and seal is the affixing of an apostille by the appropriate U.S. Competent Authority.

CENTRAL AFRICAN REPUBLIC

Official language: French

Legalization

American notarizations for production in the Central African Republic must first be legalized by its consular officers in the United States. Prior authentication of the notary's status, signature and seal by authorized U.S. state, territory and/or federal officials is required for all notarizations which are submitted for legalization.

Legalization services for the United States and its territories are provided by:

The Consular Section
Embassy of Central African Republic

1618 22nd St NW
WASHINGTON, DC 20008
Tel: (202) 483-7800
Fax: (202) 332-9893

CHAD

Official languages: More than 100 different languages are spoken in Chad. Legal and commercial documents in English or French are usually acceptable.

Legalization

American notarizations for production in the Republic of Chad must first be legalized by its consular officers in the United States. Prior authentication of the notary's status, signature and seal by authorized U.S. state, territory and/ or federal officials is required for all notarizations which are submitted for legalization.

Legalization services for the United States and its territories are provided by:

The Consular Section
Embassy of Chad

2401 Massachusetts Ave NW
WASHINGTON, DC 20008
Tel: (202) 652-1312
Fax: (202) 758-0431
Website: www.chadembassy.us

CHANNEL ISLANDS

Official language: English

Legalization

The Bailiwick of Guernsey and the Bailiwick of Jersey (generally known together as the Channel Islands) are self-governing United Kingdom Crown Dependencies. The *Hague Apostille Convention* is in force in both bailiwicks.

American notarizations for production in the Channel Islands are therefore exempt from consular legalization. The only formality that may be required to certify the authenticity of the notary's status, signature and seal is the affixing of an apostille by the appropriate U.S. Competent Authority.

CHILE

Official language: Spanish

Legalization

American notarizations for production in the Republic of Chile must first be legalized by its consular officers in the United States. Prior authentication of the notary's status, signature and seal by authorized U.S. state, territory and/ or federal officials is required for all notarizations which are submitted for legalization.

Legalization services are provided by:

The Consular Section
Embassy of Chile

1732 Massachusetts Ave NW
WASHINGTON, DC 20036
Tel: (202) 785-1746
Fax: (202) 887-5579
Website: www.chile-usa.org

Jurisdiction throughout Maryland, North Carolina, Virginia, Washington DC and West Virginia.

Consulate General of Chile

6100 Wilshire Blvd
Suites 1240
LOS ANGELES, CA 90048
Tel: (323) 933-3697
Fax: (323) 933-3842

Jurisdiction throughout Arizona, California (Southern), Colorado, Hawaii, Nevada (Southern) and Utah.

Consulate General of Chile

800 Brickell Ave
Suite 1200
MIAMI, FL 33131
Tel: (305) 373-8623
Fax: (305) 379-6613

Jurisdiction throughout Alabama, Florida, Georgia, Mississippi, South Carolina and Tennessee.

Honorary Consul of Chile

2240 Kuhio Ave
HONOLULU, HI 96815-2820
Tel: (808) 561-1772
Fax: (808) 543-0155

Jurisdiction throughout Hawaii and American Samoa.

Consulate General of Chile

1415 N Dayton St
2nd Floor
CHICAGO, IL 60642
Tel: (312) 654-8780
Fax: (312) 654-8948

Jurisdiction throughout Illinois, Indiana, Iowa, Kansas, Kentucky, Michigan, Minnesota, Missouri, Nebraska, North Dakota, Ohio, South Dakota and Wisconsin.

Honorary Consul of Chile

1 Bernardo O'Higgins Circle
Brighton
BOSTON, MA 02135
Tel: (617) 232-0416
Fax: (617) 232-0817

Jurisdiction throughout Massachusetts

Consulate General of Chile

866 United Nations Plaza
Suite 601
NEW YORK, NY 10017
Tel: (212) 355-0612
Fax: (212) 688-5288
Website: chileny.org

Jurisdiction throughout Connecticut, Maine, Massachusetts, New Hampshire,
New Jersey (North), New York, Rhode Island and Vermont.

Consulate General of Chile

Public Ledger Building
Suite 1030
6th & Chestnut St
PHILADELPHIA, PA 19106
Tel: (215) 829-9520
Fax: (215) 829-0594

Jurisdiction throughout Delaware, New Jersey (South) and Pennsylvania.

Consulate General of Chile

1509 Lopez Landron
Suite 1101
SAN JUAN, PR 00911
Tel: (787) 725-6365
Fax: (787) 721-5650

Jurisdiction throughout American Samoa, Guam, Puerto Rico, Northern
Marianas and U.S. Virgin Islands.

Consulate General of Chile

1300 Post Oak Blvd
Suite 1130
HOUSTON, TX 77056
Tel: (713) 963-9066
Fax: (713) 621-8672

Jurisdiction throughout Arkansas, Louisiana, Mississippi, New Mexico,
Oklahoma and Texas.

CHINA

Official language: Mandarin

Legalization

American notarizations for production in the People's Republic of China, other than in the Special Administrative Zones of Hong Kong and Macao, must first be legalized by its consular officers in the United States. Prior authentication of the notary's status, signature and seal by authorized U.S. state, territory and/or federal officials is required for all notarizations which are submitted for legalization.

Legalization services are provided by:

The Consular Section
Embassy of China

2201 Wisconsin Ave NW
Suite 110
WASHINGTON, DC 20007
Tel: (202) 327-1956
Fax: (202) 588-9760
Website: www.china-embassy.org/eng

Jurisdiction throughout Delaware, Idaho, Kentucky, Maryland, Montana, Nebraska, North Carolina, North Dakota, South Carolina, South Dakota, Tennessee, Utah, Virginia, Washington DC, West Virginia and Wyoming.

Consulate General of China

443 Shatto Pl
LOS ANGELES, CA 90020
Tel: (213) 807-8088
Fax: (213) 807-8091
Website: www.losangeles.china-consulate.org

Jurisdiction throughout Arizona, California (Southern), Hawaii, New Mexico and U.S. external territories.

Consulate General of China

1450 Laguna St
SAN FRANCISCO, CA 94115
Tel: (415) 852-5941
Website: www.chinaconsulatesf.org

Jurisdiction throughout Alaska, California (Northern), Nevada, Oregon and Washington.

Consulate General of China

100 W Erie St
CHICAGO, IL 60654
Tel: (312) 803-0095
Fax: (312) 803-0110
Website: www.chinaconsulatechicago.org

Jurisdiction throughout Colorado, Illinois, Indiana, Iowa, Kansas, Michigan, Minnesota, Missouri and Wisconsin.

Consulate General of China

520 12th Ave
NEW YORK, NY 10036
Tel: (212) 244-9456
Website: www.nyconsulate.prchina.org

Jurisdiction throughout Connecticut, Maine, Massachusetts, New Hampshire, New Jersey, New York, Ohio, Pennsylvania, Rhode Island and Vermont.

Consulate General of China

3417 Montrose Blvd
Suite 700
HOUSTON, TX 77006
Tel: (713) 520-1462
Fax: (713) 521-3064
Website: www.houston.china-consulate.org

Jurisdiction throughout Alabama, Arkansas, Florida, Georgia, Louisiana, Mississippi, Oklahoma and Texas.

CHRISTMAS ISLAND

Official language: English

Legalization

The Territory of Christmas Island is a non-self-governing territory of Australia and the *Hague Apostille Convention* is in force there.

American notarizations for production in Christmas Island are therefore exempt from consular legalization. The only formality that may be required to certify the authenticity of the notary's status, signature and seal is the affixing of an apostille by the appropriate U.S. Competent Authority.

COCOS (KEELING) ISLANDS

Official language: English

Legalization

The Territory of Cocos (Keeling) Islands is a non-self-governing territory of Australia and the *Hague Apostille Convention* is in force there.

American notarizations for production in the Cocos (Keeling) Islands are therefore exempt from consular legalization. The only formality that may be required to certify the authenticity of the notary's status, signature and seal is the affixing of an apostille by the appropriate U.S. Competent Authority.

COLOMBIA

Official language: Spanish

Legalization

The Republic of Columbia is party to the *Hague Apostille Convention*.

American notarizations for production in Columbia are therefore exempt from consular legalization. The only formality that may be required to certify the authenticity of the notary's status, signature and seal is the affixing of an apostille by the appropriate U.S. Competent Authority.

COMOROS

Official languages: Arabic and French

Legalization

The Union of the Comoros was formerly a French overseas territory to which the *Hague Apostille Convention* applied. Since independence on 6 July 1975, Comoros has not made a formal declaration as to the continuation in force of the Convention.

Documents for production in Comoros to which apostilles have been affixed do not seem to be rejected. Therefore, for the time being, Comoros should be treated as being subject to the Convention and the affixing of an apostille by the appropriate U.S. Competent Authority should be the only formality required to certify the authenticity of a notary's status, signature and seal.

CONGO (Brazzaville)

Official language: French

Legalization

American notarizations for production in the Republic of the Congo must first be legalized by its consular officers in the United States. Prior authentication of the notary's status, signature and seal by authorized U.S. state, territory and/or federal officials is required for all notarizations which are submitted for legalization.

Legalization services for the United States and its territories are provided by:

The Consular Section
Embassy of the Republic of Congo

4891 Colorado Ave NW
WASHINGTON, DC 20011
Tel: (202) 726-5500
Fax: (202) 726-1860
Website: www.embassyofcongo.org

CONGO (Democratic Republic)

Warning

The Democratic Republic of the Congo is subject to a U.S. Treasury Department Office of Foreign Assets Control sanctions program. Care must be taken to ensure that transactions with persons, entities or organizations in or relating to the DRC are not in violation of sanctions program regulations. (*See Appendix 2 for further information.*)

Official language: French

Legalization

American notarizations for production in the DRC, must first be legalized by its consular officers in the United States. Prior authentication of the notary's status, signature and seal by authorized U.S. state, territory and/or federal officials is required for all notarizations which are submitted for legalization.

Legalization services for the United States and its territories are provided by:

The Consular Section
Embassy of the Democratic Republic of Congo

1726 M St NW
Suite 601
WASHINGTON, DC 20036
Tel: (202) 234-7690
Fax: (202) 234-2609
website: www.ambardcusa.org

COOK ISLANDS

Official language: English

Legalization

Cook Islands is party to the *Hague Apostille Convention*.

American notarizations for production in Cook Islands are therefore exempt from consular legalization. The only formality that may be required to certify the authenticity of the notary's status, signature and seal is the affixing of an apostille by the appropriate U.S. Competent Authority.

COSTA RICA

Official language: Spanish

Legalization

The Republic of Costa Rica is a party to the *Hague Apostille Convention*.

American notarizations for production in Costa Rica are therefore exempt from consular legalization. The only formality that may be required to certify the authenticity of the notary's status, signature and seal is the affixing of an apostille by the appropriate U.S. Competent Authority.

CÔTE D'IVOIRE

Warning

The Republic of Côte d'Ivoire is subject to a U.S. Treasury Department Office of Foreign Assets Control sanctions program. Care must be taken to ensure that transactions with persons, entities or organizations in or relating to Côte d'Iviore are not in violation of sanctions program regulations. (*See Appendix 2 for further information.*)

Official language: French

Legalization

American notarizations for production in Côte d'Ivoire must first be legalized by its consular officers in the United States. Prior authentication of the notary's status, signature and seal by authorized U.S. state, territory and/or federal officials is required for all notarizations which are submitted for legalization.

Legalization services throughout the United States and its territories are provided by:

The Consular Section
Embassy of Cote d'Iviôre

2424 Massachusetts Ave NW
WASHINGTON, DC 20008
Tel: (202) 797-0300
Fax: (202) 204-3967

CROATIA

Official language: Croatian

Legalization

The Republic of Croatia is party to the *Hague Apostille Convention*.

American notarizations for production in Croatia are therefore exempt from consular legalization. The only formality that may be required to certify the authenticity of the notary's status, signature and seal is the affixing of an apostille by the appropriate U.S. Competent Authority.

CUBA

Warning

The Republic of Cuba is subject to a U.S. Treasury Department Office of Foreign Assets Control sanctions program. Care must be taken to ensure that transactions with persons, entities or organizations in or relating to Cuba are not in violation of sanctions program regulations. (*See Appendix 2 for further information.*)

Official language: Spanish

Legalization

The United States does not presently have diplomatic relations with Cuba.

American notarizations for production in Cuba must first be legalized by the Cuban Interest Section of the Swiss Embassy in Washington DC.

Prior authentication of the notary's status, signature and seal by authorized U.S. state, territory and/or federal officials is required for all notarizations which are submitted for legalization.

Legalization services for the United States and its territories are provided by:

Cuban Interests Section
Embassy of Switzerland

2630 16th St NW
WASHINGTON, DC 20009
Tel: (202) 797-8518
Fax: (202) 797-0606

CURACAO

Official language: Dutch

Legalization

Land Curacao is a constituent country of the Kingdom of the Netherlands and the *Hague Apostille Convention* is in force there.

American notarizations for production in Curacao are therefore exempt from consular legalization. The only formality that may be required to certify the authenticity of the notary's status, signature and seal is the affixing of an apostille by the appropriate U.S. Competent Authority.

CYPRUS

Official languages: Greek and Turkish

Legalization

The Republic of Cyprus is party to the *Hague Apostille Convention*.

American notarizations for production in Cyprus are therefore exempt from consular legalization. The only formality that may be required to certify the authenticity of the notary's status, signature and seal is the affixing of an apostille by the appropriate U.S. Competent Authority.

CZECH REPUBLIC

Official language: Czech

Legalization

The Czech Republic is party to the *Hague Apostille Convention*.

American notarizations for production in the Czech Republic are therefore exempt from consular legalization. The only formality that may be required to certify the authenticity of the notary's status, signature and seal is the affixing of an apostille by the appropriate U.S. Competent Authority.

DENMARK

Official language: Danish

Legalization

The Kingdom of Denmark is party to the *Hague Apostille Convention*

American notarizations for production in Denmark are therefore exempt from consular legalization. The only formality that may be required to certify the authenticity of the notary's status, signature and seal is the affixing of an apostille by the appropriate U.S. Competent Authority.

DJIBOUTI

Official language: Arabic

Legalization

The Republic of Djibouti was formerly a French overseas territory to which the *Hague Apostille Convention* applied. Since independence on 27 June 1977, Djibouti has not made a formal declaration as to the continuation in force of the Convention.

Documents for production in Djibouti to which apostilles have been affixed do not seem to be rejected. Therefore, for the time being, Djibouti should be treated as being subject to the Convention and the affixing of an apostille by the appropriate U.S. Competent Authority should be the only formality required to certify the authenticity of a notary's status, signature and seal.

DOMINICA

Official language: English

Legalization

The Commonwealth of Dominica is party to the *Hague Apostille Convention*.

American notarizations for production in Dominica are therefore exempt from consular legalization. The only formality that may be required to certify the authenticity of the notary's status, signature and seal is the affixing of an apostille by the appropriate U.S. Competent Authority.

DOMINICAN REPUBLIC

Official language: Spanish

Legalization

The Dominican Republic is party to the *Hague Apostille Convention*.

American notarizations for production in the Dominican Republic are therefore exempt from consular legalization. The only formality that may be required to certify the authenticity of the notary's status, signature and seal is the affixing of an apostille by the appropriate U.S. Competent Authority.

EAST TIMOR

See Timor-Leste

ECUADOR

Official language: Spanish

Legalization

The Republic of Ecuador is party to the *Hague Apostille Convention*.

American notarizations for production in Ecuador are therefore exempt from consular legalization. The only formality that may be required to certify the authenticity of the notary's status, signature and seal is the affixing of an apostille by the appropriate U.S. Competent Authority.

EGYPT

Official language: Arabic

Legalization

American notarizations for production in the Arab Republic of Egypt must first be legalized by its consular officers in the United States. Prior authentication of the notary's status, signature and seal by authorized U.S. state, territory and/or federal officials is required for all notarizations which are submitted for legalization.

Legalization services are provided by:

The Consular Section
Embassy of Egypt

3521 International Ct NW
WASHINGTON, DC 20008
Tel: (202) 895-5400
Fax: (202) 244-4319
Website: www.egyptembassy.net

Jurisdiction throughout Delaware, Florida, Georgia, Maryland, North Carolina, South Carolina, Virginia, Washington DC, West Virginia and U.S. external territories.

Consulate General of Egypt

3001 Pacific Ave
SAN FRANCISCO, CA 94115
Tel: (415) 346-9700

Jurisdiction throughout Alaska, Arizona, California, Hawaii, Idaho, Montana, Nevada, Oregon, Utah, Washington and Wyoming.

Consulate General of Egypt

500 N. Michigan Ave
Suite 1900
CHICAGO, IL 60611
Tel: (312) 828-9162
Fax: (312) 828 9167

Jurisdiction throughout Illinois, Indiana, Iowa, Kentucky, Michigan, Minnesota, Nebraska, North Dakota, South Dakota and Wisconsin.

Consulate General of Egypt

1110 2nd Ave
Suite 201
NEW YORK, NY 10022
Tel: (212) 759-7120
Fax: (212) 308-7643
Website: www.egyptnyc.net

Jurisdiction throughout Connecticut, Maine, Massachusetts, New Hampshire, New Jersey, New York, Ohio, Pennsylvania, Puerto Rico, Rhode Island and Vermont.

Consulate General of Egypt

1990 Post Oak Blvd
Suite 2180
HOUSTON, TX 77056
Tel: (713) 961-4915
Fax: (713) 961-3868

Jurisdiction throughout Alabama, Arkansas, Colorado, Kansas, Louisiana, Mississippi, Missouri, New Mexico, Oklahoma, Tennessee and Texas.

EL SALVADOR

Official language: Spanish

Legalization

The Republic of El Salvador is party to the *Hague Apostille Convention.*

American notarizations for production in El Salvador are therefore exempt from consular legalization. The only formality that may be required to certify the authenticity of the notary's status, signature and seal is the affixing of an apostille by the appropriate U.S. Competent Authority.

EQUATORIAL GUINEA

Official languages: Spanish and French

Legalization

American notarizations for production in the Republic of Equatorial Guinea must first be legalized by its consular officers in the United States. Prior authentication of the notary's status, signature and seal by authorized U.S. state, territory and/ or federal officials is required for all notarizations which are submitted for legalization.

Legalization services for the United States and its territories are provided by:

The Consular Section
Embassy of Equatorial Guinea

2020 16th St NW
WASHINGTON, DC 20009
Tel: (202) 518-5700
Fax: (202) 518-5252

ERITREA

Official language: No official language.

Legal and commercial documents in English are usually acceptable.

Legalization

American notarizations for production in the State of Eritrea must first be legalized by its consular officers in the United States. Prior authentication of the notary's status, signature and seal by authorized U.S. state, territory and/ or federal officials is required for all notarizations which are submitted for legalization.

Legalization services for the United States and its territories are provided by:

The Consular Section
Embassy of Eritrea

1708 New Hampshire Ave NW
WASHINGTON, DC 20009
Tel: (202) 319-1991
Fax: (202) 319-1304

ESTONIA

Official language: Estonian

Legalization

The Republic of Estonia is party to the *Hague Apostille Convention*

American notarizations for production in Estonia are therefore exempt from consular legalization. The only formality that may be required to certify the authenticity of the notary's status, signature and seal is the affixing of an apostille by the appropriate U.S. Competent Authority.

ETHIOPIA

Official language: Amharic

Legalization

American notarizations for production in the Federal Democratic Republic of Ethiopia must first be legalized by its consular officers in the United States. Prior authentication of the notary's status, signature and seal by authorized U.S. state, territory and/or federal officials is required for all notarizations which are submitted for legalization.

Legalization services for the United States and its territories are provided by:

The Consular Section
Embassy of Ethiopia

3506 International Ct NW
WASHINGTON, DC 20008
Tel: (202) 364-1200
Fax: (202) 686-9551
Website: www.ethiopiaembassy.org

FALKLAND ISLANDS

Official language: English

Legalization

The Falkland Islands constitute a self-governing United Kingdom dependency and the *Hague Apostille Convention* is in force there.

American notarizations for production in the Falkland Islands are therefore exempt from consular legalization. The only formality that may be required to certify the authenticity of the notary's status, signature and seal is the affixing of an apostille by the appropriate U.S. Competent Authority.

FAROE ISLANDS

Official languages: Danish and Faroese

Legalization

The Faroe Islands constitute a single self-governing Danish overseas administrative division. Even though the *Hague Apostille Convention* entered into force for Denmark on 29 December 2006, Denmark has declared that, for the time being, the Convention does not apply to the Faroe Islands.

American notarizations for production in the Faroe Islands must first be legalized by a Danish consular officer in the United States. Prior authentication of the notary's status, signature and seal by authorized U.S. state, territory and/or federal officials is required for all notarizations which are submitted for legalization.

Particulars of Danish consulates in the United States may be found via the Danish Embassy website, <www.ambwashington.um.dk>.

FIJI

Official language: English

Legalization

The Republic of the Fiji Islands is party to the *Hague Apostille Convention*.

American notarizations for production in Fiji are therefore exempt from consular legalization. The only formality that may be required to certify the authenticity of the notary's status, signature and seal is the affixing of an apostille by the appropriate U.S. Competent Authority.

FINLAND

Official languages: Finnish and Swedish

Legalization

The Republic of Finland is party to the *Hague Apostille Convention*.

American notarizations for production in Finland are therefore exempt from consular legalization. The only formality that may be required to certify the authenticity of the notary's status, signature and seal is the affixing of an apostille by the appropriate U.S. Competent Authority.

FRANCE

Official language: French

Legalization

The French Republic is party to the *Hague Apostille Convention*.

American notarizations for production in France are therefore exempt from consular legalization. The only formality that may be required to certify the authenticity of the notary's status, signature and seal is the affixing of an apostille by the appropriate U.S. Competent Authority.

FRENCH GUIANA

Official language: French

Legalization

French Guiana is a French overseas department.

As France is party to the *Hague Apostille Convention* American notarizations for production in French Guiana are therefore exempt from consular legalization. The only formality that may be required to certify the authenticity of the notary's status, signature and seal is the affixing of an apostille by the appropriate U.S. Competent Authority.

FRENCH POLYNESIA

Official languages: French and Tahitian

Legalization

The Overseas Lands of French Polynesia constitute a French overseas collectivity and the *Hague Apostille Convention* is in force there.

American notarizations for production in French Polynesia are therefore exempt from consular legalization. The only formality that may be required to certify the authenticity of the notary's status, signature and seal is the affixing of an apostille by the appropriate U.S. Competent Authority.

FRENCH SOUTHERN AND ANTARCTIC LANDS

Official language: French

Legalization

The Territory of the French Southern and Antarctic Lands is a French overseas territory and the *Hague Apostille Convention* is in force there.

If it were ever necessary for an American notarization to be produced in the French Southern and Antarctic Lands, the only formality that could be required to certify the authenticity of the notary's status, signature and seal would be the affixing of an apostille by the appropriate U.S. Competent Authority.

GABON

Official language: French

Legalization

American notarizations for production in the Gabonese Republic must first be legalized by its consular officers in the United States. Prior authentication of the notary's status, signature and seal by authorized U.S. state, territory and/ or federal officials is required for all notarizations which are submitted for legalization.

Legalization services for the United States and its territories are provided by:

The Consular Section
Embassy of Gabon

1630 Connecticut Ave NW
7th Floor
WASHINGTON, DC 20009
Tel: (202) 797-1000
Fax: (202) 332-0668

Consul of Gabon

18 East 41st St
Floor 9
NEW YORK, NY 10017
Tel: (212) 686-9720
Fax: (212) 683-7371

GAMBIA

Official language: English

Legalization

American notarizations for production in the Republic of the Gambia must first be legalized by its consular officers in the United States. Prior authentication of the notary's status, signature and seal by authorized U.S. state, territory and/or federal officials is required for all notarizations which are submitted for legalization.

Legalization services for the United States and its territories are provided by:

The Consular Section
Embassy of Gambia

2233 Wisconsin Ave NW
Georgetown Plaza, Suite 240
WASHINGTON, DC 20007
Tel: (202) 785-1379
Fax: (202) 785-1430
Website: www.gambiaembassy.us

GEORGIA

Official language: Georgian

Legalization

Georgia is party to the *Hague Apostille Convention*.

American notarizations for production in Georgia are therefore exempt from consular legalization. The only formality that may be required to certify the authenticity of the notary's status, signature and seal is the affixing of an apostille by the appropriate U.S. Competent Authority.

GERMANY

Official language: German

Legalization

The Federal Republic of Germany is party to the *Hague Apostille Convention*.

American notarizations for production in Germany are therefore exempt from consular legalization. The only formality that may be required to certify the authenticity of the notary's status, signature and seal is the affixing of an apostille by the appropriate U.S. Competent Authority.

GHANA

Official language: English

Legalization

American notarizations for production in the Republic of Ghana must first be legalized by its consular officers in the United States. Prior authentication of the notary's status, signature and seal by authorized U.S. state, territory and/ or federal officials is required for all notarizations which are submitted for legalization.

Legalization services for the United States and its territories are provided by:

The Consular Section
Embassy of Ghana

3512 International Drive NW
WASHINGTON, DC 20008
Tel: (202) 686-4520
Fax: (202) 686-4527
Website: www.ghanaembassy.org

Consulate General of Ghana

19 East 47th St
NEW YORK, NY 10017
Tel: (212) 832-1300
Fax: (212)751-6743

GIBRALTAR

Official language: English

Legalization

Gibraltar is a self-governing United Kingdom dependency and the *Hague Apostille Convention* is in force there.

American notarizations for production in Gibraltar are therefore exempt from consular legalization. The only formality that may be required to certify the authenticity of the notary's status, signature and seal is the affixing of an apostille by the appropriate U.S. Competent Authority.

GREECE

Official language: Greek

Legalization

The Hellenic Republic is party to the *Hague Apostille Convention*.

American notarizations for production in Greece are therefore exempt from consular legalization. The only formality that may be required to certify the authenticity of the notary's status, signature and seal is the affixing of an apostille by the appropriate U.S. Competent Authority.

GREENLAND

Official language: Danish

Legalization

Greenland is a self-governing Danish overseas administrative division. Even though the *Hague Apostille Convention* entered into force for Denmark on 29 December 2006, Denmark has declared that, for the time being, the Convention does not apply to Greenland.

American notarizations for production in Greenland must first be legalized by a Danish consular officer in the United States. Prior authentication of the notary's status, signature and seal by authorized U.S. state, territory and/or federal officials is required for all notarizations which are submitted for legalization.

Particulars of Danish consulates in the United States maybe found via the Danish Embassy website, <www.ambwashington.um.dk>.

GRENADA

Official language: English

Legalization

Grenada is party to the *Hague Apostille Convention*.

American notarizations for production in Grenada are therefore exempt from consular legalization. The only formality that may be required to certify the authenticity of the notary's status, signature and seal is the affixing of an apostille by the appropriate U.S. Competent Authority.

GUADELOUPE

Official language: French

Legalization

Guadeloupe is a French overseas department.

As France is party to the *Hague Apostille Convention* American notarizations for production in Guadeloupe are therefore exempt from consular legalization. The only formality that may be required to certify the authenticity of the notary's status, signature and seal is the affixing of an apostille by the appropriate U.S. Competent Authority.

GUATEMALA

Official language: Spanish

Legalization

American notarizations for production in the Republic of Guatemala must first be legalized by its consular officers in the United States. Prior authentication of the notary's status, signature and seal by authorized U.S. state, territory and/or federal officials is required for all notarizations which are submitted for legalization.

Legalization services are provided by:

The Consular Section
Embassy of Guatemala

2220 R St NW
WASHINGTON, DC 20008
Tel: (202) 745-4953
Fax: (202) 745-1908
Website: www.guatemala-embassy.org

Jurisdiction throughout Delaware, Kentucky, Maryland, Tennessee, Virginia, Washington DC and West Virginia.

Consulate General of Guatemala

3540 Wilshire Blvd
Suite 100
LOS ANGELES, CA 90010
Tel: (213) 365-9251
Fax: (213) 365-9245
Website: www.consulaxgt.com

Jurisdiction throughout American Samoa, Arizona, California, Hawaii, Nevada, Northern Marianas and Guam.

Consulate General of Guatemala

870 Market St
Suite 667
SAN FRANCISCO, CA 94103
Tel: (415) 788-5651
Fax: (415) 788-5653

Jurisdiction throughout Alaska, California, Idaho and Oregon.

Consulate General of Guatemala

1605 W Olympic Boulevard
Suite 422
DENVER, CO 80202.
Website: www.consulateofguatemalaindenver.org

Jurisdiction throughout Colorado, Kansas, Montana, Nebraska, New Mexico, South Dakota, Utah and Wyoming.

Consulate General of Guatemala

1101 Brickell Ave
Suite 1003-S
MIAMI, FL 33131
Tel: (305) 679-9945
Fax: (305) 679-9983

Jurisdiction throughout Alabaman, Florida, Georgia, North Carolina, South Carolina, Puerto Rico and U.S. Virgin Islands.

Consulate General of Guatemala

230 N Michigan Ave
Suite 2350
CHICAGO, IL 60601
Tel: (312) 332-1587
Fax: (312) 332-4256
Website: www.consulatechicago.org

Jurisdiction throughout Illinois, Indiana, Iowa, Michigan, Minnesota, Missouri, North Dakota, Ohio and Wisconsin.

Consulate General of Guatemala

57 Park Ave
NEW YORK, NY 10016
Tel: (212) 686-3837

Jurisdiction throughout Connecticut, Maine, Massachusetts, New Hampshire, New Jersey, New York, Pennsylvania, Rhode Island and Vermont.

Consulate General of Guatemala

3600 S Gessner Rd
Suite 200
HOUSTON, TX 77063
Tel: (713) 953-9531
Fax: (713) 953-9383

Jurisdiction throughout Arkansas, Kansas, Louisiana, Mississippi, Nebraska, Oklahoma and Texas.

Consulate General of Guatemala

2001 6th Ave
Suite 3300
SEATTLE, WA 98121
Tel: (206) 728-5920
Jurisdiction throughout Washington.

GUERNSEY

See Channel Islands

GUINEA

Official language: French

Legalization

American notarizations for production in the Republic of Guinea must first be legalized by its consular officers in the United States. Prior authentication of the notary's status, signature and seal by authorized U.S. state, territory and/ or federal officials is required for all notarizations which are submitted for legalization.

Legalization services for the United States and its territories are provided by:

The Consular Section
Embassy of Guinea

2112 Leroy Pl NW
WASHINGTON, DC 20008
Tel: (202) 986-4300
Fax: (202) 478-3010
Website: www.guineaembassy.com

GUINEA-BISSAU

Official language: Portuguese

Legalization

American notarizations for production in the Republic of Guinea-Bissau must first be legalized by its consular officers in the United States. Prior authentication of the notary's status, signature and seal by authorized U.S. state, territory and/or federal officials is required for all notarizations which are submitted for legalization.

Legalization services for the United States and its territories are provided by:

The Consular Section
Embassy of Guinea-Bissau

P.O. Box 33813 NW
WASHINGTON, DC 20033
Tel: (301) 947-3958
Fax: (301) 947-3958

GUYANA

Official language: English

Legalization

In 1965, the United Kingdom extended its coverage of the *Hague Apostille Convention* to the Co-operative Republic of Guyana which, at the time, was a British colony known as British Guiana. Since independence on 26 May 1966, Guyana has not made a formal declaration as to the continuance in force of the Convention.

Documents for production in Guyana to which apostilles have been affixed do not seem to be rejected. Therefore, for the time being, Guyana should be treated as being subject to the Convention and the affixing of an apostille by the appropriate U.S. Competent Authority should be the only formality required to certify the authenticity of a notary's status, signature and seal.

HAITI

Official language: French

Legalization

American notarizations for production in the Republic of Haiti must first be legalized by its consular officers in the United States. Prior authentication of the notary's status, signature and seal by authorized U.S. state, territory and/or federal officials is required for all notarizations which are submitted for legalization.

Legalization services are provided by:

The Consular Section
Embassy of Haiti

2311 Massachusetts Ave NW
WASHINGTON, DC 20008
Tel: (202) 332-4090
Fax: (202) 745-7215
Website: www.haiti.org

Jurisdiction throughout Alaska, Delaware, Hawaii, Maryland, North Carolina, South Carolina, Virginia and Washington DC.

Consulate General of Haiti

259 SW 13th St
MIAMI, FL 33131
Tel: (305) 859-2003
Fax: (305) 854-7441

Jurisdiction throughout American Samoa, Alabama, Florida, Georgia, Guam, Louisiana, Mississippi, Northern Marianas, Tennessee, Texas, Puerto Rico and U.S. Virgin Islands.

Consulate General of Haiti

11 E Adams St
Suite 1400
CHICAGO, IL 60603
Tel: (312) 922-4004
Fax: (312) 922-7122
Website: www.haitianconsulate.org

Jurisdiction throughout Illinois, Indiana, Iowa, Kansas, Kentucky, Michigan, Minnesota, Missouri, Ohio and Wisconsin.

Consulate General of Haiti

545 Boylston St
Suite 201
BOSTON, MA 02116
Tel: (617) 266-3660
Fax: (617) 266-4060

Jurisdiction throughout Connecticut, Maine, Massachusetts, New Hampshire, Rhode Island and Vermont.

Consulate General of Haiti

271 Madison Ave
Floor 17
NEW YORK, NY 10017
Tel: (212) 697-9767
Fax: (212) 681-6991
Website: www.haitianconsulate-nyc.org

Jurisdiction throughout New Jersey, New York and Pennsylvania.

HOLY SEE

Official languages: Italian and Latin

Legalization

American notarizations for production in The Holy See (State of the Vatican City) must first be legalized by its consular officers in the United States. Prior authentication of the notary's status, signature and seal by authorized U.S. state, territory and/or federal officials is required for all notarizations which are submitted for legalization.

Legalization services for the United States and its territories are provided by:

The Consular Office
Apostolic Nunciature

3339 Massachusetts Ave NW
WASHINGTON, DC 20008
Tel: (202) 333-7121
Fax: (202) 337-4036
Email: nuntius@worldnett.att.net

HONDURAS

Official language: Spanish

Legalization

The Republic of Honduras is party to the *Hague Apostille Convention*.

American notarizations for production in Honduras are therefore exempt from consular legalization. The only formality that may be required to certify the authenticity of the notary's status, signature and seal is the affixing of an apostille by the appropriate U.S. Competent Authority.

HONG KONG

Official languages: English and Mandarin

Legalization

Formerly a British colony to which the *Hague Apostille Convention* applied, Hong Kong Special Administrative Region is now a special administrative region of the People's Republic of China (PRC). In accordance with the Joint Declaration on the Question of Hong Kong of 19 December 1984, the Convention continued to apply to Hong Kong following the resumption of sovereignty over it by the PRC, even though it is not in force in the PRC generally.

American notarizations for production in Hong Kong are therefore exempt from consular legalization. The only formality that may be required to certify the authenticity of the notary's status, signature and seal is the affixing of an apostille by the appropriate U.S. Competent Authority.

If an American notarized document is to be used in both Hong Kong and elsewhere within the PRC (other than in Macau), then the document must also be legalized by a PRC consular officer in the United States.

HUNGARY

Official language: Hungarian

Legalization

The Republic of Hungary is party to the *Hague Apostille Convention*.

American notarizations for production in Hungary are therefore exempt from consular legalization. The only formality that may be required to certify the authenticity of the notary's status, signature and seal is the affixing of an apostille by the appropriate U.S. Competent Authority.

ICELAND

Official language: Icelandic

Legalization

The Republic of Iceland is party to the *Hague Apostille Convention*.

American notarizations for production in Iceland are therefore exempt from consular legalization. The only formality that may be required to certify the authenticity of the notary's status, signature and seal is the affixing of an apostille by the appropriate U.S. Competent Authority.

INDIA

Official languages: English and Hindi

Legalization

The Republic of India is party to the *Hague Apostille Convention*.

American notarizations for production in India are therefore exempt from consular legalization. The only formality that may be required to certify the authenticity of the notary's status, signature and seal is the affixing of an apostille by the appropriate U.S. Competent Authority.

INDONESIA

Official language: Bahasa Indonesia

Legalization

American notarizations for production in the Republic of Indonesia must first be legalized by its consular officers in the United States. Prior authentication of the notary's status, signature and seal by authorized U.S. state, territory and/or federal officials is required for all notarizations which are submitted for legalization.

Legalization services are provided by:

The Consular Section
Embassy of Indonesia

2020 Massachusetts Ave NW
WASHINGTON, DC 20036
Tel: (202) 775-5200
Fax: (202) 775-5365
Website: www.embassyofindonesia.org

Jurisdiction throughout Washington DC.

Consulate General of Indonesia

3457 Wilshire Blvd
LOS ANGELES, CA 90010
Tel: (213) 383-5126
Fax: (213) 487-3971
Website: www.kjri-la.net

Jurisdiction throughout Arizona, California (Southern), Colorado, Hawaii, Montana, Nevada (Southern), Utah, Wyoming and U.S. external territories.

Consulate General of Indonesia

1111 Columbus Ave
SAN FRANCISCO, CA 94133
Tel: (415) 474-9571
Fax: (415) 441-4320
Website: www.kjrisfo.net

Jurisdiction throughout Alaska, California (Northern), Idaho, Nevada (Northern), Oregon, and Washington.

Consulate General of Indonesia

211 W Wacker Dr
8th Floor
CHICAGO, IL 60606
Tel: (312) 920-1880
Fax: (312) 920-1881
Website: www.indonesiachicago.info

Jurisdiction throughout Illinois, Indiana, Iowa, Kansas, Kentucky, Michigan, Minnesota, Missouri, Nebraska, Ohio, North Dakota and South Dakota and Wisconsin.

Consulate General of Indonesia

5 East 68th St
NEW YORK, NY 10065
Tel: (212) 879-0600
Fax: (212) 570 6206
Website: www.indonesianewyork.org

Jurisdiction throughout Connecticut, Delaware, Maine, Maryland, Massachusetts, New Hampshire, New Jersey, New York, North Carolina, Pennsylvania, Rhode Island, South Carolina, Vermont, Virginia and West Virginia.

Consulate General of Indonesia

10900 Richmond Ave
HOUSTON, TX 77042
Tel: (713) 785-1691
Fax: (713) 780-9644
Website: www.indonesiahouston.net

Jurisdiction throughout Alabama, Arkansas, Florida, Georgia, Louisiana, Mississippi, New Mexico, Puerto Rico, Tennessee, Texas, U.S. Virgin Islands and Washington.

IRAN

Warning

The Islamic Republic of Iran is subject to a U.S. Treasury Department Office of Foreign Assets Control sanctions program. Care must be taken to ensure that transactions with persons, entities or organizations in or relating to Iran are not in violation of sanctions program regulations. (*See Appendix 2 for further information.*)

Official language: Farsi (Persian)

Legalization

The United States does not presently have diplomatic relations with Iran.

American notarizations for production in Iran must first be legalized by the Iranian Interest Section of the Pakistani Embassy in Washington DC.

Prior authentication of the notary's status, signature and seal by authorized U.S. state, territory and/or federal officials is required for all notarizations which are submitted for legalization.

Legalization services for the United States and its territories are provided by:

Iranian Interests Section
Embassy of the Islamic Republic of Pakistan

2209 Wisconsin Ave NW
WASHINGTON, DC 20007
Tel: (202) 965-4990
Fax: (202) 965-1073
Website: www.daftar.org

IRAQ

Warning

The Republic of Iraq is subject to a U.S. Treasury Department Office of Foreign Assets Control sanctions program. Care must be taken to ensure that transactions with persons, entities or organizations in or relating to Iraq are not in violation of sanctions program regulations. (*See Appendix 2 for further information.*)

Official language: Arabic

Legalization

American notarizations for production in Iraq must first be legalized by its consular officers in the United States. Prior authentication of the notary's status, signature and seal by authorized U.S. state, territory and/or federal officials is required for all notarizations which are submitted for legalization.

Legalization services for the United States and its territories are provided by:

The Consular Section
Embassy of Iraq

3421 Massachusetts Ave NW
WASHINGTON, DC 20007
Tel: (202) 742-1600
Website: www.iraqiembassy.us

IRELAND

Official languages: Irish and English

Legalization

Ireland is party to the *Hague Apostille Convention*.

American notarizations for production in Ireland are therefore exempt from consular legalization. The only formality that may be required to certify the authenticity of the notary's status, signature and seal is the affixing of an apostille by the appropriate U.S. Competent Authority.

ISLE OF MAN

Official language: English

Legalization

The Isle of Man is a self-governing United Kingdom dependency and the *Hague Apostille Convention* is in force there.

American notarizations for production in the Isle of Man are therefore exempt from consular legalization. The only formality that may be required to certify the authenticity of the notary's status, signature and seal is the affixing of an apostille by the appropriate U.S. Competent Authority.

ISRAEL

Official languages: Hebrew and Arabic

Legalization

The State of Israel is party to the *Hague Apostille Convention*.

American notarizations for production in Israel are therefore exempt from consular legalization. The only formality that may be required to certify the authenticity of the notary's status, signature and seal is the affixing of an apostille by the appropriate U.S. Competent Authority.

ITALY

Official language: Italian

Legalization

The Italian Republic is party to the *Hague Apostille Convention*.

American notarizations for production in Italy are therefore exempt from consular legalization. The only formality that may be required to certify the authenticity of the notary's status, signature and seal is the affixing of an apostille by the appropriate U.S. Competent Authority.

JAMAICA

Official language: English

Legalization

American notarizations for production in Jamaica must first be legalized by its consular officers in the United States. Prior authentication of the notary's status, signature and seal by authorized U.S. state, territory and/or federal officials is required for all notarizations which are submitted for legalization.

Legalization services are provided by:

The Consular Section
Embassy of Jamaica

1520 New Hampshire Ave NW
WASHINGTON, DC 20036
Tel: (202) 452-0660
Fax: (202) 452-0081
Website: www.embassyofjamaica.org

Jurisdiction throughout California, Maryland, Virginia, Washington DC and Washington.

Consulate General of Jamaica

842 Ingraham Building
25 SE 2nd Ave
Suite 842
MIAMI, FL 33131
Tel: (305) 374-8431

Jurisdiction throughout Alabama, Arizona, Arkansas, Florida, Georgia, Louisiana, Mississippi, New Mexico, North Carolina, Oklahoma, South Carolina, Tennessee and Texas.

Consulate General of Jamaica

767 3rd Ave
NEW YORK, NY 10017
Tel: (212) 935-9000

Jurisdiction throughout Alaska, Colorado, Connecticut, Delaware, Hawaii, Idaho, Illinois, Indiana, Iowa, Kansas, Kentucky, Maine, Massachusetts, Michigan, Minnesota, Missouri, Montana, Nebraska, Nevada, New Hampshire, New Jersey, New York, North Dakota, Ohio, Oregon, Pennsylvania, Rhode Island, South Dakota, Utah, Vermont, West Virginia, Wisconsin, Wyoming, Puerto Rico and U.S. external territories.

JAPAN

Official language: Japanese

Legalization

Japan is party to the *Hague Apostille Convention*.

American notarizations for production in Japan are therefore exempt from consular legalization. The only formality that may be required to certify the authenticity of the notary's status, signature and seal is the affixing of an apostille by the appropriate U.S. Competent Authority.

JERSEY

See Channel Islands

JORDAN

Official language: Arabic

Legalization

American notarizations for production in the Hashemite Kingdom of Jordan must first be legalized by its consular officers in the United States. Prior authentication of the notary's status, signature and seal by authorized U.S. state, territory and/or federal officials is required for all notarizations which are submitted for legalization.

Legalization services for the United States and its territories are provided by:

The Consular Section
Embassy of Jordan

3504 International Ct NW
WASHINGTON, DC 20008
Tel: (202) 966-2664
Fax: (202) 966-3110
Website: www.jordanembassyus.org

KAZAKHSTAN

Official languages: Kazakh and Russian

Legalization

The Republic of Kazakhstan is party to the *Hague Apostille Convention*.

American notarizations for production in Kazakhstan are therefore exempt from consular legalization. The only formality that may be required to certify the authenticity of the notary's status, signature and seal is the affixing of an apostille by the appropriate U.S. Competent Authority.

KENYA

Official languages: English and Swahili

Legalization

American notarizations for production in Republic of Kenya must first be legalized by its consular officers in the United States. Prior authentication of the notary's status, signature and seal by authorized U.S. state, territory and/or federal officials is required for all notarizations which are submitted for legalization.

Legalization services for the United States and its territories are provided by:

The Consular Section
Embassy of Kenya

2249 R St NW
WASHINGTON, DC 20008
Tel: (202) 387-6101
Fax: (202) 462-3829
Website: www.kenyaembassy.com

Consulate General of Kenya

Park Mile Plaza
Mezzanine Floor
4801Wilshire Blvd
LOS ANGELES, CA 90010
Tel: (323) 939-2408
Fax: (323) 932-2412
Website: www.kenyaconsulatela.com

Consul of Kenya

866 United Nations Plaza
Suite 4016
NEW YORK, NY 10017
Tel: (212) 421-4740
Fax: (212) 486-1985

KIRIBATI

Official languages: English and I-Kiribati (Gilbertese)

Legalization

In 1965, the United Kingdom extended the coverage of the *Hague Apostille Convention* to the Republic of Kiribati which, at the time, was a British colony. Since independence on 12 July 1979, Kiribati has not made a formal declaration as to the continuance in force of the Convention.

Documents for production in Kiribati to which apostilles have been affixed do not seem to be rejected. Therefore, for the time being, Kiribati should be treated as being subject to the Convention and the affixing of an apostille by the appropriate U.S. Competent Authority should be the only formality required to certify the authenticity of a notary's status, signature and seal.

KOREA (North)

Warning

The Democratic People's Republic of Korea is subject to a U.S. Treasury Department Office of Foreign Assets Control sanctions program. Care must be taken to ensure that transactions with persons, entities or organizations in or relating to North Korea are not in violation of sanctions program regulations. (*See Appendix 2 for further information.*)

Official language: Korean

Legalization

The United States does not presently have diplomatic relations with North Korea.

American notarizations for production in North Korea must first be legalized by a consular officer at its Permanent Mission to the United Nations. Prior authentication of the notary's status, signature and seal by authorized U.S. state, territory and/or federal officials is required for all notarizations which are submitted for legalization.

Legalization services for the United States and its territories are provided by:

Consulate General of North Korea
Permanent Mission to United Nations

820 Second Ave
NEW YORK, NY
Tel: (212) 972-3105
Fax: (212) 972-3154

KOREA (South)

Official language: Korean

Legalization

The Republic of South Korea is party to the *Hague Apostille Convention*.

American notarizations for production in South Korea are therefore exempt from consular legalization. The only formality that may be required to certify the authenticity of the notary's status, signature and seal is the affixing of an apostille by the appropriate U.S. Competent Authority.

KOSOVO

Official languages: Albanian and Serbian

Legalization

The Republic of Kosovo was formerly an autonomous province of Serbia which was subject to the *Hague Apostille Convention* from 27 April 1992. Since declaring independence from Serbia on 17 February 2008, Kosovo has not made a formal declaration as to the continuance in force of the Convention.

Documents for production in Kosovo to which apostilles have been affixed do not seem to be rejected. Therefore, for the time being, Kosovo should be treated as being subject to the Convention and the affixing of an apostille by the appropriate U.S. Competent Authority should be the only formality required to certify the authenticity of a notary's status, signature and seal.

If consular legalization is required, prior authentication of the notary's status, signature and seal by authorized U.S. state, territory and/or federal officials must first be obtained.

If consular legalization services are required they will be provided by:

Consulate General of The Republic of Kosovo

801 Second Ave
Suite 405
NEW YORK, NY 10017
Tel: (212) 949 1400
Fax: (212) 949 1403

KUWAIT

Official language: Arabic

Legalization

American notarizations for production in the State of Kuwait must first be legalized by its consular officers in the United States. Prior authentication of the notary's status, signature and seal by authorized U.S. state, territory and/or federal officials is required for all notarizations which are submitted for legalization.

Legalization services are provided by:

The Consular Section
Embassy of Kuwait

2940 Tilden St NW
WASHINGTON, DC 20008
Tel: (202) 966-0702
Fax: (202) 966-8468

Jurisdiction throughout the whole of the United States and its territories.

Consulate General of Kuwait

1801 Avenue of the Stars
Suite 1010
LOS ANGELES, CA 90067
Tel: (310) 556-0300
Fax: (310) 556-0400

Jurisdiction throughout Alaska, Arizona, California, Colorado, Idaho, Montana, Nevada, New Mexico, Oregon, Texas, Utah, Washington and Wyoming.

KYRGYZSTAN

Official languages: Kyrgyz and Russian

Legalization

The Kyrgyz Republic is a party to the *Hague Apostille Convention*.

American notarizations for production in Kyrgyzstan are therefore exempt from consular legalization. The only formality that may be required to certify the authenticity of the notary's status, signature and seal is the affixing of an apostille by the appropriate U.S. Competent Authority.

LAOS

Official language: Lao

Legalization

American notarizations for production in the Lao People's Democratic Republic must first be legalized by its consular officers in the United States. Prior authentication of the notary's status, signature and seal by authorized U.S. state, territory and/or federal officials is required for all notarizations which are submitted for legalization.

Legalization services for the United States and its territories are provided by:

The Consular Section
Embassy of Laos

2222 S St NW
WASHINGTON, DC 20008
Tel: (202) 332-6416
Fax: (202) 332-4923
Website: www.laoembassy.com

LATVIA

Official language: Latvian (Lettish)

Legalization

The Republic of Latvia is party to the *Hague Apostille Convention.*

American notarizations for production in Latvia are therefore exempt from consular legalization. The only formality that may be required to certify the authenticity of the notary's status, signature and seal is the affixing of an apostille by the appropriate U.S. Competent Authority.

LEBANON

Warning

Persons undermining the sovereignty of the Lebanese Republic or its democractic processes and institutions are subject to a U.S. Treasury Department Office of Foreign Assets Control sanctions program. Care must be taken to ensure that transactions with or relating to such persons, entities or organizations are not in violation of sanctions program regulations. (*See Appendix 2 for further information.*)

Official languages: Arabic and French

Legalization

American notarizations for production in Lebanon must first be legalized by its consular officers in the United States. Prior authentication of the notary's status, signature and seal by authorized U.S. state, territory and/or federal officials is required for all notarizations which are submitted for legalization.

Legalization services are provided by:

The Consular Section
Embassy of Lebanon

2560 28th St NW
WASHINGTON, DC 20008
Tel: (202) 939-6300
Fax: (202) 939-6324
Website: www.lebanonembassyus.org

Jurisdiction throughout Alabama, Arkansas, Florida, Georgia, Louisiana, Maryland, Mississippi, North Carolina, Oklahoma, South Carolina, Tennessee, Texas, Virginia, Washington DC, American Samoa, Guam, Northern Marianas, Puerto Rico and U.S. Virgin Islands.

Consulate General of Lebanon

660 S Figueroa St
Suite 1050
LOS ANGELES, CA 90017
Tel: (213) 243-0999
Fax: (213) 612-5070
Website: www.lebanonconsulatela.org

Jurisdiction throughout Alaska, Arizona, California, Colorado, Hawaii, Idaho, Montana, Nevada, New Mexico, Orgeon, Utah, Washington and Wyoming.

Consulate General of Lebanon

3031 W Grand Blvd
Suite 560
DETROIT, MI 48202
Tel : (313) 758-0753

Jurisdiction throughout Illinois, Indiana, Iowa, Kansas, Kentucky, Michigan, Minnesota, Missouri, Nebraska, North Dakota, Ohio, South Dakota, West Virginia and Wisconsin.

Consulate General of Lebanon

9 East 76th St
NEW YORK, NY 10021
Tel: (212) 744-7905
Fax: (212) 794-1510
Website: www.lebconsny.org

Jurisdiction throughout Connecticut, Delaware, Maine, Massachusetts, New Hampshire, New Jersey, New York, Pennsylvania, Rhode Island and Vermont.

LESOTHO

Official languages: English and Sesotho

Legalization

The Kingdom of Lesotho is party to the *Hague Apostille Convention*.

American notarizations for production in Lesotho are therefore exempt from consular legalization. The only formality that may be required to certify the authenticity of the notary's status, signature and seal is the affixing of an apostille by the appropriate U.S. Competent Authority.

LIBERIA

Warning

The former regime of Charles Taylor in the Republic of Liberia is subject to a U.S. Treasury Department Office of Foreign Assets Control sanctions program. Care must be taken to ensure that transactions with persons, entities or organizations relating to that regime are not in violation of sanctions program regulations. (*See Appendix 2 for further information.*)

Official language: English

Legalization

Liberia is party to the *Hague Apostille Convention*, however the United States formally objected to Liberia's accession the Convention in 1995 and the Convention is not in force between Liberia and the United States.

American notarizations for production in Liberia must first be legalized by its consular officers in the United States. Prior authentication of the notary's status, signature and seal by authorized U.S. state, territory and/or federal officials is required for all notarizations which are submitted for legalization.

Legalization services for the United States and it territories are provided by:

The Consular Office
Embassy of Liberia

5201 16th St NW
WASHINGTON, DC 20011
Tel: (202) 723-0437
Fax: (202) 723-0436
Website: www.embassyofliberia.org

Consulate General of Liberia

866 United Nations Plaza
Suite 478
NEW YORK, NY 10017
Tel: (212) 687-1025
Fax: (212) 599-3189
Website: www.liberiaconsulateny.org

LIBYA

Official language: Arabic

Legalization

American notarizations for production in the Great Socialist People's Libyan Arab Jamahiriya must first be legalized by its consular officers in the United States. Prior authentication of the notary's status, signature and seal by authorized U.S. state, territory and/or federal officials is required for all notarizations which are submitted for legalization.

Legalization services are provided by:

The Consular Section
Embassy of Libya

2600 Virginia Ave NW
Suite 705
WASHINGTON, DC 20037
Tel: (202) 944-9601
Fax:(202) 944-9606
Website: www.embassyoflibyadc.org

LIECHTENSTEIN

Official language: German

Legalization

The Principality of Liechtenstein is party to the *Hague Apostille Convention*.

American notarizations for production in Liechtenstein are therefore exempt from consular legalization. The only formality that may be required to certify the authenticity of the notary's status, signature and seal is the affixing of an apostille by the appropriate U.S. Competent Authority.

LITHUANIA

Official language: Lithuanian

Legalization

The Republic of Lithuania is party to the *Hague Apostille Convention*.

American notarizations for production in Lithuania are therefore exempt from consular legalization. The only formality that may be required to certify the authenticity of the notary's status, signature and seal is the affixing of an apostille by the appropriate U.S. Competent Authority.

LUXEMBOURG

Official languages: Letzeburgish
French (for civil administrative purposes)
German (for commercial purposes)

Legalization

The Grand Duchy of Luxembourg is party to the *Hague Apostille Convention*.

American notarizations for production in Luxembourg are therefore exempt from consular legalization. The only formality that may be required to certify the authenticity of the notary's status, signature and seal is the affixing of an apostille by the appropriate U.S. Competent Authority.

MACAU

Official languages: Portuguese and Chinese (Mandarin)

Legalization

Formerly a Portuguese colony to which the *Hague Apostille Convention* applied, Macau Special Administrative Region is now a special administrative region of the People's Republic of China (PRC). In accordance with the Joint Declaration on the Question of Macau of 13 April 1987, the Convention continued to apply to Macau following the resumption of the sovereignty over it by the PRC, even though it is not in force in the PRC generally.

American notarizations for production in Macau are therefore exempt from consular legalization. The only formality that may be required to certify the authenticity of the notary's status, signature and seal is the affixing of an apostille by the appropriate U.S. Competent Authority.

If an American notarized document is to be used both in Macau and elsewhere within the PRC (other than Hong Kong), then the document must be legalized by a PRC consular officer in the United States.

MACEDONIA

Official language: Macedonian

Legalization

The Republic of Macedonia is party to the *Hague Apostille Convention*.

American notarizations for production in Macedonia are therefore exempt from consular legalization. The only formality that may be required to certify the authenticity of the notary's status, signature and seal is the affixing of an apostille by the appropriate U.S. Competent Authority.

MADAGASCAR

Official languages: French and Malagasy

Legalization

American notarizations for production in the Republic of Madagascar must first be legalized by its consular officers in the United States. Prior authentication of the notary's status, signature and seal by authorized U.S. state, territory and/or federal officials is required for all notarizations which are submitted for legalization.

Legalization services for the United States and its territories are provided by:

The Consular Section
Embassy of Madagascar

2374 Massachusetts Ave NW
WASHINGTON, DC 20008
Tel: (202) 265-5525
Fax: (202) 265-3034
Website: www.madagascar-embassy.org

MADEIRA

Official language: Portuguese

Legalization

Madeira is an autonomous region of Portugal and the *Hague Apostille Convention* is in force there.

American notarizations for production in Madeira are therefore exempt from consular legalization. The only formality that may be required to certify the authenticity of the notary's status, signature and seal is the affixing of an apostille by the appropriate U.S. Competent Authority.

MALAWI

Official languages: English and Chichewa

Legalization

The Republic of Malawi is party to the *Hague Apostille Convention*.

American notarizations for production in Malawi are therefore exempt from consular legalization. The only formality that may be required to certify the authenticity of the notary's status, signature and seal is the affixing of an apostille by the appropriate U.S. Competent Authority.

MALAYSIA

Official language: Bahasa Malaysia

Legalization

In the absence of allegations to the contrary in a particular case, documents emanating from any jurisdiction which are to be produced in Malaysia are presumed to be authentic and do not require legalization or other authentication.

MALDIVES

Official language: Divehi

Legalization

American notarizations for production in the Republic of Maldives must first be legalized by its consular officers in the United States. Prior authentication of the notary's status, signature and seal by authorized U.S. state, territory and/or federal officials is required for all notarizations which are submitted for legalization.

Legalization services for the United States and its territories are provided by:

The Consular Section
Embassy of Maldives

800 2nd Ave
Suite 400E
NEW YORK, NY 10017
Tel: (212) 599-6195
Fax: (212) 661 -6405

MALI

Official language: French

Legalization

American notarizations for production in the Republic of Mali must first be legalized by its consular officers in the United States. Prior authentication of the notary's status, signature and seal by authorized U.S. state, territory and/or federal officials is required for all notarizations which are submitted for legalization.

Legalization services for the United States and its territories are provided by:

The Consular Section
Embassy of Mali

2130 R St NW
WASHINGTON, DC 20008
Tel: (202) 332-2249
Fax: (202) 332-6603

MALTA

Official languages: English and Maltese

Legalization

The Republic of Malta is party to the *Hague Apostille Convention*.

American notarizations for production in Malta are therefore exempt from consular legalization. The only formality that may be required to certify the authenticity of the notary's status, signature and seal is the affixing of an apostille by the appropriate U.S. Competent Authority.

MARSHALL ISLANDS

Official language: English

Legalization

The Republic of the Marshall Islands is party to the *Hague Apostille Convention*.

American notarizations for production in Marshall Islands are therefore exempt from consular legalization. The only formality that may be required to certify the authenticity of the notary's status, signature and seal is the affixing of an apostille by the appropriate U.S. Competent Authority.

MARTINIQUE

Official language: French

Legalization

Martinique is a French overseas department.

As France is party to the *Hague Apostille Convention* American notarizations for production in Martinique are therefore exempt from consular legalization. The only formality that may be required to certify the authenticity of the notary's status, signature and seal is the affixing of an apostille by the appropriate U.S. Competent Authority.

MAURITANIA

Official language: Arabic

Legalization

American notarizations for production in the Islamic Republic of Mauritania must first be legalized by its consular officers in the United States. Prior authentication of the notary's status, signature and seal by authorized U.S. state, territory and/or federal officials is required for all notarizations which are submitted for legalization.

Legalization services for the United States and its territories are provided by:

The Consular Section
Embassy of Mauritania

2129 Leroy Pl NW
WASHINGTON, DC 20008
Tel: (202) 232-5700
Fax: (202) 319-2623

MAURITIUS

Official language: English

Legalization

The Republic of Mauritius is party to the *Hague Apostille Convention.*

American notarizations for production in Mauritius are therefore exempt from consular legalization. The only formality that may be required to certify the authenticity of the notary's status, signature and seal is the affixing of an apostille by the appropriate U.S. Competent Authority.

MAYOTTE

Official languages: French and Mahorian

Legalization

Mayotte is a autonomous French territorial collectivity and the *Hague Apostille Convention* is in force there.

American notarizations for production in Mayotte are therefore exempt from consular legalization. The only formality that may be required to certify the authenticity of the notary's status, signature and seal is the affixing of an apostille by the appropriate U.S. Competent Authority.

MEXICO

Official language: Spanish

Legalization

The United Mexican States is party to the *Hague Apostille Convention*.

American notarizations for production in Mexico are therefore exempt from consular legalization. The only formality that may be required to certify the authenticity of the notary's status, signature and seal is the affixing of an apostille by the appropriate U.S. Competent Authority.

MICRONESIA

Official language: English

Legalization

American notarizations for production in the Federated States of Micronesia may only be legalized by Micronesia's Attorney General's office which is located in Micronesia's capital, Palikir.

Prior authentication of the notary's status, signature and seal by authorized U.S. state, territory and/or federal officials is required for all notarizations which are submitted for legalization.

Legalization services for the United States and its territories are provided by:

Attorney General's Office
Federated States of Micronesia

Palikir, Pohnpei
FSM, 96941
Tel: +69 1 320 2608
Fax: +69 1 320 6240

MOLDOVA

Official language: Moldovan

Legalization

The Republic of Moldova is party to the *Hague Apostille Convention*.

American notarizations for production in Moldova are therefore exempt from consular legalization. The only formality that may be required to certify the authenticity of the notary's status, signature and seal is the affixing of an apostille by the appropriate U.S. Competent Authority.

MONACO

Official language: French

Legalization

The Principality of Monaco is party to the *Hague Apostille Convention*.

American notarizations for production in Monaco are therefore exempt from consular legalization. The only formality that may be required to certify the authenticity of the notary's status, signature and seal is the affixing of an apostille by the appropriate U.S. Competent Authority.

MONGOLIA

Official language: Khalkha Mongol

Legalization

Mongolia is party to the *Hague Apostille Convention*.

American notarizations for production in Mongolia are therefore exempt from consular legalization. The only formality that may be required to certify the authenticity of the notary's status, signature and seal is the affixing of an apostille by the appropriate U.S. Competent Authority.

MONTENEGRO

Official language: Serbian

Legalization

Montenegro is party to the *Hague Apostille Convention*.

American notarizations for production in Montenegro are therefore exempt from consular legalization. The only formality that may be required to certify the authenticity of the notary's status, signature and seal is the affixing of an apostille by the appropriate U.S. Competent Authority.

MONTSERRAT

Official language: English

Legalization

Montserrat is a self-governing United Kingdom dependency and the *Hague Apostille Convention* is in force there.

American notarizations for production in Montserrat are therefore exempt from consular legalization. The only formality that may be required to certify the authenticity of the notary's status, signature and seal is the affixing of an apostille by the appropriate U.S. Competent Authority.

MOROCCO

Official language: Arabic

French is widely used as the language of commerce and government administration.

Legalization

American notarizations for production in the Kingdom of Morocco must first be legalized by its consular officers in the United States. Prior authentication of the notary's status, signature and seal by authorized U.S. state, territory and/or federal officials is required for all notarizations which are submitted for legalization.

Legalization services are provided by:

The Consular Section
Embassy of Morocco

1601 21st St NW
WASHINGTON, DC 20009
Tel: (202) 462-7980
Fax: (202) 462-7643

Jurisdiction throughout Maryland, Virginia, Washington DC.

Consulate General of Morocco

10 East 40th St
Floor 23
NEW YORK, NY 10016
Tel: (212) 758-2625
Fax: (646) 395-8077
Website: www.moroccanconsulate.com

Jurisdiction throughout the whole of the United States and its territories.

MOZAMBIQUE

Official language: Portuguese

English is becoming the language of commerce.

Legalization

In 1969, Portugal extended the coverage of the *Hague Apostille Convention* to the Republic of Mozambique which, at the time, was a Portuguese colony. Since independence on 25 June 1975, Mozambique has not made a formal declaration as to the continuation in force of the Convention.

Even though documents for use in Mozambique to which apostilles have been affixed have not been rejected in the past, it is advisable for notarized documents which are to be produced in Mozambique to be legalized by the Consular Section of the Mozambique Embassy in the United States.

Prior authentication of the notary's status, signature and seal by authorized U.S. state, territory and/or federal officials is required for all notarizations which are submitted for legalization.

Legalization services for the United States its territories are provided by:

The Consular Section
Embassy of Mozambique

1525 New Hampshire Ave NW
WASHINGTON, DC 20036
Tel: (202) 293-7146
Fax: (202) 835-0245
Website: www.embamoc-usa.org

MYANMAR

Warning

The Union of Myanmar is subject to a U.S. Treasury Department Office of Foreign Assets Control sanctions program. Care must be taken to ensure that transactions with persons, entities or organizations in or relating to Myanmar are not in violation of sanctions program regulations. (*See Appendix 2 for further information.*)

Official language: Burmese

Legalization

American notarizations for production in Myanmar must first be legalized by its consular officers in the United States. Prior authentication of the notary's status, signature and seal by authorized U.S. state, territory and/or federal officials is required for all notarizations which are submitted for legalization.

Legalization services are provided by:

The Consular Section
Embassy of the Union of Myanmar

2300 S St NW
WASHINGTON, DC 20008-4016
Tel: (202) 332-3344
Fax: (202) 332-4351
Website: www.mewashingtondc.com

Jurisdiction throughout the whole of the United States and its territories.

Consulate General of the Union of Myanmar

10 East 77th St
NEW YORK, NY 10021
Tel: (212) 535-1311
Fax: (212) 744-1290
Jurisdiction throughout Connecticut, New Jersey and New York.

NAMIBIA

Official language: English

Legalization

The Republic of Namibia is party to the *Hague Apostille Convention*.

American notarizations for production in Namibia are therefore exempt from consular legalization. The only formality that may be required to certify the authenticity of the notary's status, signature and seal is the affixing of an apostille by the appropriate U.S. Competent Authority.

NAURU

Official language: Nauruan

English is used for government and commercial purposes.

Legalization

American notarizations for production in the Republic of Nauru must first be legalized by its consular officers in the United States. Prior authentication of the notary's status, signature and seal by authorized U.S. state, territory and/ or federal officials is required for all notarizations which are submitted for legalization.

Legalization services for the United States and its territories are provided by:

The Consular Section
Embassy of Nauru

800 2nd Ave
Suite 400A
NEW YORK, NY 10017
Tel: (212) 937-0074
Fax: (212) 937-0079

NEPAL

Official language: Nepali

Legalization

American notarizations for production in the Federal Democratic Republic of Nepal must first be legalized by its consular officers in the United States. Prior authentication of the notary's status, signature and seal by authorized U.S. state, territory and/or federal officials is required for all notarizations which are submitted for legalization.

Legalization services for the United States and its territories are provided by:

The Consular Section
Embassy of Nepal

2131 Leroy Pl NW
WASHINGTON, DC 20008
Tel: (202) 667-4550
Fax: (202) 667-5534
Website: www.nepalembassyusa.org

Consulate General of Nepal

820 2nd Ave
Suite 17B
NEW YORK, NY 10017
Tel: (212) 370-3988
Fax: (212) 953-2038

NETHERLANDS

Official language: Dutch

Legalization

The Kingdom of the Netherlands is party to the *Hague Apostille Convention*.

American notarizations for production in the Netherlands are therefore exempt from consular legalization. The only formality that may be required to certify the authenticity of the notary's status, signature and seal is the affixing of an apostille by the appropriate U.S. Competent Authority.

NETHERLANDS ANTILLES

See Aruba, Bonaire, Curacao, Saba, Sint Eustatius and Sint Maarten

NEW CALEDONIA

Official language: French

Legalization

The Territory of New Caledonia and Dependencies is a French overseas territory and the *Hague Apostille Convention* is in force there.

American notarizations for production in New Caledonia are therefore exempt from consular legalization. The only formality that may be required to certify the authenticity of the notary's status, signature and seal is the affixing of an apostille by the appropriate U.S. Competent Authority.

NEW ZEALAND

Official language: English

Legalization

New Zealand is party to the *Hague Apostille Convention*.

American notarizations for production in New Zealand are therefore exempt from consular legalization. The only formality that may be required to certify the authenticity of the notary's status, signature and seal is the affixing of an apostille by the appropriate U.S. Competent Authority.

NICARAGUA

Official language: Spanish

Legalization

American notarizations for production in the Republic of Nicaragua must first be legalized by its consular officers in the United States. Prior authentication of the notary's status, signature and seal by authorized U.S. state, territory and/or federal officials is required for all notarizations which are submitted for legalization.

Legalization services are provided by:

The Consular Section
Embassy of Nicaragua

1627 New Hampshire Ave NW
WASHINGTON, DC 20009
Tel: (202) 939-6531
Fax: (202) 939-6574

Jurisdiction throughout Delaware, Illinois, Indiana, Kentucky, Maryland, North Carolina, Pennsylvania, Tennessee, Virginia, Washington DC, U.S. external territories and West Virginia.

Consulate General of Nicaragua

3550 Wilshire Blvd
Suite 200
LOS ANGELES, CA 90010
Tel: (213) 252-1170
Fax: (213) 252-1177

Jurisdiction throughout Alaska, Arizona, Nevada, Oregon, Utah and the California counties of Fresno, San Diego, Santa Barbara, San Luis, Obispo, Palm Springs, Ventura, Bakersfield, San Fernado, Santa Ana, Orange, San Bernadino and Potoma.

Consulate General of Nicaragua

870 Market St
Suite 1050
SAN FRANCISCO, CA 94102
Tel: (415) 765-6821
Fax: (415) 765-6826

Jurisdiction throughout Idaho, Wyoming and the California counties of Oakland, San Jose, Monterrey, Eureka, Redding and Napa.

Consulate General of Nicaragua

8532 SW 8th St
Suite 270
MIAMI, FL 33144
Tel: (305) 265-1415
Fax: (305) 265-1780

Jurisdiction throughout Arkansas, Alabama, Florida, Georgia, Iowa, Louisiana, Minnesota, Missouri, Mississippi and South Carolina.

Consulate General of Nicaragua

820 2nd Ave
Suite 802
NEW YORK, NY 10017
Tel: (212) 983-1981
Fax: (212) 989-5528

Jurisdiction throughout Connecticut, Maine, Massachusetts, Michigan, New Hampshire, New Jersey, New York, Ohio, Pennsylvania, Rhode Island, Vermont and Wisconsin.

Consulate General of Nicaragua

6300 Hillcroft Ave
Suite 250
HOUSTON, TX 77081
Tel: (713) 272-9628
Fax: (713) 272-7131

Jurisdiction throughout Colorado, Kansas, Montana, Nebraska, New Mexico, North Dakota, Oklahoma, South Dakota and Texas.

NIGER

Official language: French

Legalization

American notarizations for production in the Republic of Niger must first be legalized by its consular officers in the United States. Prior authentication of the notary's status, signature and seal by authorized U.S. state, territory and/ or federal officials is required for all notarizations which are submitted for legalization.

Legalization services for the United States its territories are provided by:

The Consular Section
Embassy of Niger

2204 R St NW
WASHINGTON, DC 20008
Tel: (202) 483-4224
Fax: (202) 483-3169
Website: www.embassyofniger.org

NIGERIA

Official language: English

Legalization

American notarizations for production in the Federal Republic of Nigeria must first be legalized by its consular officers in the United States. Prior authentication of the notary's status, signature and seal by authorized U.S. state, territory and/ or federal officials is required for all notarizations which are submitted for legalization.

Legalization services for the United States its territories are provided by:

The Consular Section
Embassy of Nigeria

3519 International Ct NW
WASHINGTON, DC 20008
Tel: (202) 986-8400
Fax: (202) 362-6541
Website: www.nigeriaembassyusa.org

Consulate General of Nigeria

828 2nd Ave
NEW YORK, NY 10017
Tel: (212) 808-0301
Fax: (212) 682-4789
Website: www.nigeriahouse.com

NIUE

Official language: English

Legalization

Niue is a autonomous self-governing country in free association with New Zealand and is party to the *Hague Apostille Convention*.

American notarizations for production in Niue are therefore exempt from consular legalization. The only formality that may be required to certify the authenticity of the notary's status, signature and seal is the affixing of an apostille by the appropriate U.S. Competent Authority.

NORFOLK ISLAND

Official language: English

Legalization

The Territory of Norfolk Island is a self-governing territory of Australia and the *Hague Apostille Convention* is in force.

American notarizations for production in Norfolk Island are therefore exempt from consular legalization. The only formality that may be required to certify the authenticity of the notary's status, signature and seal is the affixing of an apostille by the appropriate U.S. Competent Authority.

NORWAY

Official language: Norwegian

Legalization

The Kingdom of Norway is party to the *Hague Apostille Convention*.

American notarizations for production in Norway are therefore exempt from consular legalization. The only formality that may be required to certify the authenticity of the notary's status, signature and seal is the affixing of an apostille by the appropriate U.S. Competent Authority.

OMAN

Official language: Arabic

Legalization

With effect from 30 January 2012, the *Hague Apostille Convention* will come into force for the Sultanate of Oman.

American notarizations for production in Oman will therefore be exempt from consular legalization. The only formality that will be required to certify the authenticity of the notary's status, signature and seal will be the affixing of an apostille by the appropriate U.S. Competent Authority.

PAKISTAN

Official languages: English and Urdu

Legalization

American notarizations for production in the Islamic Republic of Pakistan must first be legalized by its consular officers in the United States. Prior authentication of the notary's status, signature and seal by authorized U.S. state, territory and/or federal officials is required for all notarizations which are submitted for legalization.

Legalization services are provided by:

The Consular Section
Embassy of Pakistan

3517 International Ct NW
WASHINGTON, DC 20008
Tel: (202) 243-6500
Fax: (202) 686-1534
Website: www.embassyofpakistanusu.org

Jurisdiction throughout Alabama, Florida, Georgia, Maryland, Mississippi, North Carolina, Pennsylvania, South Carolina, Tennessee, Virginia, Washington DC, West Virginia and U.S. external territories.

Consulate General of Pakistan

10850 Wilshire Blvd
Suite 1250
LOS ANGELES, CA 90024
Tel: (310) 441-5114
Fax: (310) 441 9256

Jurisdiction throughout Alaska, Arizona, California, Colorado, Hawaii, Idaho, Kansas, Montana, Nebraska, Nevada, Oregon, Utah, Washington and Wyoming.

Consul of Pakistan

333 N Michigan Ave
Suite 728
CHICAGO, IL 60601
Tel: (312) 781-1831
Fax: (312) 781-1839

Jurisdiction throughout Illinois, Indiana, Iowa, Minnesota, Missouri and Wisconsin.

Consulate General of Pakistan

12 East 65th St
NEW YORK, NY 10065
Tel: (212) 879-5800
Fax: (212) 517-6987

Jurisdiction throughout Connecticut, Delaware, Kentucky, Maine, Massachusetts, Michigan, New Hampshire, New Jersey, New York, North Dakota, Ohio, Rhode Island, South Dakota and Vermont.

Consul of Pakistan

11850 Jones Rd
HOUSTON, TX 77070
Tel: (281) 894-6605
Fax: (281) 890-1433

Jurisdiction throughout Arkansas, Louisiana, New Mexico, Oklahoma and Texas.

PALAU

Official languages: English and Palauan

Legalization

American notarizations for production in the Republic of Palau must first be legalized by its consular officers in the United States. Prior authentication of the notary's status, signature and seal by authorized U.S. state, territory and/ or federal officials is required for all notarizations which are submitted for legalization.

Legalization services for the United States and its territories are provided by:

**The Consular Section
Embassy of Palau**

1701 Pennsylvania Ave NW
Suite 300
WASHINGTON, DC 20006
Tel: (202) 452-6814
Fax: (202) 452-6281
Website: www.palauembassy.com

PANAMA

Official language: Spanish

Legalization

The Republic of Panama is party to the *Hague Apostille Convention.*

American notarizations for production in Panama are therefore exempt from consular legalization. The only formality that may be required to certify the authenticity of the notary's status, signature and seal is the affixing of an apostille by the appropriate U.S. Competent Authority.

PAPUA NEW GUINEA

Official languages: English, Pidgin and Motu

Legalization

American notarizations for production in the Independent State of Papua New Guinea must first be legalized by its consular officers in the United States. Prior authentication of the notary's status, signature and seal by authorized U.S. state, territory and/or federal officials is required for all notarizations which are submitted for legalization.

Legalization services for the United States its territories are provided by:

The Consular Section
Embassy of Papua New Guinea

1779 Massachusetts Ave NW
Suite 805
WASHINGTON, DC 20036
Tel: (202) 745-3680
Fax: (202) 745-3679
Website: www.pngembassy.org

PARAGUAY

Official language: Spanish

Legalization

American notarizations for production in the Republic of Paraguay must first be legalized by its consular officers in the United States. Prior authentication of the notary's status, signature and seal by authorized U.S. state, territory and/or federal officials is required for all notarizations which are submitted for legalization.

Legalization services are provided by:

The Consular Section
Embassy of Paraguay

2400 Massachusetts Ave NW
WASHINGTON, DC 20008
Tel: (202) 483-6960
Fax: (202) 234-4508
Website: www.embaparusa.gov.py

Jurisdiction throughout Delaware, Illinois, Iowa, Kansas, Maryland, Minnesota, North Dakota, South Dakota, Virginia, Washington DC and West Virginia.

Consulate General of Paraguay

9841 Airport Boulevard
Suite 820
LOS ANGELES, CA 90045
Tel: (310) 417-9500
Fax: (310) 417-9520

Jurisdiction throughout Arizona, California, Colorado, Hawaii, Idaho, Mexico, Montana, Nevada, New Mexico, North Dakota, Oregon, Texas, Utah, Washington and Wyoming.

Consulate General of Paraguay

25 SE 2nd Ave
Suite 705
MIAMI, FL 33131
Tel: (305) 374-9090
Fax: (305) 974-5522

Jurisdiction throughout Alabama, Arkansas, Florida, Georgia, Kentucky, Louisiana, Mississippi, Missouri, North Carolina, South Carolina, Tennessee and U.S. external territories.

Consulate General of Paraguay

211 East 43rd St
Suite 2101
NEW YORK, NY 10017
Tel: (212) 682-9441
Fax: (212) 682-9443

Jurisdiction throughout Connecticut, Indiana, Maine, Massachusetts, New Hampshire, Michigan, New Jersey, New York, Ohio, Pennsylvania, Rhode Island, Vermont and Wisconsin.

PERU

Official languages: Spanish and Quechua

Legalization

The Republic of Peru is a party to the *Hague Apostille Convention*.

American notarizations for production in Peru are therefore exempt from consular legalization. The only formality that may be required to certify the authenticity of the notary's status, signature and seal is the affixing of an apostille by the appropriate U.S. Competent Authority.

PHILIPPINES

Official languages: English and Filipino

Legalization

American notarizations for production in the Republic of the Philippines must first be legalized by its consular officers in the United States. Prior authentication of the notary's status, signature and seal by authorized U.S. state, territory and/ or federal officials is required for all notarizations which are submitted for legalization.

Legalization services are provided by:

The Consular Section
Embassy of the Philippines

1600 Massachusetts Ave NW
WASHINGTON, DC 20036
Tel: (202) 467-9300
Fax: (202) 467-9417
Website: www.philipineembassy-usa.org

Jurisdiction throughout Alabama, Florida, Georgia, Kentucky, Maryland, North Carolina, South Carolina, Tennessee, Washington DC, West Virginia, Virginia, Puerto Rico and U.S. Virgin Islands.

Consulate General of the Philippines

3600 Wilshire Blvd
Suite 500
LOS ANGELES, CA 90010
Tel: (213) 639-0980
Fax: (213) 639-0990
Website: www.philippineslosangeles.org

Jurisdiction throughout Arizona, California (Southern), Nevada (Southern), New Mexico and Texas.

Consulate General of the Philippines

447 Sutter St
Floor 6
SAN FRANCISCO, CA 94108
Tel: (415) 433-6666
Fax: (415) 421-2641
Website: www.philippinessanfrancisco.org

Jurisdiction throughout Alaska, California (Northern), Colorado, Idaho, Montana, Nevada (Northern), Oregon, Utah, Washington and Wyoming.

Honorary Consul General of the Philippines

1900 Commercial Boulevard
Suite 29
Fort Lauderdale NORTH MIAMI, FL 33309
Tel: (954) 729-6647
Fax: (954) 755-6367
Website: www.philippinesmiami.org

Jurisdiction throughout Florida (South).

Honorary Consul General of the Philippines

3340 Peach Tree Rd NE
Suite 1685
ATLANTA, GA 30326
Tel: (404) 239-5747
Fax: (404) 233-4041
Website: www.philippinesatlanta.org

Jurisdiction throughout Atlanta GA.

Consulate General of the Philippines

ICT Building, Marine Dr
Suite 601
TAMUNING, GU 96913
Tel: (671) 646-4620
Fax: (671) 649-1868
Website: www.philippinesguam.org

Jurisdiction throughout Guam.

Consulate General of the Philippines

2433 Pali Hwy
HONOLULU, HI 96817
Tel: (808) 595-6316
Fax: (808) 595-2581
Website: www.philippineshonolulu.org

Jurisdiction throughout Hawaii and American Samoa.

Consulate General of the Philippines

30 N Michigan Ave
Suite 2100
CHICAGO, IL 60602
Tel: (312) 332-6458
Fax: (312) 332-3657
Website: www.philippineschicago.org

Jurisdiction throughout Arkansas, Illinois, Indiana, Iowa, Kansas, Louisiana, Michigan, Minnesota, Missouri, Mississippi, Nebraska, North Dakota, Ohio, Oklahoma, South Dakota and Wisconsin.

Consulate General of the Philippines

556 5th Ave
NEW YORK, NY 10036
Tel: (212) 764-1330
Fax: (212) 764-6010
Website: www.philippinesnewyork.org

Jurisdiction throughout Connecticut, Delaware, Maine, Massachusetts, New Hampshire, New Jersey, New York, Pennsylvania, Rhode Island and Vermont.

PITCAIRN ISLANDS

Official language: English

Legalization

Pitcairn, Henderson, Ducie and Oeno Islands are an overseas territory of the United Kingdom and the *Hague Apostille Convention* is in force.

American notarizations for production in the Pitcairn Islands are therefore exempt from consular legalization. The only formality that may be required to certify the authenticity of the notary's status, signature and seal is the affixing of an apostille by the appropriate U.S. Competent Authority.

POLAND

Official language: Polish

Legalization

The Republic of Poland is party to the *Hague Apostille Convention*.

American notarizations for production in Poland are therefore exempt from consular legalization. The only formality that may be required to certify the authenticity of the notary's status, signature and seal is the affixing of an apostille by the appropriate U.S. Competent Authority.

PORTUGAL

Official language: Portuguese

Legalization

The Portuguese Republic is party to the *Hague Apostille Convention*.

American notarizations for production in Portugal are therefore exempt from consular legalization. The only formality that may be required to certify the authenticity of the notary's status, signature and seal is the affixing of an apostille by the appropriate U.S. Competent Authority.

QATAR

Official language: Arabic

Legalization

American notarizations for production in the State of Qatar must first be legalized by its consular officers in the United States. Prior authentication of the notary's status, signature and seal by authorized U.S. state, territory and/or federal officials is required for all notarizations which are submitted for legalization.

Legalization services for the United States and its territories are provided by:

The Consul General
Embassy of Qatar

2555 M St NW
WASHINGTON, DC 20037
Tel: (202) 274-1600
Fax: (202) 237-0061
Website: www.qatarembassy.net

Jurisdiction throughout the whole of the United States and its territories which are not covered by the Houston Consulate General.

The Consulate General of the State of Qatar in Houston

1990 Post Oak Blvd
Suite 810
HOUSTON, TX 77056
Tel: (713) 355-8221
Fax: (713) 355-8184

Jurisdiction throughout Alabama, Arizona, California, Colorado, Florida, Georgia, Kansas, Louisiana, Mississippi, Minnesota, New Mexico, Nevada, Oklahoma, Tennessee and Utah.

REUNION

Official language: French

Legalization

Reunion is a French overseas department.

As France is party to the *Hague Apostille Convention* American notarizations for production in Reunion are therefore exempt from consular legalization. The only formality that may be required to certify the authenticity of the notary's status, signature and seal is the affixing of an apostille by the appropriate U.S. Competent Authority.

ROMANIA

Official language: Romanian

Legalization

Romania is party to the *Hague Apostille Convention.*

American notarizations for production in Romania are therefore exempt from consular legalization. The only formality that may be required to certify the authenticity of the notary's status, signature and seal is the affixing of an apostille by the appropriate U.S. Competent Authority.

RUSSIAN FEDERATION

Official language: Russian

Legalization

The Russian Federation is party to the *Hague Apostille Convention.*

American notarizations for production in Russia are therefore exempt from consular legalization. The only formality that may be required to certify the authenticity of the notary's status, signature and seal is the affixing of an apostille by the appropriate U.S. Competent Authority.

RWANDA

Official languages: French, Kinyarwanda and English

Legalization

American notarizations for production in the Republic of Rwanda must first be legalized by its consular officers in the United States. Prior authentication of the notary's status, signature and seal by authorized U.S. state, territory and/or federal officials is required for all notarizations which are submitted for legalization.

Legalization services for the United States and its territories are provided by:

**The Consular Section
Embassy of Rwanda**

1714 New Hampshire Ave NW
WASHINGTON, DC 20009
Tel: (202) 232-2882

SAINT BARTHELEMY

Official language: French

Legalization

The Overseas Collectivity of Saint Barthelemy is a French overseas collectivity and the *Hague Apostille Convention* is in force there.

American notarizations for production in Saint Barthelemy are therefore exempt from consular legalization. The only formality that may be required to certify the authenticity of the notary's status, signature and seal is the affixing of an apostille by the appropriate U.S. Competent Authority.

SAINT HELENA

Official language: English

Legalization

Saint Helena, Ascension and Tristan de Cunha is an overseas territory of the United Kingdom and the *Hague Apostille Convention* is in force there.

American notarizations for production in Saint Helena are therefore exempt from consular legalization. The only formality that may be required to certify the authenticity of the notary's status, signature and seal is the affixing of an apostille by the appropriate U.S. Competent Authority.

SAINT KITTS AND NEVIS

Official language: English

Legalization

The Federation of Saint Kitts and Nevis is party to the *Hague Apostille Convention*.

American notarizations for production in Saint Kitts and Nevis are therefore exempt from consular legalization. The only formality that may be required to certify the authenticity of the notary's status, signature and seal is the affixing of an apostille by the appropriate U.S. Competent Authority.

SAINT LUCIA

Official language: English

Legalization

Saint Lucia is party to the *Hague Apostille Convention*.

American notarizations for production in Saint Lucia are therefore exempt from consular legalization. The only formality that may be required to certify the authenticity of the notary's status, signature and seal is the affixing of an apostille by the appropriate U.S. Competent Authority.

SAINT PIERRE AND MIQUELON

Official language: French

Legalization

The Territorial Collectivity of Saint Pierre and Miquelon is a French self-governing overseas collectivity and the *Hague Apostille Convention* is in force there.

American notarizations for production in Saint Pierre and Miquelon are therefore exempt from consular legalization. The only formality that may be required to certify the authenticity of the notary's status, signature and seal is the affixing of an apostille by the appropriate U.S. Competent Authority.

SAINT VINCENT AND THE GRENADINES

Official language: English

Legalization

In 1965, the United Kingdom extended the coverage of the *Hague Apostille Convention* to Saint Vincent and the Grenadines which at the time was a British colony. Since independence on 27 October 1979, Saint Vincent and the Grenadines has not made a formal declaration at the continuance in force of the Convention.

Documents for production in Saint Vincent and the Grenadines to which apostilles have been affixed do not seem to be rejected. Therefore, for the time being, Saint Vincent and the Grenadines should be treated as being subject to the Convention and the affixing of an apostille by the appropriate U.S. Competent Authority should be the only formality required to certify the authenticity of a notary's status, signature and seal.

SABA

Official language: Dutch

Legalization

Saba is a special municipality of the Kingdom of the Netherlands and the *Hague Apostille Convention* is in force there.

American notarizations for production in Saba are therefore exempt from consular legalization. The only formality that may be required to certify the authenticity of the notary's status, signature and seal is the affixing of an apostille by the appropriate U.S. Competent Authority.

SAMOA

Official languages: English and Samoan

Legalization

Samoa is party to the *Hague Apostille Convention*.

American notarizations for production in Samoa are therefore exempt from consular legalization. The only formality that may be required to certify the authenticity of the notary's status, signature and seal is the affixing of an apostille by the appropriate U.S. Competent Authority.

SAN MARINO

Official language: Italian

Legalization

The Republic of San Marino is party to the *Hague Apostille Convention*.

American notarizations for production in San Marino are therefore exempt from consular legalization. The only formality that may be required to certify the authenticity of the notary's status, signature and seal is the affixing of an apostille by the appropriate U.S. Competent Authority.

SAO TOME AND PRINCIPE

Official language: Portuguese

Legalization

The Democratic Republic of Sao Tome and Principe is party to the *Hague Apostille Convention*.

American notarizations for production in Sao Tome and Principe are therefore exempt from consular legalization. The only formality that may be required to certify the authenticity of the notary's status, signature and seal is the affixing of an apostille by the appropriate U.S. Competent Authority.

SAUDI ARABIA

Official language: Arabic

Legalization

American notarizations for production in the Kingdom of Saudi Arabia must first be legalized by its consular officers in the United States. Prior authentication of the notary's status, signature and seal by authorized U.S. state, territory and/or federal officials is required for all notarizations which are submitted for legalization.

Legalization services are provided by:

The Consular Section
Embassy of Saudi Arabia

601 New Hampshire Ave NW
WASHINGTON, DC 20037
Tel: (202) 342-3800
Fax: (202) 944-3113
Website: www.saudiembassy.net

Consulate General of Saudi Arabia

2045 Sawtelle Blvd
LOS ANGELES, CA 90025
Tel: (310) 479-6000

Consulate General of Saudi Arabia

866 2nd Ave
Floor 5
NEW YORK, NY 10017
Tel: (212) 752-2740

Consulate General of Saudi Arabia

5718 Westheimer Union
Suite 1500
HOUSTON, TX 77057
Tel: (713) 785-5577

SENEGAL

Official language: French

Legalization

American notarizations for production in the Republic of Senegal must first be legalized by its consular officers in the United States. Prior authentication of the notary's status, signature and seal by authorized U.S. state, territory and/ or federal officials is required for all notarizations which are submitted for legalization.

Legalization services are provided by:

The Consular Section
Embassy of Senegal

2112 Wyoming Ave NW
WASHINGTON, DC 20008
Tel: (202) 234-0540
Fax: (202) 332-6315

Consulate General of Senegal

4 West 125th St
2nd Floor
NEW YORK 10027
Tel: (917) 493-8950
Website: www.consulsenny.com

SERBIA

Official language: Serbian

Legalization

The Republic of Serbia is party to the *Hague Apostille Convention*.

American notarizations for production in Serbia are therefore exempt from consular legalization. The only formality that may be required to certify the authenticity of the notary's status, signature and seal is the affixing of an apostille by the appropriate U.S. Competent Authority.

SEYCHELLES

Official languages: English, French and Creole

Legalization

The Republic of Seychelles is party to the *Hague Apostille Convention*.

American notarizations for production in Seychelles are therefore exempt from consular legalization. The only formality that may be required to certify the authenticity of the notary's status, signature and seal is the affixing of an apostille by the appropriate U.S. Competent Authority.

SIERRA LEONE

Warning

The Republic of Sierra Leone is subject to a U.S. Treasury Department Office of Foreign Assets Control sanctions program. Care must be taken to ensure that transactions with persons, entities or organizations in or relating to Sierra Leone are not in violation of sanctions program regulations. (*See Appendix 2 for further information.*)

Official language: English

Legalization

American notarizations for production in Sierra Leone must first be legalized by its consular officers in the United States. Prior authentication of the notary's status, signature and seal by authorized U.S. state, territory and/or federal officials is required for all notarizations which are submitted for legalization.

Legalization services for the United States its territories are provided by:

The Consular Section
Embassy for Seirra Leone

1701 19th St NW
WASHINGTON, DC 20009
Tel: (202) 939-9261
Fax: (202) 483-1793
Website: www.embassyofsierraleone.net

SINGAPORE

Official language: English

Legalization

Notarized documents for production in the Republic of Singapore must first be legalized by its consular officers in the United States. Prior authentication of the notary's status, signature and seal by authorized U.S. state, territory and/ or federal officials is required for all notarizations which are submitted for legalization.

Legalization services are provided by:

The Consular Section
Embassy of Singapore

3501 International Pl NW
WASHINGTON, DC 20008
Tel: (202) 537-3100
Fax: (202) 537-0876
Website: www.mfa.gov.sg/washington

Jurisdiction throughout the whole of the United States and its territories except those states under the jurisdiction of the consulates.

Consulate General of Singapore

595 Market St
Suite 2450
SAN FRANCISCO, CA 94105
Tel: (415) 543-0474
Fax: (415) 543-4788
Website: www.mfa.gov.sg/sanfrancisco

Jurisdiction throughout Arizona, California, Colorado, Nevada, Oregon, Utah and Washington.

Honorary Consul General of Singapore

2601 S Bayshore Dr
Suite 900
MIAMI, FL 33133
Tel: (305) 858-4225
Fax: (305) 858-2334

Jurisdiction throughout Florida.

Honorary Consul General of Singapore

1 S Dearborn St
CHICAGO, IL 60603
Tel: (312) 853-7555
Fax: (312) 853-7036

Jurisdiction throughout Illinois.

Consul of Singapore

231 East 51st St
NEW YORK, NY 10022
Tel: (212) 223-3331
Fax: (212) 826-5028
Website: www.mfa.gov.sg/newyork-consul

Jurisdiction throughout Connecticut, Illinois, Indiana, Maine, Massachusetts, Michigan, Minnesota, New Hampshire, New Jersey, New York, Ohio, Pennsylvania, Rhode Island, Vermont and Wisconsin.

SINT EUSTATIUS

Official language: Dutch

Legalization

Sint Eustatius is a special municipality of the Kingdom of the Netherlands and the *Hague Apostille Convention* is in force there.

American notarizations for production in Sint Eustatius are therefore exempt from consular legalization. The only formality that may be required to certify the authenticity of the notary's status, signature and seal is the affixing of an apostille by the appropriate U.S. Competent Authority.

SINT MAARTEN

Official language: Dutch

Legalization

Land Sint Maarten is a constituent country of the Kingdom of the Netherlands and the *Hague Apostille Convention* is in force there.

American notarizations for production in Sint Maarten are therefore exempt from consular legalization. The only formality that may be required to certify the authenticity of the notary's status, signature and seal is the affixing of an apostille by the appropriate U.S. Competent Authority.

SLOVAKIA

Official language: Slovak

Legalization

The Slovak Republic is party to the *Hague Apostille Convention*.

American notarizations for production in Slovakia are therefore exempt from consular legalization. The only formality that may be required to certify the authenticity of the notary's status, signature and seal is the affixing of an apostille by the appropriate U.S. Competent Authority.

SLOVENIA

Official language: Slovenian

Legalization

The Republic of Slovenia is party to the *Hague Apostille Convention*.

American notarizations for production in Slovenia are therefore exempt from consular legalization. The only formality that may be required to certify the authenticity of the notary's status, signature and seal is the affixing of an apostille by the appropriate U.S. Competent Authority.

SOLOMON ISLANDS

Official language: English

Legalization

In 1965, the United Kingdom extended coverage of the *Hague Apostille Convention* to Solomon Islands which at the time was a British Colony. Since independence on 7 July 1978, the Solomons has not made a formal declaration as to the continuance in force of the Convention.

Documents for production in the Solomons to which apostilles have been affixed do not seem to be rejected. Therefore, for the time being, the Solomons should be treated as being subject to the Convention and the affixing of an apostille by the appropriate U.S. Competent Authority should be the only formality required to certify the authenticity of a notary's status, signature and seal.

SOMALIA

Official language: Somali

Legalization

Somalia does not have diplomatic or consular representation in the United States. Its sole diplomatic mission in the world appears to be its permanent mission to the United Nations which usually does not provide legalization services.

However, Somalia is a member of the Arab League. As a general rule, consular officers of other Arab League members which have consular or diplomatic posts in the United States will legalize American notarizations for production in Somalia. It is advisable to obtain advance confirmation from the relevant authority or organization in Somalia as to whether or not legalization by a consular officer of a specific Arab League member will be acceptable in the particular case.

Prior authentication of the notary's status, signature and seal by authorized U.S. state, territory and/or federal officials is required for all notarizations which are submitted for legalization.

SOUTH AFRICA

Official language: English, Afrikaans and various local languages.

Legalization

The Republic of South Africa is party to the *Hague Apostille Convention*.

American notarizations for production in South Africa are therefore exempt from consular legalization. The only formality that may be required to certify the authenticity of the notary's status, signature and seal is the affixing of an apostille by the appropriate U.S. Competent Authority.

SOUTH GEORGIA AND SOUTH SANDWICH ISLANDS

Official language: English

Legalization

South Georgia and the South Sandwich Islands are an overseas territory of the United Kingdom and the *Hague Apostille Convention* is in force there.

American notarizations for production in SGSSI are therefore exempt from consular legalization. The only formality that may be required to certify the authenticity of the notary's status, signature and seal is the affixing of an apostille by the appropriate U.S. Competent Authority.

SOUTH SUDAN

Official languages: English and Arabic

Legalization

American notarizations for production in the Republic of Sudan must first be legalized by its consular offices in the United States. Prior authentication of the notary's status, signature and seal by authorized U.S. state, territory and/or federal officials is required for all notarizations which are submitted for legalization.

Legalization services for the United States and its territories are provided by:

Government of South Sudan Mission to the United States of America

1233 20th St NW
Suite 602
WASHINGTON, DC 20036
Tel: (202) 293-7940
Fax: (202) 293-7941
Website: www.gossmission.org

SPAIN

Official language: Spanish

Legalization

The Kingdom of Spain is party to the *Hague Apostille Convention*.

American notarizations for production in Spain are therefore exempt from consular legalization. The only formality that may be required to certify the authenticity of the notary's status, signature and seal is the affixing of an apostille by the appropriate U.S. Competent Authority.

SRI LANKA

Official language: Sinhala

English is used for governmental administration purposes.

Legalization

American notarizations for production in the Democratic Socialist Republic of Sri Lanka must first be legalized by its consular officers in the United States. Prior authentication of the notary's status, signature and seal by authorized U.S. state, territory and/or federal officials is required for all notarizations which are submitted for legalization.

Legalization services are provided by:

The Consular Section
Embassy of Sri Lanka

2148 Wyoming Ave NW
WASHINGTON, DC 20008
Tel: (202) 483-4025
Fax: (202) 232-7181
Website: www.slembassyusa.org

Jurisdiction throughout the whole of the United States and its territories except those states within the jurisdiction of the Consulates in Los Angeles and New York.

Consulate General of Sri Lanka

3250 Wilshire Blvd
Suite 1405
LOS ANGELES, CA 90010
Tel: (213) 387-0213
Fax: (213) 387-0216
Website: www.srilankaconsulatela.com

Jurisdiction throughout Arizona, California, Colorado, Idaho, Montana, Nevada, New Mexico, Oregon, Utah, Washington and Wyoming.

Consulate of Sri Lanka

630 3rd Ave
Floor 20
NEW YORK, NY 10017
Tel: (212) 986-7040
Fax: (212) 986-1838
Website: www.slmission.com

Jurisdiction throughout Connecticut, New Jersey and New York.

SUDAN

Warning

The Republic of Sudan is subject to a U.S. Treasury Department Office of Foreign Assets Control sanctions program. Care must be taken to ensure that transactions with persons, entities or organizations in or relating to Sudan are not in violation of sanctions program regulations. (*See Appendix 2 for further information.*)

Official language: Arabic

Legalization

American notarizations for production in Sudan must first be legalized by its consular officers in the United States. Prior authentication of the notary's status, signature and seal by authorized U.S. state, territory and/or federal officials is required for all notarizations which are submitted for legalization.

Legalization services for the United States and its territories are provided by:

The Consular Section
Embassy of Sudan

2210 Massachusetts Ave NW
WASHINGTON, DC 20008
Tel: (202) 338-8565
Fax: (202) 667-2406
Website: www.sudanembassy.org

SURINAME

Official language: Dutch

Legalization

The Republic of Suriname is party to the *Hague Apostille Convention.*

American notarizations for production in Surinam are therefore exempt from consular legalization. The only formality that may be required to certify the authenticity of the notary's status, signature and seal is the affixing of an apostille by the appropriate U.S. Competent Authority.

SWAZILAND

Official languages: English and Swazi

Legalization

The Kingdom of Swaziland is party to the *Hague Apostille Convention.*

American notarizations for production in Swaziland are therefore exempt from consular legalization. The only formality that may be required to certify the authenticity of the notary's status, signature and seal is the affixing of an apostille by the appropriate U.S. Competent Authority.

SWEDEN

Official language: Swedish

Legalization

The Kingdom of Sweden is party to the *Hague Apostille Convention*.

American notarizations for production in Sweden are therefore exempt from consular legalization. The only formality that may be required to certify the authenticity of the notary's status, signature and seal is the affixing of an apostille by the appropriate U.S. Competent Authority.

SWITZERLAND

Official languages: German, French, Italian and Romansch

Legalization

The Swiss Confederation is party to the *Hague Apostille Convention*.

American notarizations for production in Switzerland are therefore exempt from consular legalization. The only formality that may be required to certify the authenticity of the notary's status, signature and seal is the affixing of an apostille by the appropriate U.S. Competent Authority.

SYRIA

Warning

The Syrian Arab Republic is subject to a U.S. Treasury Department Office of Foreign Assets Control sanctions program. Care must be taken to ensure that transactions with persons, entities or organizations in or relating to Syria are not in violation of sanctions program regulations. (*See Appendix 2 for further information.*)

Official language: Arabic

Legalization

American notarizations for production in Syria must first be legalized by its consular officers in the United States. Prior authentication of the notary's status, signature and seal by authorized U.S. state, territory and/or federal officials is required for all notarizations which are submitted for legalization.

Legalization services are provided by:

Embassy of Syrian Arab Republic

2215 Wyoming Ave NW
Washington DC, 20008
Tel: (202) 232-6316
Fax:(202) 232-4357
Website: www.syrianembassy.us

Jurisdiction throughout the whole of the United States and its territories.

Honorary Consul General of Syria

3 San Joaquin Plaza
Suite 190
NEWPORT BEACH, CA 92660
Tel: (949) 640-9888
Fax: (949) 640-9292

Jurisdiction throughout the whole of the United States and its territories.

Honorary Consul General of Syria

900 Wilshire Dr
Suite 202
TROY, MI 48084
Tel: (248) 519-2496
Fax: (248) 519-2399
Website: www.syrianconsulate.org

Jurisdiction throughout Michigan and throughout the whole of the United States and its territories if necessary.

Honorary Consul General of Syria

1022 Wirt Rd
Suite 300
HOUSTON, TX 77055
Tel: (713) 622-8860
Fax: (713) 965-8872

Jurisdiction throughout Texas and throughout the whole of the United States and its territories if necessary.

TAIWAN

Official language: Mandarin

Legalization

There is a long-standing special relationship between the United States and the Republic of China (Taiwan) even though they do not have diplomatic relations. The Taipei Economic and Cultural Offices in the USA act as *de facto* consular posts.

American notarizations for production in Taiwan must first be legalized by the appropriate Taipei Economic and Cultural Office. Prior authentication of the notary's status, signature and seal by authorized U.S. state, territory and/ or federal officials is required for all notarizations which are submitted for legalization.

Legalization services are provided by:

Taipei Economic and Cultural Office

4201 Wisconsin Ave NW
WASHINGTON, DC 20016
Tel: (202) 895-1800
Fax: (202) 895-0017
Website: www.taiwanembassy.org

This office services Delaware, Maryland, Virginia, Washington DC and West Virginia.

Taipei Economic and Cultural Office

1180 West Peachtree St
Suite 800
Atlantic Center Plaza
ATLANTA, GA 30309
Tel: (404) 870-9375
Fax: (404) 870-9376
Website: www.teco.org

This office services Alabama, Georgia, Kentucky, North Carolina, South Carolina and Tennessee.

Taipei Economic and Cultural Office

Bank of Guam Bldg
111 Chalan Santo Papa Rd
Suite 505
HAGATNA, GU 96910
Tel: (671) 472-5865
Fax: (671) 472-5869
Website: www.taiwanembassy.org

This office services Guam and Northern Marianas.

Taipci Economic and Cultural Office

99 Summer St
Suite 801
BOSTON, MA 02110
Tel: (617) 737-2050
Fax: (617) 737-1260
Website: www.taiwanembassy.org

This office services Maine, Massachusetts, New Hampshire, Rhode Island and Vermont.

Taipei Economic and Cultural Office

180 North Stetson Ave
Two Prudential Plaza
57th & 58th Floor
CHICAGO, IL 60601
Tel: (312) 616-0100
Fax: (312) 616-1486

This office services Illinois, Indiana, Ohio, Iowa, Michigan, Minnesota and Wisconsin.

Taipei Economic and Cultural Office

2333 Ponce de Leon Blvd
Suite 610
CORAL GABLES, FL 33134
Tel: (305) 443-8917

This office services Florida, Puerto Rico and U.S. Virgin Islands.

Taipei Economic and Cultural Office

2746 Pali Hwy
HONOLULU, HI 96817
Tel: (808) 595-6347
Fax: (808) 595-6542

This office services American Samoa and Hawaii.

Taipei Economic and Cultural Office

11 Greenway Plaza
Suite 2006
HOUSTON, TX 77046
Tel: (713) 626-7445
Fax: (713) 626-1202

This office services Arkansas, Louisiana, Mississippi, Oklahoma and Texas.

Taipei Economic and Cultural Office

3100 Broadway
Suite 800
KANSAS CITY, MO 64111
Tel: (816) 531-1298
Fax: (816) 531-3066

This office services Colorado, Kansas, Missouri, Nebraska, North Dakota and South Dakota.

Taipei Economic and Cultural Office

3731 Wilshire Blvd
Suite 700
LOS ANGELES, CA 90010
Tel: (213) 389-1215
Fax: (213) 389-1676

This office services Arizona, New Mexico and Southern California.

Taipei Economic and Cultural Office

555 Montgomery St
Suite 501
SAN FRANCISCO, CA 94111
Tel: (415) 362-7680
Fax: (415) 362-5382

This office services Nevada, Northern California and Utah.

Taipei Economic and Cultural Office

1 East 42nd St
4th Floor
NEW YORK, NY 10017
Tel: (212) 317-7300
Fax: (212) 754-1549

This office services Connecticut, New Jersey, New York and Pennsylvania.

Taipei Economic and Cultural Office

One Union Square
Suite 2020
600 University St
SEATTLE, WA 98101
Tel: (206) 441-4586
Fax: (206) 441-4320

This office services Alaska, Montana, Idaho, Oregon, Washington and Wyoming.

TAJIKISTAN

Official language: No official languages but Tajik and Russian are widely used.

Legalization

American notarizations for production in the Republic of Tajikistan must first be legalized by its consular officers in the United States. Prior authentication of the notary's status, signature and seal by authorized U.S. state, territory and/or federal officials is required for all notarizations which are submitted for legalization.

Legalization services for the United States and its territories are provided by:

The Consular Section
Embassy of Tajikistan

1005 New Hampshire Ave NW
WASHINGTON, DC 20037
Tel: (202) 223-6090
Fax: (202) 223-6091
Website: www.tjus.org

TANZANIA

Official languages: English and Kiswahili

Legalization

American notarizations for production in the United Republic of Tanzania must first be legalized by its consular officers in the United States. Prior authentication of the notary's status, signature and seal by authorized U.S. state, territory and/ or federal officials is required for all notarizations which are submitted for legalization.

Legalization services for the United States and its territories are provided by:

The Consular Section
Embassy of Tanzania

1232 22nd St NW
WASHINGTON, DC 20037
Tel: (202) 939-6125
Fax: (202) 797-7408
Website: www.tanzaniaembassy-us.org

THAILAND

Official language: Thai

Legalization

American notarizations for production in the Kingdom of Thailand must first be legalized by its consular officers in the United States. Prior authentication of the notary's status, signature and seal by authorized U.S. state, territory and/or federal officials is required for all notarizations which are submitted for legalization.

Legalization services are provided by:

The Consular Section
Embassy of Thailand

1024 Wisconsin Ave NW
WASHINGTON, DC 20007
Tel: (202) 944-3600
Fax: (202) 944-3611
Website: www.thaiembdc.org

Jurisdiction throughout the whole of the United States and its territories.

Honorary Consul General of Thailand

P.O. Box 4504
MONTGOMERY, AL 36103-4504
Tel: (334) 269-2518
Fax: (334) 269-4678

Jurisdiction throughout Alabama.

Consulate General of Thailand

611 N Larchmont Blvd
Floor 2
LOS ANGELES, CA 90004
Tel: (323) 962-9574
Fax: (323) 962-2128
Website: www.thai-la.net

Jurisdiction throughout Alaska, Arizona, California, Idaho, Nevada, Oregon, Utah and Washington.

Consulate General of Thailand

700 N Rush St
CHICAGO, IL 60611
Tel: (312) 664-3129
Fax: (312) 664-3230
Website: www.thaiconsulatechicago.org

Jurisdiction throughout Illinois, Indiana, Iowa, Kansas, Kentucky, Michigan, Minnesota, Missouri, Nebraska, North Dakota, South Dakota and Wisconsin.

Consulate General of Thailand

351 East 52nd St
New York , NY 10022
Tel: (212) 754-1770
Fax: (212) 754-1907
Website: www.thaiconsulnewyork.com

Jurisdiction throughout Connecticut, Maine, Massachusetts, New Hampshire, New Jersey, New York, Ohio, Pennsylvania, Rhode Island and Vermont.

TIMOR-LESTE

Official languages: Tetum and Portuguese
English and Indonesian are widely used

Legalization

American notarizations for production in the Democratic Republic of Timor-Leste must first be legalized by its consular officers in the United States. Prior authentication of the notary's status, signature and seal by authorized U.S. state, territory and/or federal officials is required for all notarizations which are submitted for legalization.

Legalization services for the United States and its territories are provided by:

The Consular Section
Embassy of Timor-Leste

4201Connecticut Ave NW
Suite 504
WASHINGTON, DC 20008
Tel: (202) 966-3202
Fax: (202) 966-3205
Website: www.timorlesteembassy.org

TOGO

Official language: French

Legalization

American notarizations for production in the Togolese Republic must first be legalized by its consular officers in the United States. Prior authentication of the notary's status, signature and seal by authorized U.S. state, territory and/ or federal officials is required for all notarizations which are submitted for legalization.

Legalization services for the United States and its territories are provided by:

**The Consular Section
Embassy of Togo**

2208 Massachusetts Ave NW
WASHINGTON, DC 20008
Tel: (202) 234-4212
Fax: (202) 232-3190
Website: www.togoembassy.us

Consulate General of Togo

100 Fifth Ave
Suite 902
NEW YORK, NY 10011
Tel: (212) 647-1122
Fax: (212) 366-0690

TONGA

Official languages: English and Tongan

Legalization

The Kingdom of Tonga is party to the *Hague Apostille Convention*.

American notarizations for production in Tonga are therefore exempt from consular legalization. The only formality that may be required to certify the authenticity of the notary's status, signature and seal is the affixing of an apostille by the appropriate U.S. Competent Authority.

TRINIDAD AND TOBAGO

Official language: English

Legalization

The Republic of Trinidad and Tobago is party to the *Hague Apostille Convention*.

American notarizations for production in Trinidad and Tobago are therefore exempt from consular legalization. The only formality that may be required to certify the authenticity of the notary's status, signature and seal is the affixing of an apostille by the appropriate U.S. Competent Authority.

TUNISIA

Official language: Arabic

Legalization

American notarizations for production in the Tunisian Republic must first be legalized by its consular officers in the United States. Prior authentication of the notary's status, signature and seal by authorized U.S. state, territory and/ or federal officials is required for all notarizations which are submitted for legalization.

Legalization services for the United States and its territories are provided by:

The Consular Section
Embassy of Tunisia

1515 Massachusetts Ave NW
WASHINGTON, DC 20005
Tel: (202) 862-1850
Fax: (202) 862-1858

TURKMENISTAN

Official language: Turkmen

Legalization

American notarizations for production in Turkmenistan must first be legalized by its consular officers in the United States. Prior authentication of the notary's status, signature and seal by authorized U.S. state, territory and/or federal officials is required for all notarizations which are submitted for legalization.

Legalization services for the United States and its territories are provided by:

The Consular Section
Embassy of Turkmenistan

2207 Massachusetts Ave NW
WASHINGTON, DC 20008
Tel: (202) 588-1500
Website: www.turkmenistanembassy.org

TURKEY

Official language: Turkish

Legalization

The Republic of Turkey is party to the *Hague Apostille Convention*.

American notarizations for production in Turkey are therefore exempt from consular legalization. The only formality that may be required to certify the authenticity of the notary's status, signature and seal is the affixing of an apostille by the appropriate U.S. Competent Authority.

TURKS AND CAICOS ISLANDS

Official language: English

Legalization

The Turks and Caicos Islands constitute a single self-governing United Kingdom dependency and the *Hague Apostille Convention* is in force there.

American notarizations for production in the Turks and Caicos Islands are therefore exempt from consular legalization. The only formality that may be required to certify the authenticity of the notary's status, signature and seal is the affixing of an apostille by the appropriate U.S. Competent Authority.

TUVALU

Official languages: English and Tuvaluan

Legalization

In 1965, the United Kingdom extended the coverage of the *Hague Apostille Convention* to Tuvalu (then called the Ellice Islands) which, at the time, was a British colony. Since independence on 10 October 1978, Tuvalu has not made a formal declaration as to the continuance in force of the Convention.

Documents for production in Tuvalu to which apostilles have been affixed do not seem to be rejected. Therefore, for the time being, Tuvalu should be treated as being subject to the Convention and the affixing of an apostille by the appropriate U.S. Competent Authority should be the only formality required to certify the authenticity of a notary's status, signature and seal.

UGANDA

Official language: English

Legalization

American notarizations for production in the Republic of Uganda must first be legalized by its consular officers in the United States. Prior authentication of the notary's status, signature and seal by authorized U.S. state, territory and/ or federal officials is required for all notarizations which are submitted for legalization.

Legalization services for the United States and its territories are provided by:

The Consular Section
Embassy of Uganda

5911 16th St NW
WASHINGTON, DC 20011
Tel: (202) 726-7100
Fax: (202) 726-1727
Website: www.ugandaembassy.com

UKRAINE

Official language: Ukrainian

Legalization

Ukraine is party to the *Hague Apostille Convention*.

American notarizations for production in Ukraine are therefore exempt from consular legalization. The only formality that may be required to certify the authenticity of the notary's status, signature and seal is the affixing of an apostille by the appropriate U.S. Competent Authority.

UNITED ARAB EMIRATES

Official language: Arabic

Legalization

American notarizations for production in the United Arab Emirates must first be legalized by its consular officers in the United States. Prior authentication of the notary's status, signature and seal by authorized U.S. state, territory and/or federal officials is required for all notarizations which are submitted for legalization.

Legalization services for the United States and its territories are provided by:

The Consular Section
Embassy of United Arab Emirates

3522 International Ct NW
Suite 100
WASHINGTON DC, 20008
Tel: (202) 243-2400
Fax: (202) 243-1029
Website: www.uae-embassy.org

UNITED KINGDOM

Official language: English

Legalization

The United Kingdom of Great Britain and Northern Ireland is party to the *Hague Apostille Convention*.

American notarizations for production in the United Kingdom are therefore exempt from consular legalization. The only formality that may be required to certify the authenticity of the notary's status, signature and seal is the affixing of an apostille by the appropriate U.S. Competent Authority.

URUGUAY

Official language: Spanish

Legalization

American notarizations for production in the Oriental Republic of Uraguay must first be legalized by its consular officers in the United States. Prior authentication of the notary's status, signature and seal by authorized U.S. state, territory and/or federal officials is required for all notarizations which are submitted for legalization.

Legalization services are provided by:

The Consular Section
Embassy of Uruguay

1913 I St NW
WASHINGTON, DC 20006
Tel: (202) 331 -1313
Fax: (202) 331 -8142
Website: www.uruwashi.org

Jurisdiction throughout Kentucky, Maryland, Ohio, Virginia, Washington DC, West Virginia and U.S. external territories except Puerto Rico.

Consulate General of Uruguay

429 Santa Monica Blvd
Suite 400
LOS ANGELES, CA Santa Monica, 90401
Tel: (310) 394-5777
Fax: (310) 394-5140

Jurisdiction throughout Alaska, Arizona, California, Colorado, Hawaii, Idaho, Montana, New Mexico, Nevada, Oregon, Utah, Washington and Wyoming.

Consulate General of Uruguay

1077 Ponce de Leon Blvd
Suite B
MIAMI, FL Coral Gables 33134
Tel: (305) 443-9764
Fax: (305) 443-7802

Jurisdiction throughout Alabama, Florida, Georgia, North Carolina, South Carolina and Tennessee.

Consulate General of Uruguay

875 N Michigan Ave
Suite 1318
CHICAGO, IL 60611
Tel: (312) 642-3430
Fax: (312) 642-3470

Jurisdiction throughout Illinois, Indiana, Iowa, Kansas, Michigan, Minnesota, Missouri, Nebraska, North Carolina, South Carolina and Wisconsin.

Honorary Consul of Uruguay

540 World Trade Center
Suite 2002
2 Canal St
NEW ORLEANS, LA 70130
Tel: (504) 525-8354
Fax: (504) 200-3139

Jurisdiction throughout Arkansas, Louisiana, Mississippi, Oklahoma and Texas.

Consulate General of Uruguay

420 Madison Ave
Floor 6
NEW YORK, NY 10017
Tel: (212) 753-8191

Jurisdiction throughout Connecticut, Delaware, Maine, Massachusetts, New Hampshire, New Jersey, New York, Pennsylvania, Rhode Island and Vermont.

Consul General of Uruguay

Calle Luna 159
Viejo San Juan
San Juan
Tel: (787) 764-7941
Fax: (787) 751-9210
Jurisdiction throughout Puerto Rico.

UZBEKISTAN

Official language: Uzbek

Legalization

With effect from 15 April 2012, the *Hague Apostille Convention* will come into force for the Republic of Uzbekistan.

American notarizations for production in Uzbekistan will therefore be exempt from consular legalization. The only formality that will be required to certify the authenticity of the notary's status, signature and seal will be the affixing of an apostille by the appropriate U.S. Competent Authority.

Until 14 April 2012, American notarizations for production in must first be legalized by its consular officers in the United States. Prior authentication of the notary's status, signature and seal by authorized U.S. state, territory and/or federal officials is required for all notarizations which are submitted for legalization.

Particulars of Uzbek consulates may be obtained from the embassy of Uzbekistan via its website, <www.uzbekistan.org>.

VANUATU

Official languages: English, French, Bislama (Pidgin)

Legalization

The Republic of Vanuatu is party to the *Hague Apostille Convention*.

American notarizations for production in Vanuatu are therefore exempt from consular legalization. The only formality that may be required to certify the authenticity of the notary's status, signature and seal is the affixing of an apostille by the appropriate U.S. Competent Authority.

VATICAN CITY

See Holy See.

VENEZUELA

Official language: Spanish

Legalization

The Bolivarian Republic of Venezuela is party to the *Hague Apostille Convention*.

American notarizations for production in Venezuela are therefore exempt from consular legalization. The only formality that may be required to certify the authenticity of the notary's status, signature and seal is the affixing of an apostille by the appropriate U.S. Competent Authority.

VIETNAM

Official language: Vietnamese

Legalization

American notarizations for production in the Socialist Republic of Vietnam must first be legalized by its consular officers in the United States. Prior authentication of the notary's status, signature and seal by authorized U.S. state, territory and/or federal officials is required for all notarizations which are submitted for legalization.

Legalization services are provided by:

**The Consular Section
Embassy of Vietnam**

1233 20th St NW
Suite 400
WASHINGTON, DC 20036
Tel: (202) 861 -0737
Fax: (202) 861 -0917
Website: www.vietnamembassy-usa.org

Jurisdiction throughout the whole of the United States and its territories.

Consulate General of Vietnam

1700 California St
Suite 430
SAN FRANCISCO, CA 94109
Tel: (415) 922-1707
Fax: (415) 922-1848
Website: www.vietnamconsulate-sf.org

Jurisdiction throughout California.

WALLIS AND FUTUNA

Official languages: French and Wallisian

Legalization

The Territory of the Wallis and Futuna Island is a French overseas territory and the *Hague Apostille Convention* is in force there.

American notarizations for production in Wallis and Futuna are therefore exempt from consular legalization. The only formality that may be required to certify the authenticity of the notary's status, signature and seal is the affixing of an apostille by the appropriate U.S. Competent Authority.

WEST BANK AND GAZA STRIP

Official language: Arabic

Legalization

The current status of the West Bank and the Gaza Strip is unresolved and is subject to the Israeli-Palestinian Interim Agreement of 28 September 1995.

Neither Israel nor the Palestinian Authority provide legalization services for the West Bank and the Gaza Strip.

'Palestine' is considered by the Arab League to be one of its members. As a general rule, consular officers of other Arab League members which have consular or diplomatic posts in the United States will legalize American notarizations for production in the West Bank and Gaza Strip. It is advisable to obtain advance confirmation from the relevant department of the Palestinian Authority as to whether or not legalization by a consular officer of a specific Arab League member will be acceptable in the particular case.

Prior authentication of the notary's status, signature and seal by authorized U.S. state, territory and/or federal officials is required for all notarizations which are submitted for legalization.

WESTERN SAHARA

Official language: Arabic

Legalization

Western Sahara's legal status is unresolved. Morocco claims sovereignty and its consular officers in United States provide legalization services for Western Sahara.

Prior authentication of the notary's status, signature and seal by authorized U.S. state, territory and/or federal officials is required for all notarizations which are submitted for legalization.

See entry for Morocco for particulars of Moroccan Consular posts.

YEMEN

Official language: Arabic

Legalization

American notarizations for production in the Republic of Yemen must first be legalized by its consular officers in the United States. Prior authentication of the notary's status, signature and seal by authorized U.S. state, territory and/ or federal officials is required for all notarizations which are submitted for legalization.

Legalization services for the United States and it territories are provided by:

The Consular Section
Embassy of Yemen

2319 Wyoming Ave
WASHINGTON, DC 20008
Tel: (202) 965-4760
Fax: (202) 337-2017
Website: www.yemenembassy.org

ZAMBIA

Official Language: English

Legalization

American notarizations for production in the Republic of Zambia must first be legalized by its consular officers in the United States. Prior authentication of the notary's status, signature and seal by authorized U.S. state, territory and/ or federal officials is required for all notarizations which are submitted for legalization.

Legalization services for the United States and it territories are provided by:

The Consular Section
Embassy of Zambia

2419 Massachusetts Ave NW
WASHINGTON, DC 20008
Tel: (202) 265-9717
Fax: (202) 332-0826
Website: www.zambiaembassy.org

ZIMBABWE

Warning

The Republic of Zimbabwe is subject to a U.S. Treasury Department Office of Foreign Assets Control sanctions program. Care must be taken to ensure that transactions with persons, entities or organizations in or relating to Zimbabwe are not in violation of sanctions program regulations. (*See Appendix 2 for further information.*)

Official language: English

Legalization

In 1965, the United Kingdom extended the coverage of the *Hague Apostille Convention* to Zimbabwe which at the time was a British colony known as Rhodesia. Since independence on 18 April 1980, Zimbabwe has not made a formal declaration as to the continuance in force of the Convention.

Documents for production in Zimbabwe to which apostilles have been affixed do not seem to be rejected. Therefore, for the time being, Zimbabwe should be treated as being subject to the Convention and the affixing of an apostille by the appropriate U.S. Competent Authority should be the only formality required to certify the authenticity of a notary's status, signature and seal.

Selective Bibliography

Al-Khouri, Ali M – *An Innovative Approach for E-Government Transformation* (2011).

Altman, Rochelle – *Some Aspects of Older Writing Systems.*

Altman, Rochelle – *The Writing World of the Dead Sea Scrolls. Anderson's Manual for Notaries Public* (8th ed 1999).

Bernasconi, Christophe – *General Introduction to the e-APP and Update on the e-APP for Europe Project* (2011).

Bioren, John – *Laws of the Commonwealth of Pennsylvania from the Fourteenth Day of October One Thousand Seven Hundred on the Twentieth Day of March One Thousand Eight Hundred and Ten* (1810).

Black's Law Dictionary (9th ed) (2009).

Bruno, Klint L and Closen, Michael L – *Notaries Public and Document Signer Comprehension: a Dangerous Mirage in the Desert of Notarial Law and Practice* (1999).

Buhas, Sandra L – *Act Like a Lawyer, Be Judged Like a Lawyer: The Standard of Care for the Unlicensed Practice of Law* (2007).

Bureau of Labor Statistics – *Occupational Outlook Handbook* (2010-11), *Interpreters and Translators*

Cavalla, Gugliemo (ed) – *The Byzantines* (1997).

Central Intelligence Agency – *World Fact Book* (1981-).

Cheney, CR – *Notaries Public in England in the Thirteenth and Fourteenth Centuries* (1972).

Clanchy, Michael – *From Memory to Written Record , England 1066 – 1307* (1993).

Clarke, Roger – *Certainty of Identity: A Fundamental Misconception, and a Fundamental Threat to Security* (2001).

Clinton, William J – *Address Before a Joint Session of the Congress on the State of the Union* (2000).

Closen, Michael L – *To Swear or Not to Swear Document Signers. The Default of Notaries Public and a Proposal to Abolish Oral Notarial Oaths,* (2012).

Closen, M and Mulcahy, Thomas W – *Conflicts of Interest in Documents Authenticated by Attorney Notaries in Illinois,* (1999).

Closen, Michael, L and Faerber, Charles, N – *The Case That There is a Common Law Duty of Notaries Public to Create and Preserve Detailed Journal Records of their Official Acts* (2008-2009).

Congressional Research Service Report for Congress – *Statutory Interpretation: General Principles and Recent Trends* (2008).

Cox, Noel S – *The Notary Public – The Third Arm of the Legal Profession* (2000).

Dal, Pont, G E – *Law of Agency (2001)*.

Department of Army, Washington DC – *Army Regulation 27-55* (2003).

Department of Navy – *Air Force Instruction* (2003).

Department of Navy – *Manual of the Judge Advocate General* (2004).

Department of Navy – *United States Coast Guard Commandant Instructions* (2005).

Dunford, A G – *The General Notary* (1993).

Duranti, Luciana – *The Odyssey of Records Managers*.

Dutson, Stuart – *The Territorial Application of Statutes*, (1996).

Eder, Phanor James – *Powers of Attorney in International Practice* (1949).

Edwards Mills, John – *The American Notary and Commissioner of Deeds Manual*, (1904).

English Parliament – *Ecclesiastical Licenses Act* (1533).

Equasis Statistics – *The World Merchant Fleet in 2009*.

Eskridge, William N Jr., Frickey, Philip, P and Garrett, Elizabeth – *Legislation and Statutory Interpretation* (2006).

Faerber, Charles N – *U S Notary Reference Manual* (2010).

Faerber, Charles N – *Notary Seal & Certificate Verification Manual* (1997)

Farb, P – *Word Play – What Happens When People Talk* (1974).

Friedlander, M (ed) – *The Illustrated Jerusalem Bible*.

Geimer, Reinhold – *The Circulation of Notarial Acts and their Effect in Law*.

Hague Conference on Private International Law, sundry materials including *Convention of 5 October, 1961 Abolishing the Requirement for Legalization for Foreign Public Documents*.

Halsbury's Laws of England (1st ed).

Halsbury's Laws of England (2nd ed).

Halsbury's Laws of England (3rd ed).

Heinz, Volker G – *The French Notarial Profession*.

Holmes, O W Jr. (ed) – *Commentaries on American Law* (1873).

Housley, Norman – *The University in the Middle Ages and Reformation*.

Jacobs, Jaap – *The Colony of New Netherland* (2009).

Jackson, John H – *Status of Treaties in Domestic Legal Systems; a Policy Analysis* (1992).

Jennings, Alan, Bullock, Richard P and Johnson, Susan L – *Fundamentals of Louisiana Notarial Law and Practice* (2009).

Justice, Alexander – *General Treatise of the Dominion of the Sea and a Compleat Body of the Sea Laws*, (1707–1724).

Lamensdorf, Jose Henrique – *Almost Everything you Want to Know about Certified (Sworn) Translators in Brazil.*

Law Magazine Quarterly – *Rev Juris ns 1853.*

Law Reform Commission of Ireland – *Report on Oaths and Affirmations* (1990).

Law Reform Committee , Parliament of Victoria – *Inquiry into Oaths and Affirmations with Reference to the Multicultural Community* (2002).

Layton, Alexander and Parry, Angharad M – *Extraterritorial Jurisdiction – European Responses* (2003-2004).

MacNeil, Heather – *Trusting Records, – Legal, Historical and Diplomatic Perspectives* (2000).

Malavet, A – *Counsel for the Situation: The Latin Notary, An Historical and Comparative Model*, (1996).

Malavet, A – *The Foreign Notarial Legal Services Monopoly: Why Should We Care*, (1997).

McKitterick, Rosamond – *The Carolingians and the Written Word* (1989).

Merwick, Donna – *Death of a Notary* (2009).

Model Notary Act (2010).

Monthly Law Magazine, 225.

Murray, James M – *Notarial Instruments in Flanders between 1280 and 1452* (1995).

Nadelmann, Kurt H – *The Hague Conference on Private International Law Ninth Session*, (1960).

National Notary Association – *Notary Public Code of Professional Responsibilities* (1998).

New Shorter Oxford English Dictionary (1993).

New South Wales Law Reform Commission – *People with an intellectual Disability and the Criminal Justice System* (1994).

Notary legislation and published materials of all American states and territories.

O'Brien, James and Maraka, George M – *Introduction to Information Systems.*

Office of Foreign Asset Control materials.

Osmond, Carol S – *Granting Powers of Attorney for use in Mexico and other Practical Aspects of Establishing a Mexican Business.*

Powers of Attorney in International Practice (1949-1950).

Raff, Murray – *Private Property and Environmental Responsibility – A Comparative Study of German Real Property Law* (2003).

Ready, N P – *Brooke's Notary* (2009).

Rhode, Deborah L – *The Delivery of Legal Services by Non Lawyers* (1990-91).

Rose, Jonathan – *Unauthorized Practice of Law in Arizona; A legal and Political Problem That Won't Go Away* (2002).

Scott, Kenneth and Stryker-Rodda, Kenn – *The Register of Salomon Lachaire, Notary Public of New Amsterdam 1661-1662* (1978).

Scrutiny of Acts Committee, Parliament of Victoria, *Review of the Evidence Act 1958 (Vic) and Review of the Role and Appointment of Public Notaries,* (1999).

Seth, John E – *Notaries in the American Colonies* (1998-1999).

Shaw, Gisela – *Notaries in England and Wales: Modernising a profession Frozen in Time,* (2000).

Shin, Hyon B and Kominski, Robert, A – *Language Use in the United States* (2007-2010).

Silving, Helen – *Essays on Criminal Procedure* (1964).

Sir Zelman Cowen Centre – *Course Materials for Graduate Diploma in Notarial Practice.*

Smith, William – *Smith's Bible Dictionary.*

Sofer, Mory – *The Translator's Handbook* (2004).

Stahl, Alan M (ed) – *The Documents of Angelo de Cartura and Donato Fontanella – Venetian Notaries in Fourteenth Century Crete* (1990).

State Council of the PRC – *Interim Regulation on Public Notary Services* (1982).

State Department – *Consular List* (2011).

State Department – *Diplomatic List* (2011).

Statute of the Hague Conference.

Stein, Peter – *Roman Law in European History* (1999)

Suarez-Mendez, Alejandro – *The Agent for Service of Process in Mexico* (2006).

Tarver, J Ch – *The Royal Phraseological English-French, French-English Dictionary* (1858).

Thaw, Deborah M – *The Feminisation of the Office of Notary Public: From Female Covert to Notaire Covert* (1998).

Thaw, Deborah M – *The Notary Office and its Impact in the 21st Century.*

The Civil Code of Quebec.

The New Shorter Oxford Dictionary (1993).

The Supreme Court of Ohio – *Interpreters in the Judicial System – A Handbook for Ohio Judges.*

Turner Bushnell, Amy – *Ruling the Republic of Indians in Seventeenth Century Florida, – Powhatans Mantle* (2006).

Toulmin, Harry – *A Digest of the Laws of the State of Alabama* (1828).

UK Judicial Studies Board Benchbook.

University of Pennsylvania – *The Consular Service of the United States – its History and Activities* (1906).

U.S. Constitution.

U.S. Government – *Acquisition of the Public Domain 1781-1867.*

U.S. Census Bureau Foreign Trade Statistics.

Valera, Milton G – *New Technology and a Global Economy Demand That American Notaries Better Prepare for the Future.*

Van Alstyne, Peter J – *Van Alstyne's Notary Public Encyclopedia* (2001).

Vargas, Jorge A – *Enforcement of Judgments in Mexico* (1993).

Vienna Convention on Consular Relations, Article 5(f).

VPLR Inquiry Report (2003).

Weinberg, Mark – *The Law of Testimonial Oaths and Affirmations* (1976).

West, Roger – *Dementia Awareness for Lawyers* (2001).

Wigmore on Evidence (3rd ed).

Wilson, Ian E – *The Fine Art of Destruction* (2000).

Yearbook of the International Law Commission (1961).

Zablud, Peter – *Principles of Notarial Practice* (2005).

INDEX

Note: Page numbers followed by 'n' refer to footnotes.

Illinois
   authentication authority 150
   notaries not empowered to certify copy
      documents 61
   translation for person who does not
      speak or understand English 55
   illiterate affiants 42
India
   authentication requirements 215
   photograph certification 60
Indiana
   authentication authority 150
   certification of copy documents and
      photographs 64, 65
   translation for person who does not
      speak or understand English 55
Indonesia, authentication requirements
   215–16
ink and ink color 16
intellectual disability 103
intellectually disabled persons
   communicating with 103
   community attitudes towards 103
*1975 Inter-American Convention on the
   Legal Regime of Powers of Attorney to
   be used abroad* (1975 Inter-American
   Convention) 81, 84–5
   American notaries acceptance of 84, 85
   flexibility in certificate requirements
      84–5
   United States not a party to 84, 85
interpreter services, and notarial
   certificates 50
interpreters 48
   communicating with deaf or hearing
      impaired persons 50–1
   finding 56–7
   functions of 49
   oaths 49–50
interpreting
   fluency and literacy are not enough 48
   importance of 48
   lack of state and territory guidelines
      54–6
   what it entails 49
Iowa
   authentication authority 150
   certification of copy documents 67
   Pocketbook for Iowa Notaries Public 67
Iran
   authentication requirements 217
   subject to Office of Foreign Assets
      Control sanctions program 127, 217

Iraq
   authentication requirements 217–18
   subject to Office of Foreign Assets
      Control sanctions program 217
Ireland, authentication requirements 218
Isle of Man, authentication requirements
   218
Israel, authentication requirements 218
Italy
   authentication requirements 219
   civil code 122
   powers of attorney for use in 78

Jamaica, authentication requirements
   219–20
Japan, authentication requirements 220
Jersey *see* Channel Islands
Jordan, authentication requirements 220
Judeo-Christian oaths 36, 37, 38
jurat
   affidavit
      by a blind, sight impaired or
         illiterate person 42
      by a deaf or hearing impaired person
         42
      by a physically disabled person 43
   affirmation 40
   interpreter use 50
   statutory declarations in
      Commonwealth of Nations
      jurisdictions 45
'juristic person' certificates 30

Kansas
   authentication authority 150
   certification of copy documents 67
   Kansas Notary Public Handbook 67
Kazakhstan, authentication requirements
   221
Kentucky
   authentication authority 151
   no need for seal of office 16
   notaries limited authority to certify
      copy documents 61
Kenya, authentication requirements 221
Kiribati, authentication requirements 222
Korea (North)
   authentication requirements 222
   subject to Office of Foreign Assets
      Control sanctions program 222
Korea (South)
   authentication requirements 223
   'juristic person' certificates 30